SOLDIERS AND POLITICS IN EASTERN EUROPE, 1945–90

Soldiers and Politics in Eastern Europe, 1945–90

The Case of Hungary

Zoltan D. Barany

Assistant Professor of Government
University of Texas at Austin

St. Martin's Press

First published in Great Britain 1993 by
THE MACMILLAN PRESS LTD
Houndmills, Basingstoke, Hampshire RG21 2XS
and London
Companies and representatives
throughout the world

A catalogue record for this book is available
from the British Library.

ISBN 0–333–58821–5

Printed in Great Britain by
Ipswich Book Co Ltd
Ipswich, Suffolk

First published in the United States of America 1993 by
Scholarly and Reference Division,
ST. MARTIN'S PRESS, INC.,
175 Fifth Avenue,
New York, N.Y. 10010

ISBN 0–312–09722–0

Library of Congress Cataloging-in-Publication Data
Barany, Zoltan D.
Soldiers and politics in Eastern Europe, 1945–1990 / Zoltan D.
Barany.
p.   cm.
Includes bibliographical references (p.   ) and index.
ISBN 0–312–09722–0
1. Hungary—Politics and government—1945–1989.   2. Hungary,
Néphadsereg.—Political activity.   3. Civil–military relations-
-Hungary.   I. Title.
DB956.B37   1993
943.905—dc20   93–16624
                                                     CIP

Szüleimnek

Contents

Contents

Acknowledgements

I am pleased to acknowledge the intellectual and other debts I have taken on throughout the researching and writing of this study. S. Neil MacFarlane, my dissertation adviser at the University of Virginia, offered valuable criticisms and actively supported my academic endeavors. Daniel N. Nelson of Georgetown University and Robin Alison Remington of the University of Missouri-Columbia took the time to read and comment on some chapters as did members of my dissertation committee: Michael Joseph Smith, Paul Stephan, and Kenneth W. Thompson. I am also grateful to Peter Deak, Director of the Center for National Security and Defense Studies in Budapest, for sharing some of his insights with me.

There is hardly a more appropriate place to express my gratitude to the two teachers, mentors, and friends, whose interest and confidence in me have been sources of motivation and encouragement through the years. Teresa Rakowska-Harmstone of Carleton University aroused my interest in civil–military relations and was brave enough to entrust the preparation of a chapter in her large-scale study on the Warsaw Pact to a college senior. This project culminated in an international conference, held in Ottawa in March 1986, where I met Ivan Volgyes of the University of Nebraska-Lincoln, who became my harshest critic and a friend for all seasons. Aside from continuously stimulating my curiosity about politics and Eastern Europe, I thank him for his willingness to listen to my half-baked ideas, for offering advice, and for preparing countless scrumptious meals.

My thanks also go to the Research Institute of Radio Free Europe in Munich where I spent the summer of 1988 and the 1989–90 academic year. I am particularly grateful to Ronald Linden who served as Director of Research in 1989–91 for helping to make my stay at RFE intellectually rewarding and for supporting my all too many travel requests with good humor. My colleagues, Stephen Ashley, Barbara Donovan, Alfred Reisch, and Louisa Vinton facilitated my research by allowing me to go through their files.

During my doctoral studies I was fortunate to hold a President's Fellowship of the University of Virginia and a Doctoral Fellowship of the Social Sciences and Humanities Research Council of Canada which enabled me to concentrate on my work. A small grant from the University Research Institute of the University of Texas at Austin expedited the completion of the manuscript. In our Department of Government Suzanne Colwell offered cheerful and skillful assistance.

I also want to thank the editors of *East European Quarterly*, *Journal of Political and Military Sociology*, *Journal of Strategic Studies*, and *Sudost-Europa* for permitting me to incorporate revised portions of my articles into the manuscript.

Most importantly I thank my parents, Istvan and Lotti Barany, for more than I can say.

List of Abbreviations

ACC	Allied Control Commission
AVH	State Security Authority (Hungary)
BCP	Bulgarian Communist Party
BG	Border Guards (Hungary)
BPA	Bulgarian People's Army
BPP	Barracked People's Police (East Germany)
BSP	Bulgarian Socialist Party
CC	Central Committee
CDPP	Christian Democratic People's Party (Hungary)
CEI	Central European Initiative
CHA	Command of the Hungarian Army
CL	Central Leadership (Hungary)
CMEA	Council of Mutual Economic Assistance
CPSU	Communist Party of the Soviet Union
CSA	Czechoslovak Army
CSCE	Conference for Security and Cooperation in Europe
CSCP	Czechoslovak Communist Party
CSPA	Czechoslovak People's Army
CYL	Communist Youth League (Hungary)
DOSAAF	Soviet paramilitary organization
GDR	German Democratic Republic
HA	Hungarian Army
HDA	Hungarian Defense Association
HCP	Hungarian Communist Party
HPA	Hungarian People's Army
HSWP	Hungarian Socialist Workers' Party
HWP	Hungarian Workers' Party
ISP	Independent Smallholders' Party (Hungary)
KBW	Internal Security Police (Poland)
MBFR	Mutual Balanced Forced Reduction
MOD	Ministry of Defense
MOI	Ministry of Interior
MPA	Main Political Administration
MPD	Military-Political Department (Hungary)
NCO	non-commissioned officer

NEM	New Economic Mechanism (Hungary)
NG	National Guard (Hungary, 1956)
NKVD	Soviet security police
NPA	National People's Army (East Germany)
NPP	National Peasant Party (Hungary)
NSF	National Salvation Front (Romania)
NSWP	Non-Soviet Warsaw Pact
PB	Politburo
PCC	Political Consultative Committee (Warsaw Pact)
PPA	Polish People's Army
PU	Policing Units (Hungary, 1956–57)
PUWP	Polish United Workers' Party
RAC	Revolutionary Armed Committee (Hungary, 1956)
RC	Revolutionary Council (Hungary, 1956)
RCP	Romanian Communist Party
RPA	Romanian People's Army
SDP	Social Democratic Party (Hungary)
SED	Socialist Unity Party (East Germany)
SGSF	Southern Group of Soviet Forces
UAF	United Armed Forces (Warsaw Pact)
UOS	Unified Officers' School (Hungary, 1957–67)
WG	Workers' Guards (Hungary, 1957–89)
WTO	Warsaw Treaty Organization

Introduction

In 1989–90, Eastern Europe became independent and began to free itself from the political and socioeconomic burden of over four decades of Soviet-imposed Communism. The transformation process has been complex, the states of the region have travelled different roads to democratization. The states of East-Central Europe – Czechoslovakia, Hungary, and Poland – have already made quantum leaps toward the realization of pluralist democracies. Their Balkan neighbors, Romania and Bulgaria, have encountered more obstacles but are moving in the same direction. The boundaries separating the two Germanys were erased and Germans once again live in a single nation-state.

The political and socioeconomic tasks ahead of these newly sovereign states are enormous, tantamount to a full-scale systemic transformation. In the political realm this transition requires the dismantling of the Communist monoparty system and the establishment of pluralist democracies. One of the important aspects of the democratization process has been the comprehensive restructuring of civil–military relations.

The relationship between the polity and the armed forces has been a crucial component of politics throughout the history of the modern state. The polity needs the services of the armed forces but it must also ensure that the army does not interfere in politics. The paradox is, of course, that the army is frequently the only group in society that possesses the physical means to force the politicians to do its bidding, thus it is in the latters' interest to develop stable and agreeable relations with the former. Civil–military relations vary widely among states, depending on the given political system and political culture, on levels of economic development, prevailing ideologies, etc. Relations between the polity and the armed forces in Communist systems differ from those in other states in many respects, the most important of which is that the armed forces are subordinated not to the constitution or any given state agency, but to the ruling Marxist–Leninist party.

An important question to ask then, is how does the Communist Party gain and maintain control over the armed forces? At a time when Communist systems disintegrate, an essential area of inquiry is the nature of transformation in the relationships between soldiers and politicians. How does the transition from Communism to democracy or toward that uncertain 'something else' affect the nature and the function of the military?[1] One of the aims of this study is to seek answers to these questions.

The subject of this book is civil–military relations in Soviet-dominated Eastern Europe from the inception until the end of Communist regimes there, when the armed forces of the region were subordinated to the hegemonial Party. The Party's control, exercised through a variety of institutional mechanisms and informal channels, aimed at making the army into an instrument that would defend the regime from its internal and external enemies. A crucial question that needs to be answered is how well have the armed forces of the region carried out this task? In times of domestic crisis, was the military asked to prop up the regime and if yes, was it up to the challenge? How did the armed forces behave and why did they behave in the manner they did? Could we have reasonably expected the East European armies to perform in the manner they did in 1989? Could we have anticipated their behavior?

As in the cases of most previous treatments of the subject, this work deals extensively with the idiosyncracies of civil–military relations under communism. The focus here, however, is on the armies' role in the processes of transformation from the post-war turmoil to communism on the one hand, *and* from communism to pluralism on the other. The study begins in the immediate Communist period and ends with the demise of communism in 1989–90. Throughout the book, the utility of Western models devised to fit civil–military relations in Eastern Europe is tested by the case study. There is a dearth of country-specific studies of civil–military relations in Eastern Europe despite the profound differences of conditions across the region.[2] This work attempts to fill that gap in the literature, by analyzing civil–military relations and the evolution and devolution of Communist-dominated armed forces in Hungary.

There were many similarities between the civil–military relations of all Eastern European states, after all, Party–army relations were based on the Soviet model everywhere. The hegemonial Party maintained similar institutions of control over the armed forces and there were also analogies in the reactions of the military and the overall population to this domination. In turn, these agencies across the region shared important characteristics and often were undistinguishable from each other. Thus, the question 'have civil–military relations in Hungary been typical to those of the five other non-Soviet Warsaw Pact (NSWP) countries?' needs to be addressed.[3] The answer is an emphatic 'no'.

The underlying hypothesis of this study is that there was no 'standard' case for Party–army relations in the region since experiences in all six states had differed in many important respects. The Hungarian case, too, features several unique attributes. For instance, Hungary was the last ally of Hitler, fighting on the German side until May 1945. Until 1948 the country was ruled by a coalition government and therefore the takeover period was dissimilar in many respects to those of other NSWP states, except for Czechoslovakia. Hungary is also distinctive to the extent that it was the only NSWP state to put up armed opposition to Soviet domination in 1956. Furthermore, the slow progress of socioeconomic and domestic political liberalization began in the mid-1960s, much earlier than in the rest of the region. These factors did not fail to influence civil–military relations. In short, many similitudes *and* disparities existed between civil–military relations in all six NSWP states, and using Hungary as the basis for comparison is as good a choice as any other case would be.

This book is first and foremost an examination of the relationship between soldiers and politics in Hungary. Still, there are so many commonalities in the essential aspects – if not always in the particulars – of civil–military relations across the region that a case study of Hungary can contribute to a broader understanding of the subject in the larger East European context. In Chapter 6 and in the concluding section I explore the validity of my findings based on the Hungarian experience to the practice of civil–military relations elsewhere in the region.

Throughout the book I have attempted to focus on military politics. Civil-military relations, however, are obviously strongly affected by a great many external phenomena, such as the given country's economic situation and external relations, to mention only two obvious factors that also need to be considered. In order to gain better understanding of the Hungarian soldier's loyalties it seemed necessary to discuss the changing role Hungary had played in the Warsaw Treaty Organization (WTO). Consequently, the comparative section corresponds to the main body of the study by analyzing parallel issue areas.

This study is not about arsenals, military expenditure, strategic doctrines, or alliance politics although it was imperative to devote some attention to matters such as defense budgets and weaponry as they clearly are issues of importance to armed forces personnel. My focus throughout is on the sociopolitical side of the equation: on the Party's treatment of the armed forces, the extent of the army's participation in politics, and factors that affect civil–military relations such as the military education system, political indoctrination, the social status of the military occupation, and the armed forces' attitudes toward political change.

In Chapter 1, I briefly examine some of the Western models and theories of civil–military relations in Communist systems with particular attention to Eastern Europe. I evaluate the most influential models and attempt to determine whether they can satisfactorily explain the many differences of Party–army relations in the six NSWP states. The balance of the book seeks to substantiate my main theses through a detailed analysis of the Hungarian case and a brief comparative examination of the experiences of the other East European countries.

Chapter 2 examines civil–military relations in Hungary during the takeover period (1945–53) that has been called the era of 'satellization', 'sovietization', and 'bolshevization'. My main argument is that the Hungarian Communist Party (HCP) had extended its control over the armed forces already before the 1948 collapse of the coalition government that marked the beginning of Communist dictatorship in other areas of politics and social affairs. I also try to demonstrate that the ultimate control over Hungarian military politics lay with the Kremlin leaders.

Chapter 3 analyzes Hungarian civil–military relations from the death of Stalin (1953) to the Warsaw Pact's invasion of Czechoslovakia (1968) in which the Hungarian People's Army (HPA) participated. Special attention is devoted to the HPA's performance in the 1956 Hungarian uprising and to the post-Revolution rebuilding of the military.

In Chapter 4 the focus shifts to the 1968–88 period. The thesis here is that there was no fundamental change in civil–military relations despite the slow process of restoring more national characteristics to the HPA and the gradual democratization of the armed forces. I contend that – notwithstanding some encouraging signs of political liberalization – the Hungarian Socialist Workers' Party (HSWP) remained in firm control of the armed forces. At the same time, I study the relative deterioration of the military's social and economic status and its effects.

Chapter 5 examines the transformation of civil–military relations in 1988–90. My hypothesis is that the armed forces – in spite of the apparent reluctance of the senior officer corps – quickly embraced their new role as defender of the nation-state and did not actively oppose the transition from post-Communism to democracy.

Chapter 6 briefly analyzes civil–military relations in the six NSWP states. I consider some of the most important aspects of this relationship, such as the military's involvement in the given states' politics, the characteristics of the Communist parties' control over the armed forces, and the army's performance in political crises. I intend to show that although Party–army relations shared important attributes across the region, civil–military relations in all of the six countries were very different.

In the Conclusion, I recapitulate some of my important findings pertaining to the Hungarian case. I then contrast the Hungarian experience and that of the other NSWP states to the theoretical corpus examined in Chapter 1 and examine the utility of the models to actual behavior. Finally, I present a set of generalizations that in my view are applicable to the civil–military relations of all of the six East European systems and may inform further research in this area.

1 Civil–Military Relations in Communist Systems: Western Models Revisited

Introduction

Civil–military relations in Communist systems are crucial for our understanding of the military's role and function in such political environments. Examining military establishments in democratic polities, while paying little attention to the existing political structure might well be a fruitful undertaking. The organizational structures and basic functions of Communist armed forces, however, cannot be understood without analyzing their relationships to their respective polities. Although all military establishments have inherently strong ties to their polities, these links are far stronger and more varied in Communist systems.

In short, the main (but surely not exclusive) task of the armed forces in democratic societies is to defend the state from its external enemies, while in Communist systems its critical roles are internal *and* external. The external defensive and offensive roles of Communist armies are familiar. Their internal function was to defend the Communist regime from its domestic opponents. In democratic systems the military is not a weapon of internal political force because the system is by definition legitimate. In Communist states, however, the armed forces must play an internal political role because these systems were not brought about by democratic political processes and, as a general rule, are clearly illegitimate. Mao Zedong's famous axiom ('power grows out of the barrel of a gun') illustrates well the crux of civil–military relations in Communist systems. In such polities, the military's support is simply indispensable for the consolidation of (Communist) political power. In sum, democratic political systems can survive without supportive military establishments; Communist systems cannot.[1]

This chapter offers a brief analysis of civil military relations in Communist systems and the existing theoretical foundation thereof. First, I will

6

discuss some distinctive properties of Communist armed forces. Second, I will briefly analyze some of the theoretical constructs that were intended to explain the characteristics of civil–military relations in Soviet-type systems. It seems important to do so, since scholarly literature on civil–military relations in Communist political systems is unevenly distributed. There are many more studies dealing with the former Soviet Union than with Eastern Europe in this respect. Third, I will turn my attention to Eastern Europe and observe the differences between the Soviet and East European armies' relation to their respective political systems and then proceed to determine the applicability of some models attempting to explain them.

Scholarly and public interest in civil military relations has increased immeasurably since World War II. Samuel Huntington's pathbreaking *The Soldier and the State* was followed by a plethora of studies dealing with the subject.[2] Even a cursory perusal of this literature is sufficient to see that the most scrutinized aspect of this relationship is that of civilian control over the military. Although Huntington's work addressed many crucial and theretofore neglected aspects of the subject, students of civil–military relations correctly argued that he did not provide a universally applicable model since his conceptual notions failed to consider civil–military relations in Communist systems.[3] In the last three decades several typologies were devised to embrace the large variety of civil–military relationships in political systems.[4]

Perhaps the most common categorization distinguishes between three system types:[5] (a) those in which the military is controlled by the state and/or government institutions; (b) Communist party systems in which the military is controlled by the hegemonial Party; and (c) systems under military domination. While this typology has its critics and shortcomings, it is adequate for our purposes as it sets Communist systems apart from both democratic and praetorian structures. The distinguishing feature of civil–military relations in Communist polities is that the military in such states is subordinated to the Communist Party – for all practical purposes the monopolist of political power – and not to any other political actor. In the words of Clausewitz, 'politics is supreme to military action'.

Part I Characteristics of Communist Civil–Military Relations

One of the most glaring differences between democratic and Communist political systems was that, in the latter, the hegemonial Communist Party ruled over all political actors of the polity. To use David Easton's terminology, in classical Communist systems the Party controls not only the input and output processes of the 'political machine', but the feedback mechanism as well.[6] To be sure, as time went by, in most Communist systems the political process became less rigid as the Party opened up the input and feedback channels, but its ultimate authority over the policy-making process remained unchanged. The Communist Party's self-perceived vanguard role created a political system in which the Party was sovereign, and in practice its hegemony depended upon how successfully it was able to exert its control over the non-party political institutions of the polity.[7]

Roman Kolkowicz enumerated five significant characteristics of hegemonial political systems.[8] These included the hierarchically organized Party with its 'revolutionary' heritage; its 'rational' organizational system; and constant activism which denoted the necessity of the party–state to manipulate the population for mobilization tasks, internal and external 'revolutionary' campaigns and military aggression. Kolkowicz argued that a hegemonial system was a militant political system which contained elements of all three major 'military types' of organization: revolutionary, praetorian, and professional.

The Communist system is based on and stems from the Marxist–Leninist ideology. Nearly every facet of Communist societies was saturated by the Party in this prescriptive and combative ideology. Alexander Alexiev argued correctly that in Communist states (the Soviet Union, China) national sentiments and ideological (i.e., Marxist–Leninist) convictions might be difficult to separate.[9] (Communist systems, to be sure, are not unique in this respect as the convergence of national and religious/ideological sentiments is not alien to some other traditions either.) Of course, even before the recent revolutions, the ideological rigor of Communists in the Soviet Union and Eastern Europe had waned: clearly, Marxism-Leninism has had diminishing relevance to practice. One also needs to note that 'the Party' often did not behave as a unitary actor as intraparty squabbles and disagreements threatened unison on occasion.

Socialist systems have been found to be more militaristic than democratic ones, partly because their political culture is dominated by the values of Marxist–Leninist ideology. The fact that all Communist states maintained large military organizations is scarcely a coincidence and the 'militarism of socialist regimes is independent of their level of economic development or military threat levels'.[10] The relative militarism of some socialist states (e.g., Cuba, Vietnam) originated from their official Marxist-Leninist ideology, institutional structures, histories, traditions, and internal as well as external threat perceptions.

The militaristic tendencies of the hegemonial Party were also reflected in the militarization of society. Communist armed forces were based on conscription, a system that aside from providing the military with a consistently large pool of draftees also served as an effective vehicle for social control. Military education, stressing the progressive traditions and the important socio-political role of the indigenous army was utilized for the socialization of children long before mandatory military service. The Party also created paramilitary organizations (such as the DOSAAF in the USSR) to popularize the military as well as to equip participants with skills that were useful from the military's point of view.[11] In addition, science, technology, as well as the national economy, were militarized in Communist systems although the extent of these phenomena differed greatly by country and historical period.

Amos Perlmutter and William LeoGrande succinctly summarized some of the main differences between civil–military relations in pluralist and Communist systems when they asserted that two general assumptions confirmed in the case of democratic systems were irrelevant and invalid to Communist states: first, the clear division between civilian and military elites that makes elite conflict among them inter-institutional conflict between civilian and military structures; and second, that either or both civilian and military elites subscribe to the norm that the military ought to be apolitical.[12] Timothy Colton, among others, demonstrated how the military was *encouraged* by the Communist polity to participate in political processes in capacities such as members of and advisors to even the highest policy-making organs.[13]

The peculiar characteristics of the Soviet-type armed forces evolved largely as a result of their complex relationship with the Marxist–Leninist party. In fact, extensive control and proper utilization of the military in a revolutionary society has always been part of Communist intellectual thought.[14] Ruling parties maintained close ties with their country's military forces out of necessity: support of the armed forces was indispensable for the very survival of the regime. In many cases such as Yugoslavia, Albania, Cuba, and China, the revolutionary army at first *was* the Party.[15] Moving away from such a symbiotic relationship has been very gradual and in some cases (e.g., Cuba, Angola) incomplete.

The military in the party–state may be considered in a sense as a senior partner of the Communist regime although this was by no means an equal relationship. Rather, it was in many respects a tightly controlled interdependent alliance in which the Party was clearly in the superior position. On the one hand, the Party needed armed forces that were loyal to the regime, that could reliably discharge their important missions, one of which was the defense of the Communist regime from its external *and* internal foes. Besides this role, the armed forces were the guardians of the hegemonial Party's revolutionary-ideological heritage, acted as the agent of political socialization, offered assistance following natural disasters and in times of economic hardship, participated in the production of goods and services, etc. On the other hand, the army needed the Party for the preservation and improvement of its material status and social prestige. Just as importantly, the military wanted to exist in a stable and well-governed political system.

The relationship between the hegemonial Party and the military forces was at times conflictual. The military, as the guardian of the ultimate control of violence, was the only social force that was capable of forcefully overthrowing the Party. For this reason the Party displayed unmistakable signs of fear of the military. In fact, from their inceptions, Soviet-type governments have been obsessed by a fear of 'Bonapartism'.[16] Through the years, the Soviet regime attempted to counter this apprehension with violence (witness the decimation of the armed forces' command in the 1930s), appeasement (e.g., Marshal Zhukov's appointment to the Presidium of the Communist Party of the Soviet Union [CPSU] in 1957), and court procedures (following the August 1991 coup attempt). But one of the most important methods of dealing with real or imagined military threat to the regime was the Party's penetration of the armed forces by means of a variety of political control mechanisms, the co-optation of the armed forces personnel into political affairs, and the granting of privileges to the officer corps.

Huntington hypothesized about a 'strong, integrated, highly professional officer corps . . . immune to politics'.[17] It is questionable whether any military establishment could be indifferent to politics; in Communist systems such immunity was neither desirable nor possible. In single-party systems there is a great deal of stress on the politicization of the armed forces. In such polities the Party's firm conviction to be the vanguard of society must be accepted by the military as a fundamental principle of the system.

The thorough control of the military is a fundamental interest of the party–state as it has to insure that the armed forces remain entirely loyal to the regime. From their creation, Communist armed forces have been watched over by an entire organization of political officers whose main function was the maintenance of ideological purity within the military. The Main Political Administration (MPA), as the intramilitary organization was customarily called, was one of the most important components of the armed forces, from the Party's perspective. The hierarchy of political officers extended from the highest echelons of the military leadership down to the battalion or even company levels. Colton suggested that the actual influence of the MPA in the armed forces had been overestimated, primarily because students of the subject had readily assumed that the this organization was an effective instrument of party control.[18] To assure the reliability of the armed forces, the party also utilized the regular and military intelligence organizations.

At times, particularly when the Party was not entirely confident of the performance and reliability of the military, the system of dual command was utilized. In practical terms, a command (any command) issued by the military officer had to be counter-signed by the political officer to be a valid order. Moreover, in cases of dispute the decisive word was that of the political officer. In the Soviet Army this system was first introduced in 1918, abolished in 1934, re-introduced in 1937 and abolished in October 1942 as a result of its dire wartime consequences.

Another method through which the Party exerted its control over the military was the creation of dual elites, the co-optation of high-ranking military officers into various levels of the Party hierarchy. The military elite was well represented at almost every level of the Party leadership although they rarely advanced beyond the level of the Central Committee of the Communist Party of their country.[19] Despite its relatively strong presence in party organizations, as a general rule, the military maintained a low profile in intraparty affairs.

The military's intraparty role is of crucial significance to the ruling Communist Party. According to Perlmutter, one of the main functions of the military was to restrain intraelite conflicts to within party bounds. 'The absence of an institutionalized and autonomous military not only could magnify intraparty conflicts but could encourage systemic, structural, and ideological challenges to the party–state.'[20] The military, then, was basically forced into a political role by the Party, a role that it probably felt uncomfortable playing. The armed forces desired a Party elite that was capable of governing the system smoothly, without giving cause to or permitting the evolution of systemic crises.

Although the military had traditionally refrained from intervening in intraparty conflicts, it is important to observe that whenever it did interfere (e.g., in the Soviet Union in 1957 and 1991, or in Poland in 1981) it did so as a representative of the Party and not in a military capacity; in other words, it acted as the Party in uniform. These conflicts, more often than not, occurred at times of succession (i.e., transition of power) within the Party. One of the glaring defects of the Soviet-type political system was that a clearly-defined succession mechanism was absent from it. Indeed, at times of transition, the military could play an important role (e.g., Romania in 1989). In some cases, it opted for non-involvement thereby acting as a silent kingmaker.[21] Such conflicts were relatively rare, however. As a rule, the military seemed not to be bothered about its comparatively small political clout and sought satisfaction from concessions such as material benefits and privileges provided by the party state.

A previously often overlooked function of the militaries in Communist states was to prevent national conflicts and encourage stabilization processes. The recent political transitions made this omission all the more conspicuous. Just as in other political systems (e.g., Canada 1970), the armed forces of Communist states played a role in averting national conflicts (Soviet Union 1957, Poland 1976) and offered guarantees of stable transition processes (Czechoslovakia, Hungary, Poland, 1989).

Before we proceed further, it is important to point out some of the fundamental differences between civil–military relations in the USSR, China, and Yugoslavia on the one hand, and the six NSWP states on the other. In the former category, the armed forces were subject to the control of the indigenous Communist parties. In the latter case, however, the militaries were supervised and dominated not only by the Communist parties but also by an external force, that is, the Soviet armed forces (representing the Soviet political leadership) and the WTO, an alliance system that blatantly disregarded the national interest of these states.[22]

The WTO and the USSR were essentially extraneous 'third actors' whose relations with the East European regimes impinged on the civil–military relations in these states. The East European countries' satellite status detracted from their legitimacy and also diminished the regime's authority *vis-à-vis* the armed forces. Thus, the Party had to rely on the internal-defensive function of the armed forces and this, in turn, was an important reason why the party–state perceived the need to control the military very tightly.

Moreover, the USSR, China, and Yugoslavia organized their Communist armed forces on their own while in Eastern Europe this process was overseen by the Soviet Union. Another important distinction is, of course, that Eastern Europe's armed forces can no longer be described as Communist, given the political transitions that have been taking place since 1989. To be sure, there are important differences in the results of depoliticization across the region, none the less it is fair to say that in all of the former 'Warsaw Pact Six' the armed forces are now under constitutional (and not party) control.

Part II   Western Models of Soviet Civil–Military Relations

The first dominant model of civil–military relations in Communist systems was devised by Huntington and Morris Janowitz.[23] Their theoretical construct was largely based on the totalitarian model worked out by Hannah Arendt, Carl Friedrich and Zbigniew Brzezinski, and others in the 1950s.[24] This approach was based on the assumption 'that (1) in the process of Communist revolution, traditional militaries are replaced by (2) armed forces that have been successfully penetrated by civilian political organization and personnel, resulting in (3) an ideologically based, civilian-dominated, integration of party–army elites'.[25] It suggested the Party's control over the military as well as its domination of society. In its infrequent conflicts with the military the Party would resort to violence and weed out the actual or imagined disloyal elements from the armed forces. The problem with this model was that its rigidity could not accommodate the apparent changes within Soviet-type societies and proved to be of little value when applied to Communist countries dominated by Moscow.

Further theoretical study of civil–military relations in the Communist context was encouraged by H. Gordon Skilling's and Franklyn Griffiths' work calling attention to interest groups in the Soviet-type political systems.[26] This approach posited that there were different degrees of pluralism in Communist polities although it did not clarify how this pluralism evolved.

Kolkowicz's pioneering work on Soviet civil–military relations began the long list of theoretical studies in this area.[27] His 'institutional/conflict' or 'interest group' model described the army and the Party as two major protagonists. Both institutions espoused separate value systems and acted as distinct institutional entities. The officer corps revered values such as heroism, obedience, duty, bravery and was an elitist body that cherished its societal exclusivity. In other words, it acted in many way as a special interest group.

The Party, on the other hand, resisted some of these aims and intended to control the military to the highest degree possible. There were a number of controls at the Party's disposal. Kolkowicz stressed the role of political officers in the armed forces and suggested that they constituted a foreign and hostile element within the military that was rejected by the regular officer corps.[28] Consequently, the relationship between Party and army was characterized by permanent and multifaceted conflict resulting in political instability, adverse effects on morale, and loss of military efficiency.

Kolkowicz's interest-group model was ably criticized by William Odom on several grounds.[29] Odom's 'institutional congruence' model depicted the party–army relationship as consensual, rather than conflictual.[30] He insisted that the Party and the military espoused like value systems upholding the virtues of ideological purity, belief in the vanguard role of the Party, socialist internationalism, etc. Odom dismissed the relevance of Kolkowicz's military professionalism variable and said that the relationship between efficiency and party control was not inverse. In contrast, he suggested, political officers at times might strengthen discipline, morale, and battle-readiness. The Soviet military was portrayed by Odom as a faithful executor of the Party's policies. Instead of Kolkowicz's stress on discord between the army and the Party, Odom posits that the conflict is intra-institutional (i.e., disagreements between the various segments of the armed forces) rather than inter-institutional. Furthermore, he questioned the relevance of the interest-group approach to Soviet politics in general and to the Soviet military in particular, because of the high level of homogeneity in Soviet society.[31] He argued that the Soviet military's political life was primarily bureaucratic in character. While personal cliques and coalitions of cliques took shape in bureaucracies, they differed generically from interest groups in so far as they could not formalize themselves and thereby institutionalize the pursuit of their interests.[32]

The institutional congruence model was critical of the interest group model's underestimation of the extent of interlocking between the military and the Party. It proposed that the relationship was essentially symbiotic, that the military was, first and foremost, a political institution. Odom suggested that in case of a civil war the marshals 'would reinvent the Party or one very similar'.[33] His analysis was based on an historical/institutional approach that held that civil–military relations in the Soviet Union were rooted in the tsarist traditions of civil–military relations. Odom underscored the Russian historical experience and stated that the CPSU essentially adopted the military's organizational ethos right from the outset. It followed from his argument that there was no alienation between the armed forces and the hegemonial Party.

A third approach, Colton's 'participatory' model, fell somewhere between the two previously examined approaches, stressing not party control over the military (as Kolkowicz did) nor a symbiotic party–army relationship (as did Odom) but saw the military's participation in politics as the main feature of Soviet civil–military relations.[34] He suggested that utilizing the concept of participation rather than that of interest groups afforded analytic flexibility, left open the extent to which military officers and civilians would take part in politics as aggregates, and brought more than one level of complexity to the analysis.

Colton also called attention to another element of interpenetration that was neglected by both Kolkowicz and Odom. He suggested that co-optation worked both ways. On the one hand, the Party had drawn armed forces personnel into important positions within the party hierarchy. On the other hand, military officers could and did co-opt the political officers whose function was to supervise them. Thus, Colton argued, the Party's control over the military was far less complete than either of the other models made us believe.[35]

For Colton, then, a broad range of interactions transpired among civil–military boundaries, involving individual, group, and institutional actors and occurring at different levels and in a variety of contexts.[36] Furthermore, interaction between the Party and the military was characterized not by conflict or consensus but by the interpenetration of the two institutions. Colton's model downplayed the notion of tension in the relationship for he doubted the severity of the control problem. The participatory model posited that the military was satisfied with the political role the Party allowed it to play: it took part in decision-making, in the adoption of internal and external political goals. Significantly, the Party also permitted the military to solve its internal problems, thereby enlarging the army's sense of responsibility. While the Party obviously did have the ability to intervene by force in political affairs, Colton stressed the fact that this potential was unused.

A comparative examination of these three major models of Soviet civil–military relations convinces us that while neither is omnipotent or capable of explaining all relevant phenomena, all three of them can contribute to our understanding of the subject. If we radically simplify the three approaches, we can boil them down to key words such as 'conflict', 'consensus', and 'participation' for Kolkowicz's, Odom's, and Colton's models, respectively. From such an artificial exercise the 'participatory model' emerges as the one having the greatest explanatory power, for it is flexible enough to accommodate the largest variations in civil–military relations of the three. Both of the other models are far more rigid and would be less capable of accounting for the volatility and fluctuation in the relationship.

When taken to the task of explaining actual behavior none of the models prove to be flawless.[37] For instance, Kolkowicz's model is especially static and would be hard pressed to explain the military's relatively passive political role in some periods (for instance, in the Stalin era) of Soviet history. Odom's 'institutional congruence' model neglects to stress the tension between the Party and the army and underestimates the growing political clout of the military-industrial complex. In addition, Odom seems to belittle the Party's very real and demonstrated fear of Bonapartism.

Clearly, the military was perceived by the party as the only social group capable of unseating the regime and thus the former expended a tremendous effort to maximize its control over the latter. (The East European revolutions of 1989 illustrated how flawed this perception was.) Many would take issue with his characterization of the military as 'first and foremost a political institution'.[38] While it would serve no purpose to doubt the important political role of the military as defender of the regime and trustee of the Party's revolutionary heritage, it could also be characterized by its professionalism or its important function to project Soviet power within and outside of the USSR's boundaries.

Colton's model, in turn, is of little assistance when it is applied to the task of interpreting the absence of more extensive and more intensive military participation in party politics. While he offers a detailed examination of the military's various opportunities to participate in political life, he fails to explain the relatively low level of army involvement in political processes. Furthermore, Colton's stress on the low-level military involvement in politics cannot explain the military's support of Khrushchev in 1957, and the Soviet army leadership's active participation in the coup against Gorbachev in 1991. In addition, his model, too, is unable to explain the realities of Soviet civil–military relationship in the Stalin era.

When contrasted with the recent developments in the Soviet Union, the explanatory power of some of these models seems further weakened. The developments in Soviet civil–military relations during the early 1990s would suggest that Kolkowicz's 'interest group' model would have more relevance than previously assumed. In the tumultuous political events of 1989–91 elements of the Soviet military leadership played an increasingly significant role. Some segments of the armed forces have become more outspoken and openly voiced their disagreements with the Kremlin. On the one hand, right-wing generals and officers (e.g., Colonels Petrushenko and Alksnis), became leaders of extra-party political organizations (such as 'Soyuz' that aimed to hold the USSR together), others (e.g., General Makashov) participated in state elections (e.g., in the presidential elections of Russia), and yet others (most prominently, of course, Defense Minister Yazov) actively participated in the August 1991 coup attempt. On the other hand, reformist generals and officers (e.g., General Volkogonov) became active in liberal political organizations such as 'Communists for Democracy' and 'For Democratic Reforms'. These activities suggest that at least some important military circles were neither in agreement with the party elite (as Odom hypothesized) nor participated in party politics.

Two additional recent phenomena appeared to support Kolkowicz's arguments. The withdrawal of Soviet troops from Eastern Europe created major socioeconomic problems within the Soviet armed forces. The returning soldiers and their dependents (numbering in the hundreds of thousands) face fundamental existential problems as their jobs may well be eliminated and there are no housing facilities to accommodate them. Not surprisingly, the military leadership expressed its displeasure concerning Gorbachev's 'losing of Eastern Europe'. Furthermore, the soldiers returning from Afghanistan (the so-called *Afgantsy*) formed their own organizations and have persistently called attention to the grave errors in Soviet foreign policy and military planning.

Although the authors made no claim for their models' universal applicability to all Communist systems, one would hope that the explanatory power of these approaches could accommodate non-Soviet Communist civil–military relations as well.[39] Nonetheless, if we try to utilize these constructs for analyzing other powerful Communist armies (i.e., the Chinese, Cuban, or Vietnamese) we run into serious difficulties for they are unable to accommodate the distinctive characteristics and many varieties in civil–military relations.[40] These approaches are even less useful for the interpretation of civil–military relations in the case of the East European states. To a large extent, the additional complexity of Party–army relationship in these states is a consequence of the Soviet domination of their polities and military establishments and their drastically different histories and politico-military cultures.

Part III Civil–Military Relations in Eastern Europe

Any discussion of Eastern Europe should begin with the customary admonition about the differences within the region and the distinctiveness of its constituent states. Furthermore, it is only appropriate to note that none of these states are 'Communist' any more, although the degrees of democratization in the individual political systems differ widely. Nonetheless, the bulk of this study examines the period in which these countries were members of the Communist or Soviet bloc. Their political and military systems shared enough similarities to justify at least a low level of generalization.

To begin with one important shared attribute, all of these political systems were established with the active or tacit support of the Soviet Army following World War II.[41] In fact, Soviet military presence[42] in and politico-military domination of these regimes explains to a large extent the differences between civil–military relations in Eastern Europe and in the USSR. The Soviet army was not only instrumental in the sometimes violent birth of these political systems but it also made sure that violations against the bloc's *modus operandi* would be short-lived and duly requited.[43]

The Soviet army played a major role in the transformation of the East European armies according to Moscow's desiderata. In fact, a few years after the Communist takeovers the region's military establishments became very similar to the Soviet army and to each other. While Soviet armed forces occupied the territory of the East European states, Soviet military personnel were deployed within the native army itself. Political officers penetrated the regular forces, resulting in the evolution of dual command structures.[44] Soviet equipment and even uniforms were introduced then standardized, large-scale participation of the armed forces in post-war reconstruction began: all these and many other factors evidently reflected Soviet design.

The Soviet Union subordinated the East European military establishments and attempted, less successfully, to integrate them not with each other but with the Soviet armed forces. The creation of the WTO in 1955 sought to institutionalize the structures and mechanisms of the Soviet–East European military alliance. Within the WTO several devices were employed to assure military integration between the fraternal armies: joint exercises, shared doctrinal concepts, consolidated political administrations, and an integrated system of officer education.[45] Nevertheless, some observers have suggested that in spite of the many outward signs, there was little *genuine* integration between the East European and the Soviet armed forces.[46]

The East European armies' subordination to and integration with the Soviet forces was designed to raise their level of commitment to Marxist-Leninist ideology and to the Soviet cause. There are reasons to believe, however, that subordination and integration did not achieve their goals. Although the occupation of East European countries by the Soviet army was a precondition of the establishment of Communist regimes in the region and served Moscow's strategic interests, the people were certainly opposed to it. At the same time, Soviet occupation suggested to the people of the region that Moscow did not consider the native armies sufficiently reliable to defend the regimes should the need arise. To be sure, the extent and methods of direct Soviet supervision showed significant changes over time. While Soviet 'advisers' and political officers deeply penetrated East European militaries (although to varying degrees) until the late 1950s, from the 1960s Soviet interference adopted less obtrusive instruments and Soviet personnel were stationed only at and above division command level.[47]

Soviet domination of the East European armed forces deprived the latter of their national identities. Soldiers were expected to be loyal first and foremost to the Soviet-controlled Warsaw Pact and only then to the party–state. Threat perception was fashioned on Soviet/Communist desiderata and had little in common with national identity or historical experience. In short, Moscow's goal was to prevent the evolution of truly national armed forces in the region. In some states (e.g., Poland) a clear potential existed for civil–military conflict as subservience to Soviet interest separated the national military traditions from party policy.

Although the relationship between the ruling parties and the armed forces in the region was close – after all in want of legitimizing mechanisms, such as democratic elections, the Party had to rely to some extent on the military's support – there was a crucial difference between the Soviet and the East European systems in this respect. While in the Soviet case the ultimate guarantor of the regime's survival was the Soviet army, the East European militaries were far from being free from external domination; indeed, the East European parties and their leaders themselves were dependent on the Kremlin's goodwill. Consequently, East European regimes were not reliant on the benevolence of their respective military establishments to the degree we have seen in the Soviet example, because in a worst-case scenario the regime's last line of defense was not its own army but that of the Soviet Union. As a result, the typical East European military's intraparty role was of significantly lower profile than in the cases of the Soviet Union or other Communist countries (Romania's army after 1958 was a deviation within the WTO) where the military was not subordinated to an external force.[48] An important exception to this rule is, of course, the intensive political involvement of the Polish military establishment in the 1980s. Still, it is fair to say that aside from a few departures from the rule, the military was not a significant actor in East European politics.

Similarly to the Soviet case, one of the dominant methods through which East European ruling parties sought to ascertain the loyalty of their armed forces was political indoctrination. Military education was already introduced at the grade school level and extended to university education. Political indoctrination was more intensive in educational institutions operated by the military. From all of the East European states a selected group of officers and officer candidates were educated in Soviet military institutions of higher learning where, besides the acquisition of professional skills, students acquired a great deal of politico-ideological training. Socialization of values is a time-consuming process, however, and is exceedingly difficult when contrary agents of socialization abound. But it may be profitably argued, as did Ivan Volgyes, that party elites did not really care whether the members of the armed forces were sufficiently inculcated with the 'necessary' values. 'In fact,' he wrote, 'the possession of certain minimal non-Communist values that are not contradictory to the military desiderata seem to be far more important than the generalized inculcation of "Communist values".'[49] Clearly, the Party had a vested interest in making a serious attempt to inculcate the army with Communist values. On the one hand, the successful control of the armed forces could afford a measure of legitimacy from and approval by the Kremlin leaders, on whom the survival of the regime ultimately depended. On the other hand, the inculcation of the military with Communist values decreased the chances of civil–military conflict and made the regime less reliant on Moscow's benevolence.

Civil–military relationships were frequently strained in the region because the armed forces had to discharge socioeconomic functions they were reluctant to shoulder. In Eastern Europe conscripted soldiers routinely spent a considerable part of their service period with agricultural and industrial labor. The armed forces were evidently displeased with their image as the 'last resort labor pool'.[50] In addition, some of the region's armies were also bothered by the quality and quantity of equipment and weaponry at their disposal. In fact, party–army relations in some states of Eastern Europe were strained by the parties' reluctance to expand military budgets in the face of worsening economic crises.

Notwithstanding the fact that the degree of the army's intraparty involvement in the case of East European polities was less obtrusive than in the Soviet Union, civil–military relations in the NSWP were far closer than one would find in pluralist party systems.[51] The pattern of high level elite integration, known from the Soviet example, was also an attribute of East European civil–military relations, although again, to a lesser degree. Through the years, East European regimes attempted to insure the loyalty of the (professional component of the) armed forces with material benefits and granting the military occupation high professional status. Ross Johnson argued that the development of military professionalism in NSWP armed forces adversely affected civil–military relations in the region. He suggested that the newly professionalizing military began to act more as an interest group in the 1960s and thus the models adumbrated by Kolkowicz and even Colton were more applicable to them than Odom's.[52]

Assessing the record of four decades of East European 'communism', one arrives at the conclusion that the Party's attempt was far from being an unqualified success. Civil–military relations were not always consensual, and in conflict situations the military often sided not with the Party, but with the popular revolts it was supposed to quell.[53]

There are many more studies dealing with the former Soviet and Chinese than with East European party–army relations. Nonetheless, several theoretical attempts were made in the last two decades to explain the differences of civil–military relations between the Soviet Union and Eastern Europe. As we have seen in the case of models pertaining to Soviet civil–military relations, none of them can account for the varieties and differences of such relations in East European Communist systems; each of them, however, can contribute much to our knowledge.

Perhaps the best known of the 'East European' approaches is the work of Dale Herspring and Ivan Volgyes which stressed the applicability of the notions of political socialization and political culture to understanding civil–military relations in the region.[54] They emphasized the Party's political control over the military and the significant role political officers and the MPAs were allowed to play in this relationship. The model focused on the dynamic nature of the relationship and suggested that there were three important periods in civil–military relations that were sufficiently different to merit separate case studies. These three phases were 'transformation', 'consolidation', and 'system-maintenance'.

In essence, when the Communists came to power they were not supported by military organizations of unquestioned loyalty and their subsequent rectification efforts proceeded in three stages. In the transformation phase the aim of the Party's political apparatus was to neutralize overt hostility toward the political system in the army but commitment to Marxist–Leninist ideals was not yet crucial. In the consolidation phase the supervisory and control functions of the political officers intensified and there was a great deal of pressure on professional military cadres to internalize the Party's value system. Finally, in the system-maintenance period the military supposedly had already espoused Communist dogmas, therefore the political leadership's concern regarding further politicization had diminished and its aims were to preserve the existing situation and to raise the intellectual–professional standing of career military cadres.

The utility of this approach lay mainly in its accentuation of the forces of political socialization and stress on change through time. Still, this model assumed greater commonality among Communist states than existed and at the same time suffered from too much specificity. Its usefulness for the study of civil–military relations in the region as a whole was more limited as its contentions were not sustainable in broad comparative terms. In addition, as Herspring acknowledged, it had little relevance outside of the East European realm.

Another approach, proposed by Alexander Alexiev, 'conceived of party-military interaction in Eastern Europe as proceeding through the stages of conflict, accommodation, and participation, leading ultimately to a symbiotic relationship'.[55] He believed that while East European military establishments were able to preserve their national orientation, the region's parties remained subordinated to the Soviet Union. The domination of East European parties, in turn, affected their armed forces in the following ways: (1) subordination to the Soviet military and denial of the nation-state function; (2) diminished political role and clout; (3) divergent perceptions of national versus ideological desiderata. Alexiev enumerated these desiderata which, as he readily admitted, resulted in an 'ideal typology which is unlikely to occur in a real-life situation'. Again, while his typology can inform our study of the subject, it is by no means a satisfactory explanation of civil–military relations in all East European states. More specifically, for instance, it cannot account for the continuing subordination of East European armies in the alliance structure following the WTO's 1968–69 reorganization neither can it explicate the reasons for the absence of separate 'national-supranational' interest perceptions in cases such as Bulgaria or Czechoslovakia.

Jonathan Adelman's 'historical developmental model' deserves similar praise and criticism.[56] He suggested that the decisive factors in determining the nature of civil–military relations in the region were the nature of revolutionary development and the extent of external Soviet interference. He called attention to the existence of three major patterns in civil–military relations of the region: (1) powerful political role for the military connected with the nature of the revolutionary path to power (China, Vietnam, Yugoslavia); (2) minimal political influence (Eastern Europe); and (3) minimal but significantly increasing political role (Soviet Union). Although in the analysis that followed there was much to recommend Adelman's work, his theoretical construct fell short of reaching reasonable expectations of adaptability.[57] His most significant contribution lay perhaps in directing our focus to the analysis of the initial (post-takeover) period of civil–military relations in the region.

None of the models discussed could anticipate, much less explain the collapse of party–military relationship that characterized the NSWP states during the revolutions of 1989. Even in the most extreme case (i.e., Romania) the army quickly turned its back on Ceauşescu's Communist party and sided with the democratic forces.

Conclusion

Although the Party and the armed forces shared an essentially interdependent relationship in the Soviet Union, in Eastern Europe the case was more complex. In the USSR, the armed forces appear to have played a far more important political role than they have in Eastern Europe. It is noteworthy that at the time when the Soviet Army's political prestige and economic well being became threatened – as the events of the last few years demonstrated – the Red Army's leadership started increasingly to act as an interest group. Clearly, to a certain degree the East European parties and armies also relied on each other, but the ultimate guarantor of the East European Party's survival was not its army (as in the case of the Soviet Union) but Moscow.

When the preservation of these regimes was no longer a priority of Soviet policy toward the region, then these regimes could expect little assistance from the military in times of trouble. One could scarcely illustrate this point better than with the revolution of 1989 which demonstrated that the armies retained their national orientations and, more often than not, embraced their new role as the defenders of the democratic nation-state. In the new Eastern Europe one can already see the contours of civil–military relations that approximate those of Western democracies. Notwithstanding local disparities, the armed forces of the region are already subordinated to freely elected heads of state.

Scholarly efforts at model building did not bring to desired results (i.e., empirically testable models) primarily because civil–military relations in the region's states and in different time periods were so dissimilar that they simply could not be done justice to by an overarching model that was sufficiently flexible to accommodate all variations.[58] The important issue here, however, is not whether a model can offer an all-encompassing explanation of a given phenomenon, but whether it can offer valuable insights in illuminating it. On this score, most of these approaches succeed. In the Conclusion, based on the lessons drawn from my examination of civil–military relations in Hungary and in the other East European states, I will attempt to state and evaluate the utility of a set of generalizations that are applicable to all of these systems.

2 The First Transition: Sovietization (1945–53)

Four decades of socialism radically transformed Hungary's socio-political and economic systems. As in these areas, the most significant changes in civil–military relations occurred as a result of two comprehensive transformation processes. The first took place in the 1948–53 period, when the primary role of the armed forces shifted from the defense of the nation-state to the protection of the Communist regime. By the late 1940s Hungarian Communists were the undisputed domestic masters of the national armed forces. The second transformation, discussed in Chapter 5, was an inverse process. With the demise of Communism in 1989–90, the Communist Party's control over the military gradually weakened and in time evaporated altogether.

The main argument of this chapter is that Hungarian Communists established their firm control over the military establishment well before Stalin's death. The new regime was clearly illegitimate and Hungary's satellite status in the Soviet orbit further endangered any prospects of legitimacy. Therefore, the party–state had to supervise the armed forces closely to be able to rely on it to execute its internal-defensive function. At the same time, Hungarian military policy showed total subservience to Soviet policies and desires. This notion was reflected in all areas of Hungarian military policy and civil–military relations: variegated party control over the armed forces; doctrinal considerations; developments in manpower, expenditure, and equipment planning; etc.

This chapter examines the evolution of the Hungarian armed forces between 1945–53 and its relationship with the country's polity and society. I begin with a brief overview of the political developments of this period stressing Soviet interference in Hungarian affairs. Second, I analyze the evolution of the Hungarian armed forces and civil–military relations during these years. Finally, I turn my attention to Moscow's influence in the Hungarian military establishment and, more specifically, in civil–military relations.

Part I   Political Developments

Several authors have studied Hungary's post-World War II political history and some of the resulting books provide excellent comprehensive accounts of the subject.[1] My aim here is merely to summarize the most consequential socio-political developments of the years of coalition (1945–48) and of totalitarian dictatorship (1948–53).

The last year of the war witnessed the degeneration of Admiral Miklos Horthy's authoritarian regime into the unbridled terror of Ferenc Szalasi's fascist Arrow Cross party. The Soviet army that started to pour into the country in September 1944 *did* liberate Hungary from the Nazis and the menace of Hungarian fascism. It is equally true that despite the fact that 140,000 Soviet soldiers died freeing the country, the USSR made sure it exacted whatever it could from war-ravaged Hungary.[2]

Similarly to the other Communist parties of the region, at the end of the war the HCP was divided into two relatively isolated sections. The 'home' or 'native' Communists spent the interwar years in prisons or plotting – without notable results – against Horthy's regime which declared the HCP illegal in 1920. Membership estimates of the illegal party range from 70 or 80 to less than 3,000;[3] in any event, the movement was rather weak. During the same period the 'Muscovites' gained useful experience – that is, if they managed to survive the purges that decimated not only the ranks of Soviet but also those of foreign Communists – serving in the Soviet party and government bureaucracies, the Soviet armed forces, the NKVD, or in the Comintern. Although often ill-informed about the actual socio-political and economic conditions of Hungary, when the Muscovites returned to the country on the wings of the Soviet forces they were already in a dominant position over the home Communists for they, and not the natives, enjoyed the confidence of the Soviet leadership. From the outset, Muscovite Communists were the ones (Matyas Rakosi, Erno Gero, Mihaly Farkas, Jozsef Revai, Imre Nagy, etc.) who were to determine Hungary's fate until the Revolution of 1956.[4]

The German army still occupied much of Hungary's territory when the provisional National Assembly held its first meeting in the eastern city of Debrecen, already liberated by the Red Army. Of the 320 deputies only 32 belonged to the Communist party. The first (and, until 1990, the only free) post-war general elections were conducted in November 1945. The Communists received a mere 16.9 percent of the vote, gaining 70 of the 409 seats in the National Assembly. Over 57 percent of the voters cast their ballots for the Independent Smallholders' Party (ISP) and the Social Democrats (SDP) with 17.4 percent also fared better at the polls than the HCP, the only beneficiary of Soviet support.

Hungary's sovietization was far more gradual than that of the other East European states with the exception of Czechoslovakia. For a variety of reasons – which included foreign policy considerations, Hungary's relatively small strategic importance (especially with the Soviet Army occupying a large part of Austria), and even lesser economic or military weight, let alone the anti-Soviet sentiments of the population and the initial weakness of the Hungarian Communists – Moscow, at least for the time being, elected to take the slow route to political power in the country. To be sure, some signs of the times to come were already perceptible but not yet obvious.

Even in the 1945–48 coalition period the HCP made sure that its leaders held the government positions (ministerships of interior, transportation, welfare) crucial for its design on political power. Defense at the time was not an influential portfolio given Hungary's minimal military capability and the expected future restrictions to be imposed by the Paris Peace Treaty.[5] In addition, the HCP ensured that such popular policies as the distribution of land among the peasantry be associated with the Communists. In March 1946 the HCP initiated the creation of the 'Left-Wing Bloc' (consisting of the SDP, the National Peasant Party [NPP], and the Council of Trade Unions) in order to isolate and discredit the ISP, by far the strongest political organization. The 1947 general elections concluded with the victory of the Left-Wing Bloc (receiving altogether 60.8 percent of the vote) within which Marxist parties – aided by every imaginable kind of electoral fraud – gained 45.4 percent of the votes.[6] In spite of its unscrupulous electoral campaign methods the HCP received only 22 percent of the vote.

Nonetheless, by late 1947 it appeared clear that the HCP would not be satisfied with its role as one of the parties. At the founding meeting of the Cominform Stalin unambiguously signalled to the international Communist movement – and, more specifically, to the Czechoslovak and Hungarian Communists – a drastic turn from the 'popular front' strategy and gradualism to leftist militancy, in order to eradicate the 'incipient diversity in international communism'.[7] The HCP was ready to seize power. In June 1948 the two major leftist parties, the HCP and the SDP united to form the Hungarian Workers' Party (HWP). The SDP had little say in the matter as its right wing lost control of the party and the left wing SDP leaders enthusiastically supported the merger.

In 1948 the splintered opposition parties were either disbanded outright or absorbed into the People's Independence Front, a new political umbrella organization. In the May 1949 elections the Front received over 95 percent of the votes. On August 20, a new constitution – fashioned on the 1936 Soviet constitution – was adopted, which codified the Communist party's leading role in society and sought to legitimize the political transformation of Hungary. As Bennett Kovrig wrote, 'Aided and abetted by the Soviet Union, and through skillful destruction of the opposition forces, a handful of Communists had succeeded in acquiring dictatorial power.'[8] Corresponding to these developments was the rapid increase in the membership of the HCP reaching over half a million by October 1945.[9] Following the HCP/SDP merger, the HWP's membership was well over a million, that is, more than 12 percent of the total population.[10]

During the coalition phase all major industrial enterprises and financial institutions were nationalized. Economic hardships were exacerbated by the huge reparation payments imposed by the Soviet Union. In addition the equipment of entire plants was confiscated by the Soviets without being factored into the reparation payments. In the 1945–46 period almost 90 percent of heavy industrial production was allocated as reparations to the Soviet Union.[11] The detention and subsequent deportation of Hungarian nationals to remote parts of the USSR began on the first day Soviet troops entered Hungarian territory. The Soviet authorities deported approximately 700,000 people from Hungary (according to its 1944 borders); 150,000–160,000 of these men and women died while in Soviet captivity.[12] In 1949 the entire school system was nationalized together with the last remnants of free enterprise, forced collectivization of the agricultural sector began together with the anti-clerical propaganda campaign which culminated in the trial of Cardinal Jozsef Mindszenty.

Purges, show trials, and mass persecution were prominent features of Hungarian totalitarianism. In fact, the first violent purge in the Soviet bloc took place in Hungary with the accusation that Politburo member and Interior Minister Laszlo Rajk was an employee of Allen Dulles' CIA *and* the Yugoslav secret police. The scope and methods of purges appear to have been more comprehensive in Hungary than elsewhere in the region. Leaders of the defunct parties as well as those of the HWP were persecuted, along with tens of thousands of 'bourgeois elements', prosperous peasants, intellectuals, and ordinary citizens.[13] According to a reliable source, between 1952 and 1955 the State Security Office (*Allamvedelmi Hatosag* – AVH) investigated 1,136,434 individuals (over 10 percent of the total population) of whom 516,708 (45 percent) were sentenced.[14] To ensure the 'purity' of the HWP the party conducted a 'membership control' campaign resulting in the expulsion of close to 180,000 members in 1948–49.[15]

In 1948–53 Hungary was ruled by HWP General Secretary Rakosi and his troika of Muscovite Communists: Gero, Revai, and Farkas, responsible for the economy, culture and propaganda, and defense respectively. The cult of personality surrounding Rakosi and his lieutenants was unparalleled in the region and further alienated the population from the regime. The leadership commenced the forced collectivization of agricultural lands in the summer of 1949 (taking back from the peasants what was given to them in 1945). The regime adopted the Soviet economic model, the applicability of which to Hungarian conditions was left unquestioned.[16] Giant facilities for the heavy industry were hurriedly constructed in a country devoid of natural resources, while areas of light industry were neglected. At the same time living standards showed a long-term tendency of decrease especially after 1949. The First Five-Year Plan (1950–55) predicted a 50 percent increase of living standards but realized a 20 percent drop instead.[17] Cultural life adopted the Soviet-sponsored style of socialist realism; other artistic expressions were not tolerated. Faced with the realities of a state built on oppression and terror and isolated from the outside world, Hungarian society became apathetic.

Even though Moscow's subjugation of Hungary was gradual, the Soviet presence continued following 'liberation'. As the Soviet Ambassador to Budapest during the takeover period, Georgi M. Pushkin, once remarked, 'We have shed our blood for Hungary and we do not want to loosen our grip on her.'[18] Under the terms of the armistice Hungary was to be supervised by an Allied Control Commission (ACC) until the Peace Treaty was put into force. Dominated by its Chairman, Marshal Kliment Voroshilov and his deputy, Lieutenant-General V. P. Sviridov – the ACC was essentially a Soviet institution that acted in the name of the Soviet High Command.[19] Soviet members of the ACC were subordinated to the Soviet Ministry of Foreign Affairs and the Central Committee of the CPSU for policy, and to the Soviet Ministry of Defense for intelligence and security.[20] Although Moscow made sure that Hungarian developments followed the Kremlin's blueprint, direct Soviet intervention in the political process was relatively scarce.

During 1945–47 the HCP operated as 'a disguised branch of the Soviet administration' relying entirely on Soviet support, as the Communist leader Jozsef Revai admitted.[21] In Stalin's lifetime, leaders of each section of the HCP's Secretariat conferred directly with their Soviet counterparts who were, in fact, their superiors.[22] In Moscow's chain of command Soviet Embassy staff played an important part. Ambassadors regularly consulted with members of the HCP Central Committee. Embassy officials frequently 'visited' Budapest's Ministry of Foreign Affairs, which was relatively free of Soviet advisers.

Part II   Civil–Military Relations

Between 1945 and 1953 a spectacular transformation took place in Hungarian civil–military relations. Until 1945, it was the Hungarian government of the day that controlled the armed forces. The army's involvement in politics was officially discouraged although, because of the weakness of the political elite and the increasing clout of the war-time military lobby, at times some army leaders played considerable political roles. Following the war, and particularly after 1948, the army's role changed from that of the defender of the nation-state to that of protector and guarantor of the continued domination of the Communist party.

A.   The Pre-1945 Hungarian Armed Forces

Before examining the post-World War II Hungarian military and its role in the polity it is useful to say a few words about the army's role in earlier eras. The prestige and respect Hungarian society had afforded its military had not been in proportion to the latter's performance. In fact, while Hungarians participated in more than their fair share of armed conflicts during the last 500 years, the military came out as the defeated party from nearly all of them. The Hungarian perception of history, however, is not centered around the armed forces' actual record but is directed primarily at the ability of Hungarians to survive amidst the most adverse circumstances. Thus the blame for the lost wars was never attached to the military by the population.[23]

The military profession had been held in high esteem in Hungary until the first half of the nineteenth century, although its prestige had never equalled that in Austria or Prussia. Following the suppression of the 1848–49 War of Independence the occupation had lost much of its aura, for officers came to be regarded as supporters of the loathed Habsburg occupation.[24] The military was not to recover its lost prestige until well after the 1867 'Compromise' (or *Ausgleich*) between Austria and Hungary that paved the road to the creation of the Austro-Hungarian Monarchy. By the 1890s the profession regained its relatively high prestige and reputation.[25] The remuneration of professional soldiers, especially that of senior officers, had improved to a point where – at the turn of the century – it was equal to or somewhat better than that of civil servants with comparable length of service.[26]

Hungarian media and popular opinion enthusiastically supported World War I in its initial stages. The war was promised to be short and Hungarians looked forward to a resounding military victory at last. Under the circumstances the performance of the Hungarian troops was adequate; the officer corps earned especially high marks for bravery and valor.[27] The Peace Treaty at Trianon (June 4, 1920) put the entire population in a long lasting shock and inflicted wounds yet to be healed: Hungary lost 67.3 percent of its territory and 58.4 percent of its prewar population.[28] 'Trianon', as Hungarians still bitterly refer to *the* national tragedy, imposed severe limitations on the post-World War Hungarian military. The size of the armed forces was restricted to a maximum of 35,000 men, in which the ratio of officers could not exceed one-twentieth (1,750) and that of non-commissioned officers one-fifteenth (2,333).[29]

Given the austere judgement at Trianon, it is hardly surprising that the major goal of Hungary's inter-war policy was to achieve a redress of the conditions imposed. Admiral Horthy's regime that followed the ill-fated and brief dictatorship of Hungarian Communists in 1919, singled out Romania as the country's chief adversary, but Budapest also had territorial claims on Czechoslovakia and Yugoslavia. Not unexpectedly, the states affected by Hungary's thinly veiled irredentist designs formed an alliance, the 'Little Entente', to counter them. By the end of the decade Hungary ascertained that neither England nor France could be expected to rectify the territorial issues and Horthy turned to more sympathetic ears in Rome and Berlin.

In spite of major loans secured from Italy in the late 1920s, the conception of a well-equipped elite army that some politicians and most military leaders found desirable could not but remain a utopia given Hungary's unstable economy and geo-political conditions. At the same time, the officer corps itself represented a major problem for the government. Although the profession retained much of its prestige following the war, its material conditions had drastically deteriorated. A large cleavage developed between the high-profile social lifestyle officers were expected to lead and their severely limited income and earning potential.

The majority of officers welcomed the ascension of Gyula Gombos in the positions of State Secretary for Defense (1928), Minister of Defense (1929), and finally, Prime Minister (1932–36).[30] Gombos, a man of unharnessed political ambitions, was a former officer himself who needed the support of the armed forces. His policies were unabashedly pro-Italian and pro-German and in time he came to disregard even Horthy's directives.[31] Gombos's promises of improved working and material conditions for the army notwithstanding, the military's lot further declined until 1933.[32] Some encouraging signs became apparent by the late 1930s but the volatile state of the economy simply did not permit the realization of the Prime Minister's grandiose plans.[33]

Hungary supported Hitler's East European scheme although Budapest was not eager to underscore its territorial claims with tangible military commitment. The Führer insisted, however, that territorial gains would not come without Hungarian participation in the German campaign in the region.[34] From 1938, the limitations imposed on the size and equipment of the Hungarian forces were disregarded. Hungary participated in the Nazi occupation of Czechoslovakia (1938, taking the predominantly Hungarian-populated areas of Southern Slovakia) and the campaign against Yugoslavia (1941, regaining the Vojvodina). The most appreciated territorial concession Budapest received from German hands was Western Transylvania in 1940. The initial successes of the *Wehrmacht* in Western Europe and the territorial revisions made a profound impression on the Hungarian military establishment and further encouraged close alliance with Germany.

At the same time, Hitler was not easily satisfied with Hungary's military commitment in the war and demanded more Hungarian troops in his war with the Soviet Union.[35] Hungary's actual military involvement in the anti-Soviet campaign was fostered not least by the machinations of Prime Minister Bardossy and some elements of the top military leadership.[36] Clearly, Hungary's military significance in the war was rather limited. In July 1941 Budapest sent approximately 30,000 troops to the Eastern Front, of which Hitler permitted part to be sent home in October.[37] But as the war progressed and the Germans experienced more and more trouble, Hungary had to send large contingents to the Soviet Union. The poorly-equipped Hungarian troops suffered crushing defeats at the hands of the numerically superior and better-equipped Red Army, most prominently during the winter of 1942–43 near the River Don at Voronezh, where 200,000 Hungarians perished as the Second Army was practically annihilated.[38] Notwithstanding such defeats, widespread popular support for the termination of Hungary's war participation was not demonstrated until late 1944. The lives of most people remained largely unaffected until March 19, 1944, when Hitler decided to occupy the country whose leadership started to display signs of uncertainty about the alliance.[39] In October 1944 Horthy's regime fell victim to the short-lived Fascist rule of Szalasi and his Arrow Cross Party.[40]

In the civil–military relations of the 1919–45 period there is a pronounced duality between theory and practice, between desired and manifested behavior. Horthy's regime strongly discouraged the military's participation in politics. The army's Code of Service asserted that members of the military 'should not participate in any capacity in political organizations of any sort'. The most important criteria for the soldier's conduct were to be 'a true Hungarian; an indomitable fighter for the Hungarian national ideal; a strong, Hungarian man who is a soldier and a gentleman, free from the concerns of daily politics'.[41]

In spite of its preference for no military involvement in politics, the regime itself sent out mixed signals. At the military academies, for instance, instruction was decidedly nationalist, assigning the blame for Hungary's past and present misfortunes to the neighboring countries that benefited from the breakup of the Austro-Hungarian Monarchy. The rise of Gombos as a politician of note in the late 1920s further encouraged the politicization of the military. In an influential speech given in 1929 by his Chief-of-Staff, General Vilmos Roder, the demand for the 'closest possible cooperation between the political and military leadership for the sake of foreign policy goals' was voiced in no uncertain terms. Furthermore, Roder said, 'The political leadership must provide the instruments necessary for the realization [of these goals] while the military leadership must emphatically communicate to the politicians what the armed forces are capable of under the given circumstances.[42]

Prime Minister Count Pal Teleki, one of the few exemplary politicians of the interwar period, attempted to call Horthy's attention to the political involvement of the military elite: 'Impress upon them [the soldiers] that they should not be involved in politics', he wrote in a personal letter to Horthy.[43] Shortly before committing suicide in 1940, Teleki, in another letter to the Regent, wrote that 'Probably I am not suitable for my position because I let the soldiers dominate me.'[44] Notwithstanding the distinct political role of the military in this period, one must allow that peace seemed only to be a transition period after which the war that was expected to remedy the injustice suffered at the Paris Peace Treaty was to follow. It is by no means certain that Horthy or any other head of state would have let the military 'get away with' its prominent political role in a different historical period. The given political situation and Hungary's post-Trianon predicament provided the circumstances for the political exploits of characters such as Gombos.

As a result of the rearmament program and the meteoric rise of some politicians sympathetic to the needs of the armed forces, the prestige and social status of officers had grown by the mid-1930s. The reacquisition of more than half of the territories lost at Trianon endeared the population to the military. The interest of young men in the forces increased, consequently military schools could enrol the best and brightest the country had to offer. The remuneration of officers improved significantly: in the early 1940s the starting salary of a lieutenant was three to four times that of a teacher or skilled worker.[45] The military's relatively high social status evaporated even faster than it came. By the end of the war the armed forces were plagued by severe disciplinary problems and by large-scale defections. As far as the general population was concerned, the military ignominiously lost the war, could not prevent hostile powers from occupying Hungarian lands, and lost the territories Hitler had given back to the country.[46]

B. The Military in the Last Stages of the War and the Creation of the New Army

To say that the army totally disintegrated by the end of the war would be an exaggeration, but it is safe to posit that morale was at an all-time low and many units simply evaporated. In spite of the Arrow Cross party's December 1944 decree which authorized commanders to execute deserters without due hearing, by February 1945 200,000 of them were registered.[47] A large part of the army remained loyal to the Wehrmacht, however, and retreated with German units to Bavaria and to more remote parts of Germany. Some Hungarian units finished the war in such faraway places as northern and western Germany and Denmark, and fought against the Red Army in Poland (Stettin, Breslau) as well.[48] A significant proportion of these troops (especially their officers) chose exile instead of returning to Hungary. Many of those who did not, became prisoners of war and spent several years in forced labor camps in the Soviet Union.[49]

Other units surrendered to the Red Army and continued the war on the Soviet side. In fact, some Hungarian troops fought for the liberation of Czechoslovakia and earned the right to participate in the victory parade in Prague on May 10, 1945.[50] In addition, a few partisan groups were organized in the Soviet Union from Hungarian prisoners of war as early as 1943. Most of these units were trained in Kiev by Hungarian Muscovite Communists, among them Zoltan Vas. Their preparation was light on substantive concerns of warfare and emphasized Marxist ideology and loyalty to the Soviet Union instead.[51] Even according to Communist sources the number of Hungarian partisans could not exceed 1,200, but it is likely that the actual number was much smaller.[52] The most important resistance group that took part in the liberation of the country with the Soviet forces was the Volunteer Regiment of Buda.

On December 28, 1944 Hungary's Provisional Government declared war on Germany and a month later the armistice was signed between Hungary and the Allies in Moscow. The Hungarian side accepted responsibility to outfit and prepare eight divisions or approximately 140,000 soldiers for the fight against Germany. The pledge was far too unrealistic as Hungary had neither the material nor the human resources to make good on this commitment. In a short time, however, over 60,000 people volunteered to serve in the new army. The most visible recruiters were the local Communists who were instrumental in the organization of the partisan groups in the Soviet Union.[53] The ranks of the volunteers included 'partisans, people from the Hungarian resistance, internationalists who fought for Soviet Russia, the Hungarian Council Republic, and in the Spanish Civil War'.[54] Among them were also some of the military leaders of the 1970s and 1980s, including Karoly Csemi (Deputy Minister of Defense) and Istvan Olah (Minister).[55]

In January 1945 the government began the organization of four divisions in Debrecen, Szeged, Jaszbereny, and Miskolc. The leadership hoped that if these units could make a substantial contribution to the Soviet war effort, Hungary might receive less harsh judgement at the post-war peace conferences. Stalin obviously saw through these plans, however, and was not about to help in mitigating Hungary's real and imagined war crimes. In fact, General Janos Voros, the Minister of Defense of the Provisional Government, requested the permission of ACC Chairman Voroshilov to send the first Hungarian (Debrecen) division to the front in mid-March but never received an answer. The permission was finally given on April 7, 1945 by Stalin himself.[56]

It took the troops ten days to arrive at the front in Austria where they were subordinated to the Third Ukrainian Front under the command of Marshal Tolbukhin. The division was never deployed although it did discharge non-combat duties, such as securing railway lines.[57] Following the war most of the armed forces were disarmed save for a small contingent which performed border guard duties and assisted in the post-war reconstruction of railroad lines, roads, and bridges. At the same time, several mid-level agencies of the new armed forces (e.g., emergency units and administration) were swiftly organized.[58]

Part III   Military and Politics after Liberation

The Red Army held only about one third of Hungary's territory when the HCP began its aggressive campaign to dominate the military establishment. In an open letter published on October 28, 1944 the still illegal Communist Party called for the active support of the Soviet Army 'for the sake of our country and people'. Further, 'the organization of the army and its deployment [against the *Wehrmacht*] depends not on the officer corps but on the working class. Our most important aim is the creation of the joint battle front of the working class and the army . . . we must penetrate the barracks and gain the widest support within the military'.[59]

Ostensibly for this purpose, the party warned its members that they must enlist and aid the Soviet drive against the Germans.[60] By the end of January 1945 the HCP leadership prepared a document which called for the introduction of 'orientation officers' (*nevelotisztek*) into the armed forces.[61] The draft proposal pointed to the development of democratic attitudes in the armed forces as the main function of these officers. The new position was planned to be opened at all troop levels, down to companies. By the time of the HCP's Second Military Conference (June 2, 1946) the language referring to the by then instituted system became clearer: 'the task of the orientation officers is to make our soldiers the supporters and defenders of the people's republic; Communist orientation officers are obliged to further develop this spirit and make our best soldiers HCP members'.[62]

The HCP worked hard to achieve a dominant position in military affairs even before it seized power. The party was successful, for several reasons. The first is, of course, the tacit – and at times active – support it could draw from the Soviet forces in Hungary and from the Moscow leadership. Another significant factor contributing to the HCP's success was the inability of the other parties during the coalition phase to influence the development of the armed forces. To understand the reasons behind the HCP's rapidly evolving control over the armed forces, let us briefly examine the military policies of its two main rivals, the ISP and the SDP.

The ISP which won the 1945 election by a large margin could and would have formed its own government if it were not for the vociferous objection of ACC Chairman Marshal Voroshilov.[63] Although the ISP as the senior coalition partner gave the first four defense ministers, the party helplessly watched as the HCP gained control over the military. For the most part, the Smallholders' defense policy was quite ambiguous except for their strong opposition to the politicization of the armed forces.[64] The party recognized early that Communist policies were not only aiming at the democratization of the armed forces (to which the Smallholders did not object) but also to alienate the military establishment from the bourgeoisie and the affluent strata of the peasantry. In time, the ISP also recognized that its military policy was unsuccessful. The leadership admitted that in spite of its efforts – which, to be sure, remained rather limited – control over the armed forces was resting increasingly in the hands of its political adversaries.

In October 1946 the ISP's own Defense Committee (*Vedero Bizottsag*) reported to the party administration that 'by now all key positions in the military are occupied by Communists'.[65] Even though ISP politicians continued to hold defense ministerships until 1947 (Jeno Tombor,

Albert Bartha, Lajos Dinnyes), the party's leaders assessed the situation realistically. Clearly, then, due to the Soviet design on Hungary, the ISP's survival as a genuine political alternative could only be temporary. At the same time, the Smallholders' military policy was wanting in specifics and the implementation of its vaguely defined goals lacked direction and determination.

The Social Democrats fared better at the polls than the Communists but with the 1948 merger of the two parties the SDP became irrelevant. During and following liberation, the SDP led a propaganda campaign aiming at a dominant position in the post-war military. To some extent, the SDP's endeavors were not unlike those of the HCP. While the SDP also wanted a democratic army – although in its case 'democratic' approximated Western notions of the concept more closely – it was not against the politicization of the military. Partly because the SDP did not have the resources and the Soviet backing enjoyed by the HCP and partly because of its less aggressive campaign, the SDP was far less successful in acquiring a major role in military policy.

The SDP's defense policy included some original ideas, such as the creation of various groups within the armed forces concentrating on ideological training (*Kunfi garda*) and cultural education (*Petofi garda*). Its own National Defense Organization (*Orszagos Honvedelmi Szervezet*) attempted to realize these and other goals but was ineffective without the kind of financial and political support base the HCP could count on. Even so, until 1947, the SDP was able to exercise some influence on military affairs. The Quartermasters' Academy (*Hadbiztosi Akademia*) remained its major support base. The quartermaster corps' theoretical justification lay on the SDP's doctrine contending that war was unlikely to break out in the foreseeable future, therefore the armed forces' development should emphasize areas such as administration, supply, and services. The doctrine and the Academy itself perished with the independent SDP.

In any event, by 1947 SDP leaders resigned themselves to requesting more leniency and flexibility in various military matters from the HCP rather than pursuing their own agenda. To be sure, the SDP registered its dissatisfaction concerning the HCP's domineering position in the military on numerous occasions. For instance, a 1946 study by two SDP leaders disclosed that HCP cadres filled over 90 percent of the 'orientation officer' positions and called for the party's supporters to express more interest in the military profession to prevent the HCP's monopolization of the armed forces.[66] Nonetheless, for want of political prowess and strength, these manifestations of apparent discontent remained little more than signs of resignation that could be and were safely ignored by the HCP. To make matters worse, the SDP itself was irreparably split between left- (led by Arpad Szakasits and Gyorgy Marosan) and right-wing orientations (Anna Kethly, Imre Szelig). The fact that the gaps between the two groups could not be bridged between 1945 and 1948 made the SDP's fusion with the HCP all the more smoother.

Although the HCP became the uncontested ruler of the military only in 1948 – by the time almost 100 percent of career officers were HCP members[67] – it enjoyed a dominant position in the armed forces as early as 1945. During the coalition period the HCP held five National Military Conferences (*Orszagos Katonai Konferencia*) the main purpose of which was to provide guidance for the armed forces leadership on political, ideological, and organizational matters. The conferences themselves proved to be reliable points of reference regarding the HCP's increasing influence within the armed forces. At the first such conference (held in June 1945) the general domestic political situation was examined by such noted speakers as CC Secretary Janos Kadar. Conference reports stressed the necessity of enhanced political education of the officers and soldiers, and called on Communist party members to participate in the work of local party organizations.[68] The coalition parties agreed not to permit party organizations below the division level. They were only allowed to be organized in 1947 by which time the HCP's control of the military was firm.

At the second conference (June 2, 1946) the HCP could already celebrate an important victory. The major command positions in the armed forces were almost entirely in Communist hands including the Border Guards, the military's best-prepared component at the time. Thus, the HCP felt that it no longer had to fear potential opposition from the armed forces. The HCP's third National Military Conference (1947) did not bring radical changes into the civil–military relationship in stark contrast with the fourth and fifth conferences.

The fourth meeting (May 9–10, 1948) demonstrated a marked change from the relative neglect of the armed forces to accelerated modernization. Conference speakers recognized that until this time the military was the 'stepchild' of the party as the latter could not afford to devote the financial resources necessary for its modernization. Rakosi's words ('I hope that the organization of the democratic army will follow the tempo demanded by the rise of the Hungarian people') suggested that in the near future at least, the army would receive more than its share of state revenues. Even more importantly, at this conference Superintendent of the Armed Forces General Gyorgy Palffy announced that all party organizations – at the time coalition parties were still active and had the right to organize in the barracks – in the armed forces would be disbanded and replaced by the so-called Kossuth Circles (*Kossuth Korok*).[69] The Circles were supposed to ensure the continuous political, ideological and, to a much lesser extent, cultural development of military personnel. These groups were led by the Communist-dominated 'orientation officer' corps.

What was the motivation behind the abolition of the all-important party organizations and the introduction of Kossuth Circles? By the summer of 1948 the HCP could be certain that in a few months it would reach its goal of extending its monopoly to the entire political system. Since in the Kossuth Circles membership was mandatory for all armed forces personnel (i.e., even for the remaining non-Communists), their creation appeared to be a convenient way to terminate the direct involvement of all rival parties in the military. The organization of the Circles was started without delay. A National Center for the Kossuth Circles chaired by Palffy was hurriedly organized and work soon began on the troop level as well.

Notwithstanding the early praise Palffy received for his initiative, the Kossuth Circles were soon to perish, together with their creator. The first group of Soviet advisers terminated the Circles with the stroke of a pen providing useful pretext for the party and military elites to prosecute Palffy. At the Fifth HCP National Military Conference (November 13–14, 1948) Minister of Defense Farkas's speech marked the change in the party's involvement in the military. He said that 'certain comrades' could not understand the direction of the military's evolution. Furthermore, alluding to the performance of the orientation officers, Farkas strongly disapproved of the 'professorial objectivism' of educational work in the armed forces.[70] Faithful to Bolshevik tradition and correctly perceiving the danger that fell upon him, Palffy dutifully admitted his 'horrendous mistake' to abolish the HCP party organizations within the armed forces. But self-criticism could not help him for long as he was soon accused of sabotage and espionage for imperialist powers by the HCP leadership.

At the last meeting of orientation officers (November 1948) their work received strong criticism from party and military leaders. A few days later, on December 1, 1948, the MPA (*Politikai Focsoportfonokseg*), which was to oversee the political-ideological indoctrination of the armed forces, was created by ministerial decree. From its inception the MPA was one of the most important instruments of political control over the military. As its chief, the HCP appointed Sandor Nogradi, a trusted Muscovite Communist.[71] With the creation of the MPA the already faint line between the state and the party was erased for it was responsible as a party organization to the HCP command and as a military structure to the Ministry of Defense (MOD).[72]

The establishment of the MPA, then, represented organizational and qualitative changes from the system of orientation officers. The MPA was a massive bureaucracy that included several secretariats to supervise various aspects of political life within the armed forces. The MPA established a network of Marxism-Leninism evening courses to assure the 'ideological preparedness' of military cadres. Aside from publishing books of Marxist historical and sociological analyses, the MPA also organized reading/writing proficiency courses for illiterate soldiers and staged cultural events in the barracks. More importantly, the MPA issued guidelines and manuals which were to be followed to the letter by political officers.

The MPA's footsoldiers were the political officers, deployed at every organizational level down to the company. The role and function of political officers were duplicating those of the Red Army's commissars. From the regime's perspective their military expertise was far less important than their political reliability. Whereas orientation officers were subordinated to commanding officers in military matters (although not in areas concerning ideology and political affairs), with the introduction of political officers as co-commanders an important change took place. In the new dual-command system orders were invalid without the signature of the political officer; moreover, in cases of dispute his word not the commander's was decisive.[73] Generally, political officers did not limit their activities to the 'socialist internationalist' education of the armed forces' personnel and attempted to influence military decision-making frequently disrupting the army's routine. Not surprisingly, they aroused the spontaneous hatred of many career officers. Ill-feeling toward the commissars was especially widespread among air force officers, whose advanced training, small number, and elitist attitudes made them somewhat less vulnerable to political intrigue.[74]

In retrospect, it is fair to say that the introduction of the dual command system was counterproductive from the HCP's perspective. It fostered antagonism between career and political officers and had deleterious effects on military discipline and morale. At the same time, the notion of shared responsibility between the commander and his political officer bore undesirable results. By 1951, political officers often complained that they were held responsible for the errors of career officers who, while detesting the system of dual command, attempted to take advantage of it by putting the blame on the commissars whenever possible.[75] Nonetheless the system of dual command survived until January 20, 1953 – in the USSR it was already abolished during World War II – when the party and military leadership finally decided to lower the status of political officers by taking away their privilege to countersign orders.[76] Although it is often forgotten, at least theoretically religion could be practised in the armed forces, for until 1951 army chaplains were employed by the military.[77]

The system of orientation officers (abolished in February 1949) and the creation of the MPA were only the most visible aspects of the party's control over the military. To appreciate the comprehensive mechanism the HCP devised to control the armed forces let us briefly survey the most important institutions set up for this purpose during the 1945–53 period. Although members of the HCP's Military Committee (*Katonai Bizottsag*) were high-ranking officers, it was chaired by Mihaly Farkas and, in his absence, Janos Kadar, neither of whom had any military position at the time. Formed in 1946, the Committee sought to assemble all Communist cadres who held important positions within the armed forces. The Military Committee was responsible for the direct supervision of political work in the military.

The Military Committee was united with its counterpart in the sphere of police affairs – the Internal Affairs Committee (*Belugyi Bizottsag*) – and thus became the State Defense Committee (*Allamvedelmi Bizottsag*) under the chairmanship of Matyas Rakosi. This administrative change was decided by the HWP leadership and announced on Defense Minister Farkas' first day in the job, on September 10, 1948. According to the new minister, the Military Subcommittee, now subordinated to the State Defense Committee, was charged only with the task of preparing proposals in important military matters.[78] Thus, the scope of authority of the original Military Committee became much more limited. The State Defense Committee, together with its component parts, fell victim to the rigid sovietization of the armed forces and was abolished in February 1949.

The Defense Committee (*Honvedelmi Bizottsag*) was called to life at Soviet urging in November 1950, soon after the Korean War broke out.[79] Ostensibly, the reason for its creation was to coordinate the variegated defense tasks. The three-member Committee was composed of the most powerful politicians: Rakosi, his deputy Erno Gero, and Defense Minister Farkas. It was established without the expressed approval of the HWP's Central Leadership (CL – *Kozponti Vezetoseg*) and operated entirely in secret.[80] From 1948 until the death of Stalin all important political, economic, and military decisions were made by this threesome.[81]

Aside from these organizations, it is important to consider the party's control of the military on the personnel level as well. Several military leaders were also party functionaries. The best example is Mihaly Farkas who was the HCP leader responsible for the military even before he became Minister of Defense in 1948. Starting with the return of the Muscovite

Communists to Hungary in 1944, Farkas's political clout was immense, third only after Rakosi and Gero. He served as the HCP's Deputy General Secretary, and was a member of the Politburo as well as of the Orgburo. He was dropped from the latter body in 1951 although his exclusion did not mean that he fell out of Rakosi's favor, rather it signalled even more intensive involvement in military affairs on his part.[82] Several military leaders were also high party functionaries, including Nogradi, Istvan Bata, and Geza Revesz. More often than not, these individuals were Muscovite Communists, known to the Budapest and Moscow leaderships from the years they spent in the Soviet Union during the interwar period.

Another important aspect of civil–military relations in this period was the purges that had their effects felt in all other social groups as well. The military dimension of the phenomenon can be explained in several ways. First, an underground military organization was discovered in 1946 along with some genuine spies sharing information with Western powers.[83] Second, Defense Minister Farkas, ever the faithful executor of Soviet policies and careful not to fall behind the show trials orchestrated by the Ministry of Interior (MOI) and the AVH, probably wanted to assure the Soviets and the HCP leaders of his unfailing vigilance. Third, the anti-Yugoslav campaign had an important military component and therefore it was almost expected of the military to immolate its own sacrificial lambs on the altar of totalitarianism. Fourth, Farkas, a tyrant in his own right, wanted to eliminate army leaders who could have potentially threaten his position within the armed forces.

From early 1945 on, the HCP demanded the removal of officers from the military who served in Horthy's army. On December 1, 1945 Laszlo Rajk, speaking on the HCP's behalf in the National Assembly, said that 'a significant proportion of the officer corps was unreliable' and called for their replacement with cadres of peasant and worker origin.[84] To facilitate this process, special committees were set up to investigate the professional and political records of officers. Many of them did not choose to subject themselves to the process, but of those who did 27 percent (29) of the generals and 22 percent (1838) of the officers were found to have blemishes in their backgrounds that ruled out their employment in the new army.[85] (Even before the verification committees began to work, hundreds of officers were executed or given stiff prison sentences as war criminals.)[86] In January 1946 the HCP and the SDP agreed on the expulsion of 10,000–12,000 officers from the armed forces and charged the Political State Secretary for Defense, Vilmos Zentai, to oversee the execution of the plan. The subsequent process, called 'B-listing', eliminated thousands of officers from the armed forces. Ironically, after the rearmament campaign began in late 1948, many 'B-listed' officers were recalled to fill up the military. This move was justified with reference to Lenin's own invitation to tsarist officers to aid the Bolshevik effort in the Civil War.[87] Once the HCP produced its own officers most of the recalled cadres were again dismissed.

In 1947 a small underground group of anti-Communist military officers – seeking to halt Communist influence in the armed forces – was discovered by the MOI and the Military Political Department (MPD – *Katonapolitikai Osztaly*) of the MOD. The aim of this group, led by General Lajos Veres and his 'Underground General Staff', was to prevent the further communization of the armed forces and the creation of a genuinely democratic government.[88] The subsequent investigation revealed that Veres' group had strong ties with the right-wing of the ISP and thereby provided a further pretext for a campaign against the Smallholders. In 1945–53 scores of actual espionage cases were discovered by army authorities. As a general rule, the unveiled operatives were in the employ of emigre organizations connected to Western intelligence services.

The initial purge in the military was organized by the MPD under the able guidance of General Palffy.[89] The MPD was charged with the tasks of military counter-intelligence, the uncovering and prosecution of anti-regime activities, and the maintenance of high morale within the armed forces.[90] Palffy, who was also the Commander of the Border Guards and became the Inspector of the armed forces in 1947, ruled the MPD with an iron hand. Following the arrest of Veres's underground group, Palffy had 93 individuals executed or imprisoned without court procedure. When Defense Minister Bartha was informed about Palffy's arbitrary action and wanted to hold his subordinate responsible, Marshal Voroshilov quickly placed the MPD under ACC supervision and thus prevented any action against Palffy.[91]

One familiar with the political history of the period is not surprised that Palffy himself was soon sent to the gallows. The 'reasons' were his enthusiastic support for the introduction of the Kossuth Circles and his ambitions to become the chief of the armed forces, which probably made the newly-appointed Defense Minister uncomfortable. Following Palffy's execution in early 1949 the purges did not stop in the military. In 1950 Farkas's agents 'discovered' yet another Titoist conspiracy; the culprits this time were the military leaders who were Palffy's rivals a few months before. Those arrested, executed, or imprisoned included Chief of the General Staff General Laszlo Solyom; General Gusztav Illy, the recently retired Deputy Inspector of the Armed Forces; the national commanders of the infantry and armored units, and many other top military leaders.

In addition to being Titoist spies, some of the generals were accused of sabotaging the military's development in reference to Solyom's and others' disagreement with the Soviet-inspired decision to construct a huge fortification system near the Yugoslav border.[92] Between 1949 and 1950 twelve generals and 1,100 high-ranking officers were removed from the armed forces as a consequence of the purges which affected lower-ranked military cadres as well.[93] Military courts sentenced approximately 10,000 individuals in 1951, 6,500 in 1952, and 4,600 and 1953.[94]

Part IV   Military Education and Soviet Interference

The evolution of the post-war armed forces – its manpower, equipment, educational system, etc. – reflected the gradual expansion of Communist domination over the military. Military developments were profoundly affected not only by the HWP's control but also by direct and indirect Soviet interference in Hungarian domestic affairs. This section deals primarily with factors that influenced civil–military relations the most profoundly: education, prestige, and Soviet interference.

A.   Education, Training, and Prestige

In 1945– 48, when the military was not one of the HCP's investment priorities the most important military education institutions were the orientation officer schools staffed largely by HCP-member instructors. Initially, the courses were relatively brief and provided only the fundamentals of political indoctrination techniques. The first of these was organized by the HCP and held between March 15– 30, 1945.[95] Institutionalized orientation officer training began only in the fall of 1946; after graduation, students received officer ranks. The education of regular officers commenced only in 1947 at the Kossuth Military Academy organized in October 1947. This institution existed for only two years; with the beginning of the army's sovietization it was abolished. The Kossuth was only one of several military training institutions that, because of the ongoing reorganization schemes in the armed forces, operated only for a short time.

Another one worth mentioning is the Defense War Academy in existence between December 1947 and January 1949. This was a very selective institution that offered quality education to the few officers (18 out of a pool of 350 well-qualified individuals) admitted. The faculty and student body of the institution were almost exclusively HCP members: of the first entering class, 14 were members of the HCP, two each of the SDP and NPP but by the end of the academic year all were HCP affiliated.[96] As in all educational institutions of the time, aside from military subjects the students received a rigorous political education. The Academy was disbanded on the suggestion of MPA Chief Sandor Nogradi before the introduction of the dual command system.

The Petofi Political Officer Academy, established in December 1948, was a product of the changes that took place in the armed forces. As its name suggests, political indoctrination was the main profile of this school that graduated officers on an annual and later semi-annual schedule in order to accelerate the filling of many open positions created by the rapid increase of the armed forces' size. A similar college was the Stalin Political Officer Academy organized in 1951 for the same purpose. Until 1952 it offered a two-year program, starting with the 1952–53 academic year the course was three years long.

In all of these institutions after the launching of the army's sovietization process, the curricula, training methods, and politico-ideological education were organized by Soviet-trained or Soviet political officers. Ideological training was emphasized at the expense of technical and military subjects.[97] The professional level of graduates left a great deal to be desired; many graduates were ill-prepared to assume responsibility in their new positions of command, as subsequent training and organizational difficulties indicated. According to one recent account, in 1953 there were no more than 500 officers and non-commissioned officers (NCOs) in the HPA whose professional preparedness was adequate.[98]

Not unexpectedly, conscript training was deficient, soldiers were infused with large doses of political and ideological 'knowledge' at the expense of military skills. At the same time, the terms of service contradicted the interests of the armed forces. Soldiers who were not promoted during the first two years of their mandatory service were discharged but those who received some rank had to serve an additional year. Since the overwhelming majority of conscripts considered military service an unavoidable waste of time, the brighter soldiers did their best not to be promoted. Consequently, the armed forces deprived itself of valuable human resources.[99]

While in November 1948 there were only 2,707 officers serving in the HPA, by 1953, as a result of the unprecedented military buildup, they numbered over 30,000. In 1952 the officer corps comprised 32 percent workers, 38.7 percent peasants, 16.8 percent employees, 9.9 percent small tradesmen, and 2.5 percent intellectuals.[100] By 1948, 80 percent, by 1953, 91.3 percent of the officers were trained after 1945.[101] After the army's sovietization began, the proportion of HWP-member working class and peasant youths among officer candidates was nearly 100 percent.[102]

Military training itself increasingly reflected Soviet desiderata with the abolition of such subjects as Hungarian history. The 200-year-old tradition of Hungarian officer training was totally rejected. Instead, Russian and Soviet military heroes such as Peter the Great, Suvorov, Kutuzov, let alone Stalin, were glorified in colleges while their Hungarian counterparts were left unmentioned. Politico-ideological training continued to be stressed but by the early 1950s, partly as a result of the Soviet advisers deployed in the colleges, the professional component of the training improved greatly. The West European states – especially West Germany and Britain – and the United States were portrayed as the enemy ready to attack the emerging people's democracies. In sum, the Hungarian armed forces emulated the Red Army's educational methods as far as possible. In an article published in February 1949 General Palffy wrote that 'the stronger military we organize and the more similar we make it to the that of our great ally, the Soviet Army, the better we demonstrate our gratitude to our liberator . . . ' [103]

As in other areas of social life, the new kind of human being, 'homo sovieticus', was heroized and held up as the example all should emulate.[104] To make sure that Hungarian soldiers properly imitated their Soviet colleagues, uniforms, meals, and even military language were altered. In 1951 Hungarian soldiers were supplied with Soviet-style 'Budyonniy' trousers, 'gimnastorka' shirts, and 'pilotka' hats; words of command were changed to reflect those in the Russian language. Training methods also changed, although the practicability of such alterations was left unquestioned. For instance, Hungarian troops had to camp on terrain often only a few miles away from their barracks for the summer months without leave. In the Soviet Union such training could yield results as units camped often thousands of miles away from their 'natural habitat', in different geographical and climatic conditions. In Hungary, however, it made no sense and had adverse effects on the morale and personal relations of officers and men who frequently were just a stone's throw away from their homes yet forbidden contact with their families.[105]

After 1945 the prestige of the military occupation sank to an all-time low. Since the armed forces were identified from the very beginning with the unpopular HCP and the Soviet Union, few youths were attracted to a military career. This was particularly the case after 1948. Until that year, the manpower of the armed forces was small and there seemed to be somewhat more enthusiasm for joining as the military provided shelter, clothing, and meals that were often scarce immediately after the war, and the political atmosphere was somewhat less oppressive than in the years to follow.[106] Nonetheless, after the sovietization of the armed forces began, the military career was an even less desirable alternative to young men. Command positions afforded little independence to line officers as they were showered with directives from the Ministry and closely supervised by their political officers.[107] Pay was very low, certainly not above the average income at the time. As a consequence of frequent reorganizations officers had to move with their families annually, which had a negative effect not only on their personal lives and finances but also on morale in the forces. Furthermore, family problems caused by the summer camps, Soviet-designed training and uniforms, the total neglect of national traditions, and the ongoing purges did little to endear even otherwise interested young men to the service, and embittered many who were already in it. As a rule, only those with no other career choices applied to officer schools. Consequently, the intellectual level of officers was low.[108]

Because of the accelerated expansion of military manpower, shortages of basic materials and equipment occurred frequently. Particularly from the fall of 1950, such scarcities became pervasive. Fresh conscripts were often forced to sleep in tents for months as the dearth of available beds reached 50 percent at times.[109] Accidents were commonplace due to lack of safety regulations and outdated equipment in need of repair. The living standards of professional military personnel – together with those of the general population – fell drastically after 1949 and the resulting financial problems sometimes led to unpublicized scandals that nonetheless soon became common knowledge and further undermined the army's reputation.[110]

B.   Soviet Influence in the Armed Forces

In the preceding parts of this chapter I have already mentioned various aspects of Soviet influence in Hungarian political, socioeconomic, and military affairs. This section is devoted to a more detailed examination of Soviet domination of the armed forces. The Red Army's occupation of Hungary had little direct effect on civil–military relations in this period. Unsupervised contact between members of the Soviet Army and the HPA, let alone with the general population was strongly discouraged.[111] The Soviet High Command did not want Red Army soldiers to develop attachments to their Hungarian colleagues and for this reason regular recruits were restricted to their bases while advisers and high-ranking officers were rotated at short intervals. Hungarian soldiers – particularly officers – were affected far more by the ubiquitous presence of Soviet military advisers.

1. The Soviet Advisers

With the beginning of the flow of Soviet weapons to Hungary, the first group of Soviet military advisers, led by Lieutenant General Prokoffiev, arrived in November 1948. The primary functions of these individuals were to reorganize the army's supreme command along Soviet lines and to initiate and assist in the expansion of officer training.[112] All but a few of these men had gained experience in the art of 'advising' during World War II, supporting the Chinese nationalists in Chunking.[113] The first contingent of Soviet advisers conducted themselves in a diplomatic manner, were generally helpful, and offered advice only when it was requested, pleasantly surprising Hungarian officers, who expected the worst.[114]

The second group of advisers who took over in the fall of 1949, headed by Lieutenant General Boyko, represented a marked contrast to their predecessors. Their primary aim was to sovietize thoroughly the Hungarian army and eradicate the little that was left of its national character.[115] Their behavior was reportedly determined by Boyko's deputy, General S. S. Sergei, who discharged his functions with brutality.[116] In 1951 the Kremlin sent wartime commander of Moscow, General Tsvetaev – whose position in Budapest was similar to that of Marshal Rokossovsky in Warsaw – to take over full command of the rapidly expanding HPA. Tsvetaev's arrival was followed by a new wave of terror in the Hungarian Army and a comprehensive reorganization of the General Staff.[117] In addition to the Russian-style uniforms and training, Soviet professional manuals, military regulations and Codes of Service were made compulsory in 1950.[118] In the meantime, the number of Soviet military advisers increased and by late 1951 they were installed even in regimental staff-commands. Soviet advisers 'assisted' all top- and medium-level officers. General Boyko, for instance, accompanied Defense Minister Farkas to all important meetings and conferences and was seated directly beside him.[119] The size of the advisory body continued to grow until 1953.[120]

A further important distinction between the two teams of advisers was their dissimilar command affiliations. The first group was subordinated to the Command of the Soviet Commander-in-Chief in Austria, headquartered in Austria's Burgenland province. The second detachment, however, maintained no official contact with the Soviet occupying forces in Austria since it was subordinated to the Soviet High Command in Moscow.[121] This organizational change appeared to underscore the sharp differences in the conduct of the two Soviet contingents. The introduction of the dual command structure in the HPA coincided with the arrival of the first group of advisers. The professional emphasis of the advisory groups was differentiated between political officers and 'D-[military security police] officers'.

The latter generally engaged in espionage, counter-intelligence, or political investigation activities while the former concentrated on ideological and political indoctrination.

As a general rule, Hungarian officers were not entitled to make weighty decisions or even to inspect their troops without the consent of the advisers who were, on the other hand, free to go wherever they wished for the purpose of surprise inspections.[122] On every level, Hungarian officers were subordinated to Soviet advisers and were effectively controlled by them. During the 1948–53 period the Hungarian army, through its command structure and general organization, was practically integrated into the Red Army. Through this system of advisers the Soviet High Command could administer the East European forces as branches of the Soviet army.[123]

The role of Soviet advisers is evaluated entirely negatively in the Western and contemporary Hungarian literature. Nonetheless, some advisers and some aspects of their activities affected the armed forces beneficially. Most of those, whose function was to assist in professional education, were experienced and highly skilled military officers. At the regimental level especially, Soviet officers served as technical rather than political advisers.[124] Those in the first group operated with tact, offering much-needed help to younger and inexperienced commanders while remaining only as true advisers to cadres with more qualifications.[125] In other words, aside from the intrigue and mindless political indoctrination many Soviet officers served as real teachers and certainly accelerated the professional development of the Hungarian officer corps. There is, of course, no sense in denying that many, if not most, advisers took advantage of their privileged status and were instrumental in the deterioration of morale in the HPA.

2.   The Training of Hungarian Officers in the USSR

Officer training in the Soviet Union was yet another important facet of Moscow's control of the Hungarian armed forces. Military education in the USSR attempted to create the most reliable component of the Hungarian officer corps that was clearly selected to fill the most important positions in the future armed forces.

The training of Hungarian officers in the Soviet Union commenced in late 1948. Candidates for study were screened according to several criteria in order to assure that they would not become an embarrassment to Budapest. The cadres were selected not by their commanders but by the MPA – the new administrative body organized according to the directives of Soviet advisers – and the Personnel Department of the HWP with which the former worked closely.[126] The most important yardstick in the selection of officers was loyalty to the HWP and to the Soviet Union.[127] Most of those sent to the USSR were in their twenties and thirties and, as a general rule, had already received some form of military education in Hungary.

Authors in the West have probably overestimated the rigidity of the Soviet program and the number of Hungarians that participated in it until 1953. General Kiraly wrote that departing officers were seen off by relatives who wept like mourners, as candidates were not allowed to return to Hungary until they completed the three- or four-year courses. Further, he says that officers did not voluntarily go to the USSR as they were arbitrarily chosen and had no say in the matter.[128] In the face of new evidence it seems more probable that the overwhelming proportion of officers who were sent to the USSR were asked and went voluntarily, well aware of the great career opportunities that could reasonably be expected following their return. Officers had and used the opportunity to return to Hungary during summer holidays. There is data to prove that the Personnel Department could select from a large number of candidates who desired the option of Soviet education.[129] It is probably true that some officers did not dare decline the offer. At the same time higher military education was an attractive alternative for ambitious officers, given that at the time no such training was offered in Hungary.

Although some analysts have suggested that there were thousands of officers who received Soviet education in this period,[130] it appears that no more than a few hundred did so. According to Miklos Szucs, who was an HPA General Staff Colonel during these years, the majority of top army leaders had no military qualifications at all. 'The various Soviet military academies (Voroshilov [General Staff Academy], Frunze Political Officer Academy, and the service academies) graduated only a few' Hungarian officers until 1956; the Voroshilov, for instance, only eleven.[131] In short, higher education in the Soviet Union was an appealing career opportunity to the few participating officers. Soviet military academies imbued their Hungarian students with technical proficiency and the *Weltanschauung* that qualified them both in Soviet and in Hungarian eyes as the leaders who could ensure the reliability and professionalism of the HPA.

Summary

This chapter portrayed the evolution of the Hungarian military establishment between 1945 and 1953 and delineated the military's relationship to the political elite. We have seen that the military's influence in the political domain was well-nigh insignificant, supporting Adelman's hypothesis pertaining to the armies of Eastern Europe. Although high-ranking military leaders did participate in the most important decision-making bodies, they were either clearly Communist party functionaries first and soldiers second or career soldiers who could be and were disposed of when the regime's real or perceived interests so desired. It is important to note the preponderance of *Muscovite* Communists not only in the HCP/HWP leadership, but also in the top military command positions – Minister, MPA Chief – following the 1948 takeover. The purges that affected the political as well as the military sphere were more often than not directed against 'homegrown' Communist political and military leaders (e.g., Rajk, Kadar, Palffy, Solyom, etc.).

I have attempted to show the methods the Communist party utilized to gain control of the armed forces. The army did not display the characteristics of an interest group as Kolkowicz suggested, but his model's contention of the antagonistic relationship between 'political' and 'professional' officers seems to apply to the Hungarian army in this period. After the Communists established their rule, no conflict transpired between the armed forces and the political elite, and the military did not foster political instability. Odom's 'institutional congruence' approach accommodates the Hungarian experience of the period rather neatly, stressing consensus between the army and the party. Colton's emphasis on the participation of military leaders in high politics is also borne out by the Hungarian case in this period. All three theoretical constructs dealing with Eastern Europe were useful – insofar as their descriptions of the takeover period applied to the case study – in this examination of civil–military relations. The evidence presented above supports the contentions of the Herspring–Volgyes model. The 'transformation phase', when the political apparatus played a 'largely loose supervisory role' was very brief in Hungary, as the political elite switched into the consolidation mode as early as 1948, exerting immense pressure on the military to internalize the Communists' value system.

A substantial portion of this chapter dealt with the influence of the Soviet Union in Hungarian affairs, for without the USSR's role it would be impossible to understand Hungary's (and Eastern Europe's) transition to communism. The determination and unbridled ambition of the HCP/HWP would have been unrewarded without Moscow's effective support. Soviet backing became especially overt and direct after the fateful year 1948 when the HCP managed to seize all political power in the country. The Hungary of the 1948–53 period may well be considered as a servile client state of the USSR whose real autonomy was probably no greater than that of any of the Soviet republics. The survival of the HCP/HWP depended in a very real sense on the CPSU leadership which was, ultimately, the master of the Hungarian armed forces as well.

3   Subordination (1953–68)

The bulk of this chapter analyzes the one and half decades of Hungarian politico-military relations that began with the demise of Stalin and ended with the Warsaw Pact invasion of Czechoslovakia. I argue that although no sweeping changes comparable to the 1945–53 period took place, after 1956 Budapest began cautiously to explore the limits of Moscow's tolerance. The best examples of this phenomenon are the introduction of the New Economic Mechanism (NEM) and Hungary's reluctant participation in the political isolation and subsequent military invasion of Czechoslovakia. My underlying argument throughout this chapter is that the Hungarian experience disproves several contentions of the models examined in Chapter 1. More specifically, the military's influence on politics was negligible, it did not act as an interest group opposing the Party, neither was there any perceptible conflict between the armed forces and the Party.

The political history of this period has received ample attention in the literature thus I offer only a brief background to the civil–military relations of the period.[1] Due to the distinctiveness of Party–army relations in 1953–56 and 1956–68, I deal with them separately in Parts II and III. Part IV examines Soviet influence on the HPA and Hungary's participation in the Warsaw Pact.

Part I   Political Background

A.   1953–56

After the death of Stalin criticisms of the personality cult surrounding Rakosi and other top leaders and the reassessment of the events of the past five years soon began. Nevertheless, the political struggle between the Stalinists and the advocates of liberalization was not easily decided. In June 1953, four members of the Hungarian party leadership (Rakosi, Farkas, Gero, and Nagy) and the non-Communist Istvan Dobi were summoned to Moscow for a major dressing-down by Kremlin leaders.[2] Khrushchev, Malenkov, and Molotov accused them – particularly Rakosi – of dogmatism, sectarianism, and of being out of touch with Hungarian realities. Moscow demanded changes in the composition of the leadership:

Rakosi, while allowed to retain the top Party position, was replaced by Nagy as Prime Minister.[3]

During his premiership (July 1953–April 1955) Nagy's 'New Course' attempted to undo some of the harmful policies of the previous years. The June 1953 Resolution of the HWP CL reflected not only the intentions of Nagy and the populist group of politicians and intellectuals around him but, clearly, Soviet design as well.[4] The purges were halted and the process of rehabilitation commenced. By October 1954 more than one hundred Communists – including Janos Kadar – were released from prison.[5] Light industry and the production of consumer goods received more attention than previously. Nagy ensured that collectivization proceeded on the basis of voluntarism and permitted the dismantling of already established collective farms provided that a majority of their membership so desired.[6] To a certain extent Nagy was also able to liberalize cultural life and applied fewer restrictions to creative work and publishing. In sum, as Zoltan Vas wrote, 'The people were relieved . . . The new government's measures inspired confidence and hope in a better present and future in the population.'[7]

Nagy's ascent to the top government position marked the beginning of a political struggle between two competing centers of power for the first time since 1948. Although at the May 1954 Third Congress of the HWP the delegates – and Marshal Voroshilov, representing Moscow – endorsed the Premier's program, neither his appointment nor the Soviets' approval was to be enduring. At the October 1954 session of the CL disagreements between the Nagy group and the Rakosi–Gero faction emerged openly.[8] On November 30, shortly after he returned from a two-month sojourn in the USSR, Rakosi briefed the CL of the message of the CPSU Presidium.[9] Likely to have been strongly influenced by Rakosi himself, the message suggested that right-wing tendencies were on the rise in Hungary and for the undesirable economic developments Nagy was to be blamed.[10] The December session of the HWP Politburo turned into a forum of verbal attacks against Nagy.

In January 1955 members of a HWP delegation informed the Kremlin leaders about the profound disagreements in the Hungarian leadership. The Soviets now also castigated Nagy and his political line. In March he was forced into retirement and was stripped of all Party positions and his HWP membership. To be sure, the Moscow leadership itself was divided by factional fights – centering around Khrushchev and Malenkov – and the temporary victory of conservative views in the Soviet Politburo supported the Rakosi–Gero group. Moreover, new developments in the cold war, particularly the integration of West Germany into NATO, also favored

Rakosi and convinced the Kremlin leaders that this was not the time to show weakness (i.e., liberalization) on the domestic front or in the bloc. The decision regarding Hungary's political direction was once again made in Moscow.[11]

The March 1955 turnabout in Hungarian politics had profound consequences. It demonstrated that the HWP was incapable of renewal and it set the two opposing groups in the Party further apart. Rakosi and his associates did not learn from the lessons of the past and followed the policies left off in 1953.[12] For the first time, however, the leadership met with considerable popular dissatisfaction manifested primarily by intellectual dissent. By the fall of 1955 dozens of thinly-veiled attacks appeared in the press against the leadership and in support of Nagy's 'New Course'.[13] The regime answered with the dismissal of the dissenting publications' editorial boards and began to persecute intellectuals. The tides in Moscow changed once again, however, and Khrushchev's anti-Stalin speech at the CPSU's Twentieth Congress in February 1956 caused a great deal of uncertainty in Budapest. At the Congress Khrushchev made it part of the Soviet canon that each socialist country would pursue its own road to socialism, a dictum with which Rakosi and his group could not easily identify.

Seeing obvious signs of opposition, Rakosi continued his struggle to retain power. The disturbances in Poznan, Poland in June and July played into Rakosi's hands and further strengthened his resolve to 're-establish order'. By this time, however, the Soviets realized that Rakosi could in no way consolidate his power and steer the country according to Moscow's wishes. At the July 1956 session of the HWP's Politburo Rakosi was 'talked into' surrendering his position to Erno Gero by CPSU Presidium member Anastas Mikoyan, flown in from Moscow for the occasion.[14] In a few days Rakosi left for the Soviet Union, never to return.

Gero, who supported his predecessor to the end, was the worst choice possible. As expected, the new Party leader implemented no important change in policy. In mid-October, at Tito's invitation and Moscow's urging, Gero, Kadar, and other HWP leaders visited Yugoslavia to cement the renewed relations. The trip was preceded by the reburial of Laszlo Rajk and several other Communist leaders who fell victim to the purges of the late 1940s. This was the first large-scale spontaneous gathering since 1948 and it clearly reflected the widespread popular disenchantment with the regime. According to some observers, the revolution would easily have erupted on this day if it were not for the rainy weather.[15] Gero and his colleagues returned from Belgrade only on the 23rd when the Revolution had already intoxicated many and had left the leadership in utter confusion.

My purpose is not to provide an historical analysis of the Revolution on these pages; such studies could fill a sizeable library.[16] Instead, my focus here is on the transformation of the political situation from Revolution to consolidation, associated with the leadership of Janos Kadar. The Kadar succession, if indeed one can call it that, is a case study in Soviet problem-solving.

The Hungarian political leadership was unable to stay on top of the political and military developments during the Revolution. Upon returning from Yugoslavia, Gero, intending to appease the population, appointed Nagy Prime Minister. Nagy promised reforms along the lines of his 1953 program but such an agenda was no longer sufficient to placate the population. In the meantime the Kremlin dispatched Mikoyan and Suslov who replaced HWP First Secretary Gero with Janos Kadar on October 25. In the first days of the Revolution the Communist party, particularly its provincial centers, simply disintegrated.[17] A new Communist party, the Hungarian Socialist Workers' Party (HSWP), that distanced itself from the crimes of the HWP, was formed by Nagy, Kadar, and others . On October 30, Nagy announced the abolition of the single-party system and promised democratic elections, thereby probably giving the *real* reason for Moscow to suppress the revolt. On November 1, a few hours before he was to defect to the Russians, Kadar said to Soviet Ambassador Yuri Andropov that as a Hungarian he would fight Soviet tanks with his bare hands if necessary.[18]

Once again, the Kremlin played the midwife at the birth of the new Hungarian regime. Before Kadar was selected, Khrushchev went on a whirlwind tour to consult the leaders of the bloc. Only Poland's Gomulka appeared sympathetic to Hungary,[19] while Romania and Bulgaria offered military assistance to the Soviet Army in the repression of the Revolution.[20] Although Moscow preferred Ferenc Munnich, an old Muscovite Communist for the top position in Hungary, it appears that Tito's suggestion to have Kadar appointed instead convinced the Soviets.[21]

B.   1956–68

On November 4, 1956 Radio Szolnok announced the formation of the new government and its request of Red Army units to help re-establish order in the country.[22] The popular mood was at an all-time low, industrial production was at a standstill, strikes were widespread in the capital and in the countryside. Approximately 210,000 people took advantage of the relatively open borders and left Hungary between October 1956 and January 1957.[23] Initially, the Kadar government did not have a clear conception of how to deal with the situation at hand and made promises few of which were to be delivered. Despite repeated assurances, the rounding up of revolutionaries by the new government's armed detachments began almost immediately. The Presidential Council decreed the introduction of summary and accelerated proceedings against the insurgents, the scope of which was expanded in a follow-up decree on January 13, 1957.[24] Although in his speech to the United Nations General Assembly on October 3, 1960 Kadar stressed that all criminal procedures concerning crimes of the 'counter-revolution' were completed, there is evidence that executions took place as late as November 1961.[25] Over 20,000 individuals were arrested, 2,000 executed – among them Nagy and his close associates in 1958 – and thousands more deported to the Soviet Union.[26]

The period of retaliation lasted until 1960, but the signs of a better future surfaced earlier. In the political domain, the de-Stalinization campaign continued after the Revolution even in the face of opposition from the Stalinist contingents within the HSWP.[27] By the early 1960s the domestic political situation became stable and Kadar's famous dictum ('Who is not against us, is with us') indicated the new alliance policy. In fact, a tacit social contract emerged between the leadership and the population: the former took it upon itself to improve living conditions in return for the latter's political acquiescence. The HSWP's membership increased rapidly, exceeding 600,000 by December 1967.[28] In February 1957 the HSWP Central Committee decided to create the Communist Youth League (CYL) to replace the defunct Workers' Youth League of the Rakosi regime that disintegrated during the Revolution. Starting with the early 1960s the leadership was confident enough to permit large-scale travel to the West and a cautious cultural liberalization.[29]

The economic priorities of the 1948–56 period were re-evaluated by the Kadar regime. Light industry and the satisfaction of consumer preferences received more attention, while emphasis on economic growth and investment in mammoth industrial projects continued with less vigor. The first extensive socio-economic project of the Kadar-regime was the collectivization of agriculture. This project lasted from 1959–62 and proceeded discreetly, relying on incentives instead of coercion.[30] By the Eighth Congress of the HSWP (November 1962) 93.5 percent of agricultural lands were either in collective or in state ownership.[31] The preparation of the NEM was the regime's last major undertaking in this period. The main features of the NEM were decentralization of decision-making, a new pricing system, more rational schemes of distribution, etc. After much debate and checking with bloc leaders, the NEM was introduced in January 1968.[32] Hungary's partners in the Council of Mutual Economic Assistance (CMEA) expressed no enthusiasm toward the project, indeed, CPSU General Secretary Leonid I. Brezhnev had failed to endorse it.

Despite his initial misgivings about Kadar, Khrushchev became his strong supporter and official relations between the two countries were probably at their closest ever.[33] Following Khrushchev's ouster, relations became somewhat cooler, perhaps due to Kadar's enthusiastic backing of his mentor to the end. Nonetheless, Hungary was firmly ensconced in the Soviet realm and Brezhnev probably did not see any reason to tamper with the Budapest leadership. By the end of the 1956–68 period, however, some clouds appeared in Hungary's relations with its allies. Although Moscow did not openly criticize the NEM, it also did not offer the endorsement Budapest hoped for. The differences between Hungary and the USSR concerning the Prague Spring were even more evident.

Part II   Soldiers and the Revolution

During the three years that elapsed between the death of Stalin and the eruption of the Revolution, the HPA had gone through important changes. Although the fundamental political relationship between the army and the Party retained its basic characteristics, with the passing of the 'Yugoslav threat', the different investment priorities of Nagy's government, and lessening Soviet demands of militarization affected the HPA profoundly. The most important test of the HPA came with the outbreak of the Revolution in October 1956. Clearly, the army, and particularly its leadership, could not measure up to this challenge. Generals were unprepared, unskilled, and lacked the professional stamina and ideological convictions needed to master the situation. In short, the extensive Communist effort to establish a combat-worthy and reliable army that would come to the aid of the regime failed miserably. Following the revolt the HPA had to be thoroughly reorganized.

A.   The Army before the Revolution

Despite the perceptible democratization in other areas, the rigid Stalinist political line survived in the military until the Revolution. The MPA, headed by General Sandor Nogradi, effectively controlled the armed forces. All-army party conferences were held annually, although party meetings on the division level and for the various military organizations and institutes were conducted three or four times a year.[34] The HPA leadership continued to enforce unyielding political-ideological discipline even though at times MPA leaders complained that this effort did not always meet with unqualified success.[35] Istvan Bata, who replaced Mihaly Farkas in June 1953 as Minister of Defense, followed his predecessor's policies.[36] With Bata at the helm, professional incompetence and ideological rigidity remained the trade marks of the HPA's top command.

In his position as MPA Chief Nogradi was followed by General Jeno Hazai, a party worker with no military background, who was unable to keep his grip on the emerging political situation. Political officers received no guidance from the MPA in interpreting the political developments. Many of them fell under the influence of the intellectual dissidents and became Nagy's supporters.[37] Events at the CPSU's Twentieth Congress shocked political officers: they were still left in the dark by their superiors concerning suitable commentary for the troops yet received a great deal of criticism for their shortcomings.

At the time of the Revolution about 80–85 percent of the officers were members of the Party while the majority of conscripts belonged to the HWP's youth organization.[38] Soldiers were relatively well informed about the political changes from the media (domestic and Western) and through their personal contacts.[39] During this period, Radio Belgrade broadcast in Hungarian several hours a day, analyzing the political situation in the Soviet bloc, including Khrushchev's 'Secret Speech'. According to the recollections of a fighter pilot, 'by 1954 everyone [in the armed forces] listened to these programs'.[40] The grave disparity between the political messages received from the outside and the continued ideological rigidity and obscurantism in the armed forces confused conscripts and career soldiers alike.

Political life was most active in the military colleges. Situated in or near Budapest, in spite of the wholesome discipline, cadets – living in a far less structured environment than career soldiers – could more easily familiarize themselves with the political situation. Army leaders often visited the colleges but their muddled evaluations of political developments failed to impress the soldiers. For instance, Defense Minister Bata visited the Miklos Zrinyi Military Academy in early July 1956 and declared in front of the entire student body that Rakosi should retain his position because his dismissal would be 'tragic' for the country.[41] A few days later Rakosi was dismissed.

Soviet influence on the HPA remained pervasive. Advisers were still deployed in regiments, and at times even in battalions, although their activities were most important at the HPA Headquarters in Budapest where reportedly 200 served.[42] The number of Soviet troops stationed in Hungary increased dramatically after May 1955. Until the withdrawal of the Red

Army from Austria in the summer of 1955, approximately 20,000 Soviet troops were based on Hungarian soil.[43] It appears that most, if not all, of the Soviet troops deployed in Austria until the signing of the Austrian State Treaty in May 1955 were transferred in Hungary. According to Western sources, with the arrival of this additional contingent to Hungary, the size of the Soviet occupying force increased to approximately 80,000.[44] By all official accounts, the relationship between the HPA and the Red Army in Hungary was 'comradely.' In many cases Hungarian and Soviet bases were located in close proximity and visits between the units were frequent. Sports competitions between the conscripts of the two fraternal armies were just as common as officers getting together for drinks and conversation.[45]

The length of courses at military colleges was increased somewhat and the leadership attempted to pay more attention to the selection of students. The training of some Hungarian officer candidates and officers in the Soviet Union continued. Approximately 150–200 individuals left for the USSR annually after the rigorous selection process, that included putting the applicants' files through the security clearance twelve times on occasion.[46] In spite of the careful screening, errors were made and some students had to be recalled on the recommendation of the military's counter-intelligence and personnel departments.[47] Those who managed to stay in the USSR for the full duration of the program recall that they had received world-class training from the Soviets.[48]

Once in the USSR, foreign officers lived and studied apart from the Russians. Their classrooms were better equipped and their accommodation was of higher quality although they were quite isolated not only from Soviet civilians but also from their Soviet cohorts. Following Stalin's death, restrictions on the movements of East European officers were somewhat relaxed: they were occasionally invited to civilian social functions and the ban on Soviet women marrying satellite officers was lifted.[49]

Nagy's most important policy concerning the armed forces was the reduction of the HPA's size. This effort already began during the tenure of the previous administration. There was certainly no good reason for Hungary to maintain the sort of gigantic armed forces it did in the late 1940s and early 1950s. Since the Yugoslav 'threat' no longer existed and Soviet demands for the expansion of the satellite militaries stopped after 1953, the government implemented a cut of 15,000 soldiers in August 1953, and a much larger cut in the following fall.[50] The MOD announced further troop reductions ranging between 15,000 and 20,000 in September 1955, July and August 1956.[51] In the fall of 1956 the HPA's size was approximately 120,000. Most of the troops were stationed near the southern and western borders. In Budapest there were only 6,000 soldiers (most of them in administrative and support capacities, and the student bodies of military colleges); 11,000 troops were based within a 35-mile radius from the capital, 17,000 within 70 miles.[52]

Although it was necessary to decrease the HPA's size, the implementation of this policy caused serious problems. Most of the discharged were career soldiers but neither the army nor the political leadership thought to smooth their transition to civilian life. Their military education was useless outside of the HPA due to its inferior quality and lack of transferability. Many officers found themselves on the street from one day to the next as they received no advanced warning. The prestige of the profession decreased further for other reasons as well. Officers were frequently transferred, pay was extremely low, the demands of the service high and the hours irregular.[53] During the summer of 1956 the entire HPA (with the exception of the air force) was reorganized for the umpteenth time within a few years causing further discontent in the troops.

In 1953–56 the military's share from the national budget significantly diminished. The smaller size of the HPA and the enormous investments of the previous period permitted the transfer of funds from defense to other sectors; the military budget – until 1953 as high as 30–40 percent of the GNP[54] – decreased precipitously. The HPA's arsenal showed practically no change in this period.[55]

In July 1956 the Administrative Department of the HWP Central Committee – one of the Party's main instruments of control over the military – prepared a lengthy report on the state of the HPA for the Party leadership. The document concluded that between 1953 and 1956 the HPA was morally crushed to death. The report, submitted by Lajos Czinege who was to become Defense Minister in 1960, described the situation of the thousands of officers booted out of the forces at a moment's notice. It also noted the abject failure of the military leadership in the performance of its tasks.[56] The report received a great deal of criticism and then was quickly forgotten.

B. The Military's Role in the Revolution

In this section my main hypothesis is that the HPA's record reflected much less the disenchantment of the armed forces with the regime than the confusion, lack of professionalism, and opportunism of its leaders. The army's overall performance mirrored the disintegration of the political leadership. But even in the heady days of the Revolution, the military did not act as an interest group as Kolkowicz's model would lead us to believe, and certainly was no participant in policy-making as contended by Colton.

Essentially, the military did not get involved in the disputes at either the elite or mass levels. Instead, the armed forces' leadership had simply waited for and reacted to instructions from the Party headquarters and when it did not receive clear directives it was unable to stand on its own. None of the models devised to pertain to Eastern Europe allowed for the possibility of such dramatic turns in civil–military relations.

During the Revolution the astounding deficiencies of Hungary's military leadership were clearly revealed. The MOD and the high military leadership was virtually paralyzed from the beginning of the uprising. Due to disagreements within the HPA leadership, conflicting orders, and the frequent breakdown of communication lines, army units either did not receive any guidance from the center, were given ambiguous orders that made their lot even more difficult, or were simply ignored by their leaders. In this situation few individuals were burdened with more responsibility than military officers. If they were fortunate enough to hold their troops together, could prevent them from firing on the Soviets, *and* could also avoid being elected to one of the Revolutionary Soldiers' Councils, their reward was scarcely more than escaping prosecution. Those who were not so blessed faced stiff prison terms and even execution.[57]

The signs of the military leadership's wavering were already apparent on October 23, the day the Revolution erupted. Cadets at the Petofi and Zrinyi academies asked for and received permission to participate in the demonstrations.[58] Many officers agreed with the demands of the protesters.[59] Seeing the uniformed soldiers in their ranks, the demonstrators drew the conclusion that the 'army is with us'. The inference was certainly incorrect. Although an insignificant number of soldiers joined the demonstrators on the spot, nearly all of them returned to their barracks.

The paralysis of the Party leadership strongly affected the military high command. In spite of the social ferment of the preceding months, both groups of leaders were caught entirely unprepared by the events, incapable of making rational decisions. Receiving no direction from Party headquarters, army leaders were reduced to being impotent observers of the swiftly unfolding events. Some regiments based in the provinces petitioned the military leadership to order them to the capital so they could re-establish order. The command either did not arrive or when it did reach the units it called for the troops to come un-armed.[60] Defense Minister Bata, for instance, called several thousand soldiers to Budapest from the countryside to defend buildings of strategic importance. But he and his staff forgot about the order as soon as it was released – no briefings or guidance were given, no provisions were made for housing and meals – and, as a result, thousands of troops were left to fend for themselves in the capital. Many of them either disappeared, went home, or joined the insurgents.[61]

In the evening of October 23, Lieutenant General Tikhonov, the principal Soviet adviser to Bata, after receiving the approval of the HPA leaders, ordered some of the Soviet troops stationed nearby to enter the capital.[62] In the meantime, HWP leader Gero also appealed for Soviet military assistance. By next morning some 6,000 Soviet troops arrived. Neither the size nor the actions of the first Soviet intervention suggested a massive assault on the uprising but the appearance of the Soviet troops in the capital was oil to the fire of the Revolution.

In the meantime, armed groups organized spontaneously in Budapest and in the provinces. In the ranks of the freedom-fighters there were a few non-Hungarians, such as the Yugoslav partisan Kemal Ekren, dozens of Soviet soldiers who defected from their units, North Korean students and Greek Communists living in exile in Hungary.[63] The insurgents, unaware that the functions of the Soviet troops were merely policing and the maintenance of order, resisted them with arms.[64] Although the Soviet troops were ordered not to shoot they returned fire when fired upon. They were clearly surprised upon encountering spirited resistance and suffered heavy casualties. On October 25 Mikoyan and Suslov arrived from Moscow and agreed with the Hungarian leaders to the immediate withdrawal of Red Army units from Budapest. The Soviet pull-out from the capital was completed only on October 30.

Cooperation between the government, Party, and military leaderships was accidental. In order to improve communication, the HWP Central Committee sent its own permanent committee (comprised of Politburo member Antal Apro [Chair], Lajos Czinege, Lajos Feher, Laszlo Foldes, Istvan Kovacs, and Imre Mezo) to the MOD. Apro ordered high-ranking officers on October 25 and 26 to distribute thousands of weapons among workers – so 'they could stabilize the situation' – despite the government's efforts to collect weapons in civilian hands. Thus thousands of weapons were given out to workers who promptly joined the Revolution.[65] In Nagy's government (formed on October 27) the defense portfolio went to General Karoly Janza, who served as Deputy Minister since 1950. Janza, like his predecessor, never mastered the situation and the practice of conflicting orders and messages from the MOD to the troops continued.

The HSWP Military Committee dispatched to the MOD quickly became dissatisfied with the Nagy Government's lack of clear direction and attempted to quell the Revolution on its own. On October 27, the Committee devised a plan to destroy with a decisive military action one of the major insurgent groups based at Budapest's Corvin movie theatre. Since Nagy opposed the plan, Apro's group prepared another one that was even more audacious. This called not only for the attack on the Corvin group but also the isolation of Imre Nagy and the establishment of a provisional military dictatorship.[66] According to Foldes, order could have been re-established within 48 hours.[67] The plan was vetoed by the HSWP Politburo and on October 31 the Military Committee ceased to exist.[68]

During the Revolution, more than 95 percent of the HPA units were stationed and remained in the provincial towns.[69] Although in want of adequate communication and central guidance they did not see clearly what was taking place in the political arena; the majority of *professional* cadres sided with the Communist Party.[70] The example of the division headquartered at Kecskemet (approximately 50 miles south of Budapest) illustrates well the predicament of many a provincial unit.[71] The division preserved its structural cohesion thanks to its commander, Major General Gyurko. On October 25 the division staff organized a meeting for officers who sent a telegram expressing loyalty to the HSWP. A day later, one of the division's units, the 37th Motorized Infantry Regiment stationed in Kiskunhalas, was alerted and called to Budapest by the MOD. In a Budapest suburb insurgents opened fire on the Regiment and a six-hour battle ensued resulting in 100 dead and many injured. It is telling sign of the military leadership confusion that when the Regiment's commander reported the arrival of his unit to the MOD, Janza was dumbfounded as he had no knowledge about the order.

Many army units in the provinces threw in their lot with the Revolutionary Councils (*Forradalmi Tanacs* – RC) that were being organized in towns and cities. Some of the smaller units completely disintegrated as officers and soldiers alike went home, joined the Revolution, or left the country. The majority of troops, however, remained in their barracks and adopted a 'wait and see' attitude.[72] As in Budapest, one of the provincial officers' problems was that they received 'guidance' from several sources – civilians, RCs, Soviet advisers – except from their own superiors at the MOD and Division Headquarters who were afraid of giving the 'wrong order' and tried to avoid taking stands in order to preserve their careers for the future.[73] Not surprisingly, discipline and morale in many bases quickly plummeted and some units melted away.

On October 28 the Nagy government called for a cease-fire and ordered the armed forces to use their weapons *only* when fired upon.[74] While the army observed the terms of the cease-fire, many if not most insurgent groups ignored it. In a speech broadcast on radio, the Prime Minister called the uprising a 'revolution'. For those military units that supported the government and the Party during the preceding days, the news of Nagy's declaration came as a shock. Officers, who had been explaining to their soldiers that a counter-revolution was going on, now had to tell them that the uprising was really a revolution and thus further accelerated confusion and the erosion of the troops' confidence in their superiors. By October 29 in many areas insurgents and the RCs attempted to persecute military officers loyal to the government and the Party during October 23–28. Until October 29, the HPA could probably have been used to re-establish order.[75] In the preceding days the number of deserters was relatively small, and that of soldiers who joined the ranks of the insurgents even smaller. After this day, however, confusion ruled in the army. A further step hastening the disorganization of the armed forces was the government's October 30 decree calling for the formation of Revolutionary Soldiers' Councils. These Councils – staffed by HPA officers and soldiers as well as freedom fighters – simply dismissed or arrested many a military commander and political officer.[76]

The organization of the National Guard (NG) began on October 28. The NG was supposed to rally all the armed bodies – including selected HPA and police units as well as insurgent groups – together and foster the consolidation of the political situation and observance of the cease-fire. Again, the MOD's attitude toward the NG was ambivalent: it did not order the troops to collaborate with the NG but merely took cognizance of such cooperation if and when it occurred. The creation of the Revolutionary Armed Committee (RAC, *Forradalmi Karhatalmi Bizottsag*) was another step that added to the confusion at the MOD's headquarters. The RAC's manpower was made up of 25 percent each of HPA and police personnel, and 50 percent from the insurgent groups. Through the RAC, freedom-fighters intended to take control of all armed forces in Hungary.

On October 30 Nagy made the historic announcement that abolished the one-party system and formed a coalition government. The decision was discussed with Anastas Mikoyan who was apparently in agreement.[77] On October 31, Nagy received reports that not only were the Soviet Army units not leaving but they were being complemented with additional troops entering from the Ukraine and Romania. On the next day news of a massive Soviet troop buildup in Hungarian territory continued despite assurances from Soviet Ambassador Andropov to the contrary. In the evening Nagy called a meeting of the HSWP leadership and suggested Hungary's withdrawal from the WTO (the text of which stated clearly that stationing Warsaw Pact forces on another member's territory was based strictly on mutual agreement).[78] Only two of the assembled objected: Gyorgy Lukacs and Zoltan Szanto.[79] Shortly before 8 p.m. Nagy proclaimed Hungary's neutrality on national radio.

On November 2, giving no more credence to Andropov's pledges, Nagy turned to the United Nations for help he never received. The next day he once again reorganized his cabinet replacing Janza with the hastily promoted General Pal Maleter, the commander of one of the largest armed units in Budapest made up of regular troops and freedom-fighters. In the meantime the NG's leadership had realized that the NG could not extend its authority over the entire HPA. In order to create a body to oversee the operational questions of the armed forces loyal to the Revolution, the NG established a High Command with General Bela Kiraly as its head on November 3. The new body made recommendations to Maleter about the character of the future military establishment. Maleter accepted the NG's suggestions that called for depoliticized armed forces, the rehabilitation of the insurgents, and for the clarification of relations between the NG, the HPA, and the police.[80] Nonetheless, all of these plans and aspirations were cancelled out by the Soviet invasion that commenced at dawn on November 4. It appears that the onslaught was decided in Moscow already on October 30 when Nagy gave up the Communist Party's monopoly on political power.[81]

International developments, especially the Suez Crisis and the Eisenhower government's decision not to interfere in the Hungarian events, dispersed the remaining doubts of the Soviet leadership concerning the invasion. The Soviet military command took no chances, using 11 divisions and 2,000 tanks.[82] In order to strengthen pro-Soviet lines of command, Moscow also sent back Hungarian officers studying in the USSR as part of the invading forces.[83] The uncoordinated Hungarian defense against the overwhelming force produced some individual acts of heroism, Nagy's refusal to call the armed forces to battle, however, limited such acts to the discretion of individual commanders.[84]

Most of the sporadic resistance to the second Soviet invasion was put up not by HPA units but by NG troops and independent groups of armed insurgents. In the MOD, General Gyula Uszta, a Communist officer who arrived from the USSR a few days before, seized the initiative and ordered all HPA units not to fire on the Soviet troops.[85] Most units followed this command although limited resistance by HPA troops did occur. In any event, by the second half of November all armed opposition to the Soviet Army was abandoned. The clashes between the revolutionaries and the Soviet Army resulted in heavy casualties: 2,502 Hungarians lost their lives (1,945 in Budapest), 19,226 were injured. The Soviet Army lost between 1,600 and 2,000 officers and men, including those shot for fraternizing with Hungarians.[86] Physical damages were particularly serious in the capital although several provincial cities also suffered.

The Revolution can be considered as a consequence of the major factional conflict that arose within the political elite, that is, between Nagy and the liberalizers on the one hand, and Rakosi and the hardliners on the other. The army played no appreciable political role in this conflict. In sum, the HPA did not disintegrate during the events, although the demoralization of the army in general, and the disintegration of *some* units after October 28, cannot be denied. The overwhelming majority of the armed forces remained loyal to the government and Party leadership and did not 'side with the Revolution' as some earlier studies have concluded.[87] In fact, the reason for the persecution of many military officers following the uprising was that they *followed* the often conflicting and irrational orders of the military and government leaderships (i.e., to distribute weapons among workers, etc.). Imre Nagy *was* the leader of the lawful government and whatever their shortcomings, those in the MOD who gave the orders *were* the superiors of the troops.

This confused state of the HPA was clearly the result of the incompetence and stupefaction of the top military leadership, and ultimately, that of the Party and government leaders. In many cases line officers were left to their own devices, given discretion by their superiors who wanted nothing more than to shed their responsibilities. Few officers could see through the swiftly unfolding events as rational analysis of the situation was further frustrated by their relative isolation in the provincial bases. Civil–military relations, then, broke down during the first crisis situation the HPA faced. The reasons for this fact are manifold. The Communist Party, the most important constant of the relationship, had simply melted away in the first few days of the uprising. Military leaders, in part due to the fact that they were political appointments and had little military expertise, were incapable of grasping the situation and offering leadership. Preceding the Revolution they rarely had the opportunity to make independent decisions and they were not prepared to make them when the time came.

Part III   From the Revolution to the Invasion of Czechoslovakia

Following the suppression of the Revolution the most important task of the HSWP in the domain of military policy was to rebuild the HPA. After the years of consolidation, the party leaders demonstrated that the lessons of the 1948–56 years had not been entirely lost on them. A more sensible and rational approach was adopted to civil–military relations: on the one hand, the Party demanded and received – at least to all appearances – the loyalty and ideological rigor of the armed forces; on the other hand, the HSWP provided the military with existential and financial stability and steady political guidance. Reliability remains an elusive concept and one can only speculate about the HPA's behavior in a hypothetical scenario. In any event, the Hungarian military establishment has never again had to discharge its internal-defensive function.

The models examined in Chapter 1 hardly accommodate actual Hungarian civil–military relations in this period. The armed forces' role in politics was negligible. Odom's model with its heavy emphasis on consensus between the Party and the military seems to come closest to the mark. Adapted to the Hungarian case, Adelman's approach correctly points to the minimal political influence of the armed forces. None of the models, however, posited the military profession's loss of social esteem and the resultant recruitment problems that affected civil–military relations. The Soviet domination of the East European armies stated by all of the theoretical constructs concerning Eastern Europe is clearly observable in the Hungarian case although the occasional acts of recalcitrance are left ignored.

A. Repression and Rebuilding

Kadar's Hungarian Revolutionary Workers' and Peasants' Government was still in the city of Szolnok waiting for the Soviet Army to quell the revolt when it ordered General Uszta to organize armed detachments to re-establish order. The new government, aware of the need to create a new armed force for its defense, organized armed groups (called *karhatalom* or 'policing units', PU) to repress strikes, capture freedom-fighters still at large, and to ensure unhindered communication and transportation lines in addition to conventional police work.[88] Admission to the PU was strictly voluntary but there was no shortage of applicants most of whom (75 percent) were professional military cadres.[89] By late November the PUs' manpower was well over 10,000 and by April 1957 it exceeded 18,000.[90]

The PUs collaborated closely with the Soviet forces. Although they were most active in Budapest, by the spring of 1957 the PU was a nationwide armed organization, supplied and housed by the HPA. Made up of loyal Communists, it was a ruthless executor of the HSWP's objectives and for many it seemed that PU units were out to avenge themselves for the humiliation they suffered during the uprising. Put simply, PU details provided the leadership with the armed support it needed until the reorganization of the army could begin in earnest. The entire PU organization was disbanded in mid-1957: some of its members returned to their places of work (HPA, police), others entered the Party's new paramilitary organization, the Workers' Guard (WG).

Preparations for the WG's organization commenced in February 1957.[91] Although financed by the government, the WG was nothing but the private army of the HSWP. Called to life as a voluntary organization to replace PU personnel (who were, of course, badly needed by the army and the police), the WG's main function was the defense of the HSWP's rule from any challenge. In a 1965 speech Kadar stated that 'the mere existence of the WG had given a great deal of courage to the working class' and observed that 'the greatest fortune of our generation is that we can be Communists'.[92] The WG had been the staunchest ally of the HSWP until it was disbanded by the National Assembly in October 1989.[93]

The post-Revolution repression did not bypass the military. Indeed, one of the first tasks of the new regime was to 'purge the entire army and specifically the officer corps of traitors, those who had taken part in the counterrevolutionary events, who were politically unstable, and who were cowards'.[94] The Party's revenge resulted in the prosecution of two generals, 276 officers, 35 NCOs, and 57 conscripts by military courts.[95] Many received sentences ranging from 5 years to life imprisonment; 26 were executed. The HSWP's reprisal against the HPA was all the more contemptible for the army's leaders who were accountable for the confusion within the ranks were not condemned. The ultimate responsibility for the HPA's performance lay, of course, with the Party's leaders who discussed and approved the decisions of the Nagy government.[96]

The first step of the army's reorganization was the drafting of an 'Officer's Declaration' in November 1956 to be signed by all intending to remain in the HPA. Rejoining the new HPA was voluntary although the Military Council of the HPA, and particularly its chairman, General Uszta, made a concerted effort to enlist the services of the officers.[97] Those who did, pledged to serve the new government unconditionally and to carry out its measures unfailingly against the regime's external *and* internal foes.[98] About 80 percent of the officers (8,865) chose to sign the declaration, 2,435 elected not to. It is worth noting that with the 200,000 people who left the country went thousands of conscripted soldiers as well as 1,448 officers.[99] Those officers who did not accept the conditions set out in the 'Declaration' were dismissed. As a result, according to Nikita Khrushchev at least, the Hungarian army diminished in size but improved in quality.[100]

Another significant aspect of the HPA's reorganization was the further strengthening of party control over the armed forces. Party organizations in the HPA units were rebuilt soon after the Revolution. In February

1957 the HSWP Central Committee issued a resolution regarding the 'guiding principles of party and political organs within the military'.[101] The document categorically rejected the notion of a depoliticized army and stressed that only properly functioning party organizations could enable the HPA to complete its tasks. The resolution confirmed the system of political officers and emphasized the role of the MPA as the coordinator and supervisor of political work within the armed forces.[102]

These aspects of continuation notwithstanding, the HSWP leadership took certain steps to appease the soldiers. In early 1957 the army's command broke with the Soviet-style battle dress and introduced new uniforms. Accommodation was improved for officers and conscripts alike.[103] By the mid-1960s HPA personnel, but particularly the professional cadres, experienced a tangible rise in their living standards. According to a contemporary article, the 'government is making sure that soldiers are motivated to handle their weapons well'.[104]

B. Civil–Military Relations in 1958–68

Party–army relations in this period were quite different from that of the years preceding the Revolution. On the one hand, while the HSWP maintained firm control over the military it was far more attentive to the needs of the HPA as an organization and to the material desires of armed forces personnel. On the other hand, the military's morale improved because the Kadar regime, in spite of its brutal reprisals following the Revolution, proved itself to be more accommodating and liberal than not only the pre-Revolution political leadership, but also the regimes of the rest of Eastern Europe. The Party's tacit social contract managed first to pacify and then to appease the general population; this positive societal mood also benefited the HPA.

To be sure, the HSWP left no ambiguity about who determined Hungarian defense policy. The Party made all important decisions regarding the HPA. The long-term principles of military policy were prepared and approved by the 7th Congress of the HSWP in 1959. A 1960 HSWP resolution granted more authority to commanders to control the party life of their units. Commanding officers were given the power to question, and if necessary, hold their subordinates responsible for the failings of party work.[105] A 1967 Politburo directive extended the power of military leaders to supervise party life in the armed forces but they were also made accountable for the discipline and morale of the troops. The HSWP considered the army's political organs to have dual functions as political and military organizations. The resolution declared that the most important task of the HPA Party organizations was to ensure high morale and preparedness.

According to Lajos Czinege, Minister of Defense from 1960 to 1984, all major proposals concerning the armed forces needed Politburo approval. The Party leadership's most direct control over the HPA was exercised by the responsible secretary of the HSWP Central Committee. During Czinege's quarter-century-long tenure the secretaries of the Administrative Department of the HSWP Central Committee were Bela Biszku and Mihaly Korom, both close associates of Kadar.[106] Although the Central Committee could not control the MOD's activities to the smallest detail, there was no need for such close supervision as the Administrative Department maintained day-to-day contact with the MPA and the HPA's HSWP Committee, the top level Party organ within the armed forces. Even so, the Administrative Department effectively decided issues concerning cadre policy, matters relating to promotion, political indoctrination, etc. Naturally, these decisions were duly approved and codified by the government.[107]

A recent inquiry about the armed forces revealed that the actual Commander-in-Chief of the HPA was none other than HSWP First Secretary Kadar whose highest state position was as an ordinary member of the Presidential Council.[108] This practice was unconstitutional since the 1949 Constitution prescribed that the Commander-in-Chief of the armed forces was the Chairman of the Presidential Council. Moreover, issues of critical importance, such as the Party's relationship to the armed forces, the scope of authority the MOD and the HSWP would have had in cases of emergency, were never regulated by law. These issues were determined by custom.

The government also maintained agencies charged with controlling the armed forces. There would be nothing unusual in this if it were not for the Communist practice of overlapping functions and authorities. The government's Defense Council (active between 1949–62) was also chaired by Kadar. The task of this body was to settle issues of military and domestic security relevance that were binding not only for the ministries but also for the Council of Ministers. The members of this body were the Deputy Prime Minister, the Ministers of Industry and Defense, the Chief of Staff, *in addition to* the secretary of the HSWP's Administrative Department. The Party's control over the military, then, was many-faceted and included the thorough infiltration of government organizations. As a result of organizational changes in 1962 the Defense Council was subordinated to the Council of Ministers and its scope of authority diminished.[109]

To make matters even more complex, the MOD itself had a Military

Council made up of military leaders who generally held positions in the upper party hierarchy as well. Military leaders, however, never 'made it' to the Politburo after Mihaly Farkas. One exception is Ferenc Munnich, who was Minister of Defense between November 1956 and March 1957. His ministership was clearly transitional, however, and lasted only until a suitable candidate could be found in the post-Revolution political turmoil. While none of the ministers of the period received a seat in the Politburo, none of them were 'military men' either. Munnich was followed by Geza Revesz, a 'Muscovite Communist'.[110]

The appointment of Czinege, a mid-level party apparatchik, selected to head the MOD over several loyal army generals in 1960, surprised the defense establishment.[111] It was probably not his sixth-grade education nor the lack of military skills that clinched the job for Czinege but his political credentials and excellent contacts. There is circumstantial evidence that he was Moscow's favorite. Khrushchev met Czinege during his 1958 visit to Hungary and apparently took a liking to the provincial party secretary who was paraded in front of him.[112]

The MPA remained the highest political organ of the HPA even after its 1967 reorganization. The purpose of this structural change was to establish alongside the MPA a system of party committees corresponding to every level of the MPA hierarchy. As a result of this alteration, the HPA party committees were no longer subordinated to the MPA but to the HPA Party Committee which, in turn, was directly subordinated to the HSWP Central Committee.[113] The rationale behind this measure was the HSWP leadership's objective to lessen the political-ideological isolation of the army's party organizations and encourage them to develop contacts with local civilian party organs.[114]

Lower level political officers could interfere with the decisions of the regular officers because, while the dual-command system was abolished, the spheres of authority were not clearly demarcated. Political officers were responsible not only for the ideological but also for the ethical and cultural education of professional cadres and conscripts. Despite their efforts, party life in most units was lethargic. Party meetings on the unit level were mere formalities where members did little more than show up. Delegates for party conferences continued to be selected rather than elected. In many places the secretary of the base party organization committee was chaired by the commander.[115] These problems notwithstanding, reports and memoranda regarding the army's 'political awareness' and 'ideological preparedness' were always positive, after all, the *manifested* behavior of HPA personnel approximated the desires of the HSWP. Party and CYL membership in the armed forces continued to be very high: in 1966, 78 percent of the professional cadres were HSWP members, 60 percent of the conscripts were members of the CYL.[116]

C. Education and Training

Education and training are two important aspects of civil–military relations through which the Party could influence the socialization of professional soldiers. During this period the HPA made significant progress in these areas. While in 1960 only 20 percent of the officers gained a degree from a military college and an additional 25 percent possessed a high school diploma (meaning that 55 percent did not finish secondary education), by 1966 the corresponding figures were 33 percent for both.[117] In addition, the HPA successfully completed its large retraining project necessitated by the change instituted in the relative weight of the services.

Several reforms were introduced in the structure of higher military institutions.[118] In 1957 the Unified Officers' School (UOS) was established in Budapest. Until 1967, students of all branches of military service received their officers' training under the auspices of this institution. During the 1960s, the selection process for prospective professional soldiers became more rigorous, reflecting the increased requirements regarding the political-ideological dependability of the applicant.[119] Despite the strict admission criteria, the army had no problems recruiting candidates. As a matter of fact, the UOS often received twice as many applications as it was able to accommodate.[120] One reason for the profession's relative popularity during these years was the improved remuneration of military personnel. In 1967, the UOS was replaced by separate military colleges in order to keep up with the higher technical requirements and increased specialization of modern warfare.

The reforms established three separate military colleges: Gyorgy Killian Air Force College (Szolnok) to train air and ground crews and focus on aviation and aircraft maintenance; Lajos Kossuth Military College (Szentendre) to offer instruction in command and teaching, mechanized infantry, surface-to-surface artillery, engineering, military economics, and border security; and Mate Zalka Military Technical College (Budapest) specializing in anti-aircraft defense, artillery, radar technology, signalling, telecommunications, engineering, and ABC defense and warfare.[121] As a result of the 1967 reform, upon graduation students received both a commission and two college degrees: one attesting their military education, the other to be used in civilian life should the officer resign his commission following the mandatory five years of service. Admission requirements to the Miklos Zrinyi Military Academy (Budapest), the only institution providing graduate level military education, were an undergraduate degree from a military college and, at the minimum, the rank of captain.

Some prospective officers, specializing in certain types of aviation and in other areas for which preparation was unavailable in Hungary, were trained in the USSR. To the usual admission criteria these candidates had to pass a tough Russian language examination. Officers selected for advanced training in the Soviet Union generally studied at the Frunze Military Academy or the Voroshilov General Staff Academy in Moscow.[122] The former specialized in combined arms command and training, while the latter focused on strategic combined arms command for large formations.[123]

D. Manpower, Expenditure, and Equipment

The HPA's size never reached the level of the pre-Revolution era, in the mid-1960s it stabilized at around 100,000.[124] According to the 1960 Defense Law, maximum conscription age was 23 and the duration of service could not exceed three years.[125] Soon after the Revolution the term of service was reduced from three to two years and from 1966 the usual age of conscription was changed from 20 to 18, thereby allowing the HPA to train young men immediately after they completed high school or trade school and not interrupt their careers. Those accepted to universities and colleges were obliged to serve one year before beginning their studies, while during the second year they were permitted to attend school. Labor battalions for 'politically unreliable' draftees were organized in 1960 and abolished in 1967.[126]

The completion of the post-war reconstruction did not signal the end of the HPA's participation in the national economy. The army continued to devote significant amounts of training time and large contingents to various economic projects. In fact the 1960 Defense Law identified contribution to the national economy as one of the fundamental tasks of the armed forces. As a general rule, soldiers spent as much as 25 percent of their service time with agricultural or construction work.[127] In 1964 a special organization of construction units was established to work on military as well as on civilian projects.[128]

The social composition of the HPA had changed in accord with that of Hungarian society. The educational level of the cadets entering military colleges improved immeasurably. As a result of the HSWP's increased attention to the living standards of the HPA's professional personnel, the prestige of the military occupation showed a modest increase. Although the overall economic situation did not allow a drastic amelioration in the remuneration and material conditions of HPA officers and NCOs, the change was nonetheless perceptible. The income of professional personnel was increased several times and housing conditions improved perceptibly. The relatively sophisticated equipment the HPA acquired in this period certainly helped to boost the *esprit de corps*. Some problems persisted, however. Line officers and NCOs were still required to spend 100–130 days away from home, their vacation needs at military holiday houses and cottages were not satisfied, and they – in contrast to the general population – were not permitted to visit the West. As a result, while 'morale in the HPA was good, it could have been better' and the negative effects of 'individualism and materialism' were at times noted in domestic analyses.[129]

During the 1960s the largest part of the HPA's budget was spent on the arsenal. The most important element of the Party's military program was the principle of modernization of certain components of the HPA, particularly air defense.[130] This policy corresponded with the overall modernization scheme of the Warsaw Pact whose leadership stressed integration (standardization of equipment, consolidation of battle tasks, assimilation of the international troops) in the 1960s.

Between the late 1950s and the late 1960s the HPA's air defense contingent increased by fifty percent, the proportion of infantry decreased by the same amount, that of the chemical defense and communications troops doubled, and at the same time the army's fire power quadrupled.[131] Hungarian leaders asserted on countless occasions that the improvement of the HPA was only possible within the framework of the WTO.[132] The arsenal of the HPA since the early 1950s had been almost exclusively made up of Soviet weaponry. In the 1950s, the domestic defense industry's production was restricted to the manufacturing of small arms.[133] Starting with the late 1950s, however, the production of armored personnel carriers, trucks, and anti-tank weapons contributed to the rearmament of the HPA. The quality of these arms was decidedly inferior even in the initial years of production.[134]

The large-scale modernization of the HPA's weaponry began in 1959. For the next decade, the aim of the HSWP and HPA leaderships was to close the gap between the arsenals of the HPA and those of other Pact armies.[135] In the 1960s the HPA acquired T-55 tanks, surface-to-air missiles, MiG-21 aircraft, 'Dvina' air defense rockets, delivery vehicles for ground-to-ground missiles capable of carrying nuclear warheads (the warheads themselves remained under Soviet control), and other weapon systems.[136] Purchasing these arms was not without its difficulties and pernicious consequences. Even though the HSWP devoted large resources for the modernization of the army, the economy could not pay for all that was needed. According to Hungarian sources, the country's defense budget during the 1960s amounted to 4.4–5.0 percent of the GNP.[137] It is likely, however, that a far larger share of the GNP was spent on the armed forces. The estimation of real military expenditure in Hungary – as in all socialist systems – has been hindered by the lack of reliable information, the practice of accounting military investments in the budget of non-military sectors, etc.[138] According to a recent American analysis, Hungary's military outlays more than doubled between 1960–68 with no comparable increase in GNP.[139]

Few politicians called attention to the growing proportion of defense spending in the state budget. In 1965 Miklos Ajtai, Chairman of the National Planning Office, warned that 'we must not allow a larger increase in military outlays than the growth of the national income'.[140] He was ignored. Another trait of defense spending in the 1960s was that it resulted in a very unbalanced picture. While great amounts were expended on new weaponry, the army lacked the additional financial resources for infrastructure and support facilities. In one celebrated case, the HPA's facility in the vicinity of the north-central town of Tata served as a homebase for 300 tanks and armored vehicles yet only 100 of them had adequate garage and service support.[141]

The process of determining the defense budget and investment priorities in Hungary shows a great many idiosyncrasies worth exploring. The HPA's development plans were prepared for five-year periods, corresponding with the five-year plan cycles of the national economy. Drafting the plan started approximately two to two and a half years before it would actually take effect, for good reasons: the bargaining and negotiation between the HPA and the Warsaw Pact on the one hand, and the HPA and the HSWP on the other, were not unlike the process familiar to us from the classical Soviet-type economic planning.[142]

First, the Combined Armed Forces Headquarters of the WTO would pass its 'suggestions' to the Hungarian MOD (say 100 new tanks). Second, the MOD would negotiate with them and drive the figure down (e.g., 90 tanks) which it would present to the HSWP-government leadership. (The actual decision was made by the HSWP's Defense Council.) Another bargaining session would ensue concluding in a further reduction of the plan target (e.g., 75 tanks). With this number the MOD would confront the WTO and supposedly they would come to an accord. But because of the inefficiencies of the Soviet economy and the many uncontrollable variables (e.g., more urgent need for tanks in the Third World) a significantly smaller number of weapons would be actually delivered (say, 50 tanks). The final decision about the nation's defense budget was made by the Party leadership. Its stance was routinely approved by the government leadership (for the most part, the same individuals) that apportioned the agreed-upon sum to the MOD.

Deputies of the National Assembly, let alone the general population, were left in the dark by the leaders concerning the details of military expenditure. As it was customary in the bloc, parliamentary deputies were provided with a single figure that included only direct defense expenses, which was actually the sum of monies projected for the MOD, the Ministry of Interior, and all other security and paramilitary agencies. To make matters worse, accounting practices were astoundingly licentious. For instance, according to a decree of the Council of Ministers, MOD investments under 200 million forint (approximately US $70 million at the official exchange rate in the mid-1960s) were free of any control or central restriction. As a result, corrupt military leaders, led by Czinege himself, were able to and did handle the HPA's resources liberally.[143]

At the same time Czinege, whose name is synonymous with the 1960–84 HPA, was not the entirely evil character the post-Communist Hungarian press would lead us to believe. His apparently excellent rapport with Soviet leaders (particularly with Khrushchev) was of considerable benefit for the HPA's modernization. In a recent publication he described how the Hungarian armed forces received 200 well-conserved T-34 tanks free of charge in the early 1960s.[144] Frustrated by the inadequate equipment of the HPA, Czinege invited Soviet Defense Minister Andrei A. Grechko and following a 'little hunting and an enormous Hungarian feast' the Hungarian minister popped the question: 'Could you give us a few hundred of your T-34s you no longer need?' Czinege explained to the startled Grechko that these tanks could do wonders for the HPA's morale and if they could not agree, Czinege was on good enough terms with Khrushchev to 'write him a heartrending letter that he could not resist'. Two days after Grechko's departure Czinege received a message from Colonel General Shafranov, the chief Soviet adviser in Budapest: 'Andrei Antonovich says 200.'

Part IV The Soviet Factor and the Warsaw Pact

The Warsaw Pact (and the Soviet Union) influenced the Hungarian political leadership and the HPA in many ways, and this dependent relationship, in turn, affected civil–military relations. Hungary's satellite status not only detracted from the regime's legitimacy, but also from the HSWP's relationship with the armed forces. In the 1956–68 period Soviet domination of Hungary was pervasive and many-faceted yet by the mid-1960s some signs suggested that Moscow's grip on Hungary might be weakening. After 1956 Budapest had gradually wrestled increasing flexibility and autonomy from the USSR, a notion that had lasting effects on Hungarian civil–military relations.

A. Soviet Influence in Civil–Military Relations

Although following the Revolution the Soviet troops remained in Hungary it was unclear how many and for how long. The HSWP Central Committee discussed the possible withdrawal of the Soviet Army from Hungary already in December 1956 but failed to reach a decision.[145] In May 1957, Hungarian hopes for a Soviet troop pull-out were dashed as newly-appointed Soviet Foreign Minister Andrei A. Gromyko and Defense Minister Marshal Georgi K. Zhukov concluded a bilateral treaty with their Hungarian counterparts – Imre Horvath and General Geza Revesz, respectively – which regulated the legal aspects of the Red Army's stationing in Hungary.[146]

The recurrent rumors regarding the Soviet Army's withdrawal (in the fall of 1959, for instance) were not entirely unfounded. In fact, after 1956 Moscow twice offered to pull out its troops from Hungary and Romania. Khrushchev, who considered maintaining Soviet forces in both countries costly and counterproductive, made these proposals in 1958. Romanian Defense Minister Emil Bodnaras intimated his government's wish for the Soviet troops to leave soon after Stalin's death. When Khrushchev brought up the matter a few years later, Bucharest seized the opportunity.[147] Moscow made the same offer to Budapest in 1958 but Kadar flatly refused, saying 'there is absolutely no resentment in our country against the presence of your troops on our territory'.[148] Thus, Kadar rejected the offers, referring to 'the danger of Western provocation', which he maintained could well result in another 'counter-revolution'.[149] His reasons notwithstanding, it seems that Kadar was far more afraid of internal dissension than of 'Western provocation'. Not quite two years after the Revolution, he could not feel comfortable without the Soviet troops.

The pre-Revolution size of the Soviet occupying troops (80,000 to 90,000) had swollen up during and immediately after the uprising to a reported 300,000.[150] By March 1957, 50,000 Soviet soldiers were withdrawn and periodic troop reductions had continued until 1960 when the size of the occupying force stabilized at around 60,000.[151] Soviet troops in Hungary adopted a low profile; they were rarely seen in the cities, especially in Budapest. Relations between the HPA and the Soviet troops appeared to be cordial and comradely by all official accounts. Especially in the higher echelons, inter-army relations benefited from the contacts Hungarian officers made while studying in the Soviet Union.

B. The Warsaw Pact and the Hungarian Armed Forces

The founding document of the WTO reflected the foreign policy principles of the Khrushchev-Bulganin leadership but the actual hierarchy and structure of the Pact was left relatively unregulated.[152] It is fair to say that in the first few years of the Pact's existence, it added little to the bilateral military agreements between the member states already in place. Still, the WTO had a great deal of political significance in the bloc to the extent that it (1) provided a formal framework of binding the Communist states together; (2) limited the sovereignty of individual member states by forbidding their participation in other alliances; and (3) served as a useful forum for the expression of the bloc's support of various Soviet foreign policy positions and initiatives.[153]

The conventional wisdom of Western analysts has long suggested that the primary goal of the WTO was to unite Soviet forces with their East European counterparts in a military campaign. Christopher Jones and others have convincingly argued, however, that the Pact had other equally important missions as well. First, to maintain the Soviet capability for rapid military intervention in Eastern Europe, and second, to pre-empt the capabilities of East European armies to put up sustained resistance against the Soviet occupation forces.[154]

One could argue that another important function of the WTO was the maintenance of military preparedness in the NSWP states. During the late 1940s and early 1950s Stalin and his East European puppets portrayed Yugoslavia as an enemy ready to take on its neighbors with the help of its 'imperialist patrons'. Once the perceived threat of Belgrade was gone, however, there were no more real or imagined adversaries that *East European* countries could possibly accuse of bellicose designs and defense expenditures declined along with morale. The creation of the Pact eliminated the dearth of potential enemy problem, making the enemies of the USSR those of the entire bloc.

Except for the meetings of the Political Consultative Committee (PCC), the WTO was basically ignored as a military organization until the early 1960s. According to Jeffrey Simon, the real birth of the WTO as a military organization did not occur until the creation of the Central Group of Soviet Forces (CGSF) and the reform of the Pact's organizational structure in 1969.[155] Even the PCC's meetings were rhapsodic, despite the initial declaration that it was to meet semi-annually. The first joint exercise was held only in late 1961.

The alleged purpose of joint maneuvers was to drill the armies in various, usually large-scale, military tasks, but combined exercises also served Soviet attempts to fragment national control over the individual armed forces.[156] Joint maneuvers were, as a general rule, directed by WTO and not national staffs. In addition, the Pact's virtual monopoly for conducting joint exercises robbed the national armies of the opportunity to drill large formations of national troops for action on national territory.[157]

All members of the Warsaw Pact shared a Soviet-inspired military doctrine that had no relevance to the defense needs of the individual countries in the alliance. In other words, the *'national military doctrines of the NSWP countries* were obligatory systems of thought . . . regarding the fulfillment of the portion of WTO military doctrine that related to the particular country and its armed forces'.[158] These national doctrines, then, differed from the overall WTO doctrine in scope and detail only. From the mid-1960s the Soviet high command forced its new 'coalition warfare' doctrine on the NSWP that prescribed a massive and rapid offensive onto enemy territory.[159]

The 1960s was a decade marked by several contingencies. Starting in 1963 Romania became a reluctant participant of the WTO, and its unorthodox military and foreign policies rendered the country a liability rather than an asset for the alliance. For instance, in the mid-1960s Bucharest repeatedly called for the 'liquidation of military blocs' as anachronisms to national sovereignty and refused to take part in the invasion against Czechoslovakia in 1968. Following the invasion Romania abandoned the WTO's 'coalition warfare' strategy and adopted a 'people's war' doctrine (in many ways similar to that of Yugoslavia) thereby upsetting the doctrinal uniformity within the Pact. Another, albeit less consequential, turning point occurred with Albania's unilateral withdrawal from the WTO in September 1968, in response to the invasion.

Throughout the existence of the Pact, Hungary has been an obedient, if not always content, member participating in all alliance institutions as well as in combined exercises. After the Revolution, the HPA was given a few years for reorganization and the improvement of morale in the ranks. The HPA took part in only seven of the 32 joint maneuvers between 1961–68. Only two of these were held on Hungarian territory and none of them was commanded by a Hungarian officer – the reason was, perhaps, Czinege's apparent incompetence – even though all other WTO defense ministers led more than one exercise.[160]

By all accounts the performance of Hungarian troops in the joint maneuvers was exemplary. The HPA's engineering and construction troops, and bridge-builders in support of amphibious operations, earned particularly high marks consistently.[161] Hungary's military weight within the WTO had been far less than those of the northern tier states (Czechoslovakia, Poland, East Germany). Hungary's limited role in WTO doctrine in an offensive scenario would have been to make advances to north-eastern Italy, build up bridgeheads and wait for the Soviet forces to decide the battle. Once the Soviets had arrived, the HPA's function would have been rearguard support. The large number of military engineer exercises and water crossings as part of the maneuvers indicated the HPA's supposed role.[162]

C. The Invasion of Czechoslovakia: Hungary's Role

Although Hungary did participate in the Warsaw Pact invasion of Czechoslovakia, Budapest was clearly reluctant to do so.[163] Kadar and the Hungarian leaders did have the alternative of not taking part but the costs of that decision were perceived as prohibitively high. Still, the Hungarian leadership was divided until the last minute on the issue of participation.[164] The country was embarking on its new and unorthodox economic program that did not make her any friends anywhere in the bloc. It was felt that the NEM – that just started to show some faint signs of success by August – would have been jeopardized. Rezso Nyers, a HSWP Politburo member at the time, recalled that 'we were already sticking out of the bunch, thus the argument to take part held more weight'.[165] According to then Prime Minister Jeno Fock, some leaders feared that if Hungary did not participate the Soviets might go into Czechoslovakia through Hungary, killing two birds with one stone. 'We were jerked into the conflict by our hair,' Fock said recently.[166]

The invasion that commenced in the early hours of August 20 did not involve the Warsaw Pact Combined Command in either the logistics or the command and control exercises. It was not WTO Commander-in-Chief (CiC) Marshal Yakubovskiy who led the invasion but General I. G. Pavlovskiy, CiC of the Soviet Group of Forces. The invasionary force of about 650,000 Soviet, Polish, East German, Hungarian, and Bulgarian troops encountered little opposition, partly because General Ludvik Svoboda, the CiC of the Czechoslovak army ordered the CPA to remain in their barracks. The East European detachment was not too significant, it had a decidedly political function.

The actual involvement of the HPA was limited (approximately 5,000 troops), only the Bulgarian contingent was smaller. In early July one Hungarian division – filled up with reservists – was mobilized under the pretext of a future exercise, codenamed 'Zala'. The division received its marching orders on the evening of August 19. (The command originated in the Soviet leadership and reached the troops through the MOD, in blatant disregard of the Hungarian Constitution.)[167] The HPA did not identify itself with the decision but did not oppose it either. The Zalaegerszeg-based division was an average unit, no attempts were made to improve it to 'show' level.[168] The troops were deployed in an area of 500 square kilometers, around Presov in eastern Slovakia, neither inflicting nor suffering any casualties aside from a few traffic accidents.[169] There were few provocations from the local population – some name-calling, and, as one eyewitness recalls, a few natives painted 'Budapest' on the pavement with an arrow pointing to the appropriate direction – but HPA troops acted with restraint without fail.[170]

According to recently published eyewitness reports, during the invasion the deficiencies of the HPA were clearly demonstrated. The HPA's T-52 and T-55 tanks could not exceed the speed of 30 miles per hour and they took three days to get to their destination less than 350 miles from their home base. The road to Presov was lined with the broken-down tanks and vehicles of the HPA. The troops were housed in their own tents in Czechoslovak People's Army (CSPA) bases. All of their supplies arrived daily from Hungary. The troops' morale was low to begin with and the months of idleness did not help at all. HPA officers spent a great deal of time with their Czechoslovak colleagues, who remained in their bases, drinking beer and marking time. For the conscripted men the three months in Czechoslovakia was an uneventful and, according to all published recollections, utterly boring period of time. The Hungarian 'invaders' returned home on October 23, 1968.[171]

Summary

What does the practice of Hungarian civil–military relations in the 1953–68 period tell us about the models considered in Chapter 1? First of all, there was no conflict – such as Kolkowicz suggested – between the Party and the armed forces, not even during the 1956 Revolution. The military, according to all appearances, seemed to have espoused the value system of the Party and did not turn its back on the HSWP even after the repression of the uprising. There was no major friction between political and regular officers in this period either. The interpenetration between the Party and the army did not take place in Hungary to the extent indicated by Colton's model.

A good illustration of this point is that Defense Minister Czinege was the only one among his NSWP colleagues who was not a Politburo member, furthermore, military representation in high Party bodies was lowest in the region.[172]

The three models concerning civil–military relations in the East European context do stress the Party's political control over the armed forces and this certainly seems to be a valid point for the Hungarian case. Nonetheless, it appears that the HPA's advancement through the successive developmental stages propounded by Herspring and Volgyes was frustrated by the Revolution which necessitated the comprehensive rehabilitation of the military's political constitution. Alexiev's model suggesting the gradual evolution of divergent perceptions of national versus ideological desiderata seems to approximate my findings. Although barely noticeable, 'nativization', that is, the tendency of paying increasing attention to national traditions and even national interests, did begin after 1956.

Although Moscow's influence remained pervasive, Soviet control diminished following Stalin's death, but especially after 1957. The presence of advisers became less obtrusive, their interference in Hungary's domestic affairs less pronounced. One of the major arguments of this study is that this trend had strengthened throughout the balance of Hungarian communism.

4 Accommodation and Recalcitrance (1968–88)

The chronological parameters of this chapter are the 1968 invasion of Czechoslovakia and the replacement of Janos Kadar as Party leader in May 1988. In this period the initially cautious shift away from the Soviet line that originated in the late 1960s gained a great deal of strength. By the mid-1980s, Hungary's domestic, foreign, and military policies became increasingly attentive to national desiderata.

This chapter is divided into four sections. Part I briefly examines the political and socioeconomic developments of the 1968–88 period. Part II analyzes civil–military relations. The remainder of this chapter investigates some of the issue areas that impacted upon civil–military relations. Part III evaluates politico-military training in the school system and in the HPA while Part IV surveys the changes in Hungary's relationship to the Warsaw Pact.

Part I Political, Economic, and Social Affairs

Drawing a line of distinction between Hungary's political, economic, and social developments during the 1968–88 period proves particularly difficult, for these areas were interrelated in many complex ways. Until the late 1970s Budapest's economic policy was the center of Hungarian unorthodoxy *vis-à-vis* the Soviet bloc. At the same time, the political and social phenomena that were taking shape in the early 1980s were in no small part elicited by the deterioration of the overall economic situation.

A. Increasing Autonomy in Domestic and Foreign Policy

In the 1968–88 period Kadar made few political changes. He chose his associates with care, making sure that they shared his ideas for the future. In this period, particularly in the 1980s, the extent of Soviet interference in Hungary's domestic affairs showed a marked decline. The Hungarian case reveals the lack of a consistent Soviet policy toward Eastern Europe in this period. The Kremlin's attention to the region had been erratic, wavering between permissiveness and retrenchment, reflecting both the diversity of Soviet interests and uncertainty concerning the ways of dealing with the bloc.

The tension in Soviet–Hungarian relations generated by Budapest's reluctant participation in the invasion of Czechoslovakia soon dissipated. Although relations appeared to be close, conflicts of interest between Hungary and the Soviet Union did emerge on several occasions. For instance, following the Sino-Soviet crisis of March 1969, Hungary (along with Poland and Romania) resisted Moscow's efforts to involve NSWP states in the quandary.[1] Hungary did not, as the other WTO states did, link China to 'Western imperialist forces' nor label the Chinese CP a 'military bureaucratic regime'.[2] Throughout the intraparty controversies of the World Communist movement, Hungary maintained a decidedly low profile.

Brezhnev and his colleagues viewed the Hungarian economic adventure with increasing skepticism and were instrumental in its deceleration in the early 1970s. The Kremlin refused to make a long-term commitment for the delivery of raw materials and thereby thwarted the Hungarian planning process. Discords between Budapest and Moscow were chronicled by numerous Soviet articles which expressed misgivings about the NEM. By the mid-1970s serious disputes regarding Hungary's economic reform impaired the atmosphere of Hungarian–Soviet relations. Moscow presumably saw no good reason to subsidize the Hungarian economy with cheap raw materials (especially fuels) as Hungarians already enjoyed one of the highest living standards in the region.

In the early 1970s, then, mounting Soviet and East European pressures forced Kadar to reconsider some of the most controversial aspects of the NEM. The working class and middle-level party functionaries, whose support the regime desperately needed, also strongly opposed further reforms as they had little to gain from them. At a March 1974 Central Committee session Kadar replaced a few key colleagues – most prominently Rezso Nyers, the 'father of the reform' – to appease Moscow, the bloc, and the alienated domestic groups. The regime halted some reform programs, restricted entrepreneurial opportunities, and adopted a more conservative economic policy. At the same time, the general liberalization continued. Hungarians were allowed to travel to the West in ever-increasing numbers, while political and economic contacts with capitalist countries expanded rapidly.

Romania's treatment of ethnic Hungarians had figured prominently in the public consciousness but Kadar was reluctant to jeopardize the already volatile relationship with his neighbor.[3] In the late 1980s Budapest's long-standing problems with Bucharest finally received the attention of not only the population, but for the first time since 1945 – due to mounting public pressure – that of the leadership as well. Animosities flared up in 1987 and turned into a virtual cold war between the two Warsaw Pact allies.

One significant aspect of the Kadar regime's tacit 'social contract' with the population was the relative loosening of ideological exactitude, expressed by Kadar's 'who is not against us, is with us' maxim. The relaxed ideological orthodoxy had its effects felt in the HSWP organization as well. Articles and speeches decried the discipline problems in the HSWP during the 1970s. One remedial measure was the party card exchange in 1976 resulting in the expulsion or resignation of 6.4 percent of the membership.[4] The political and ideological disinterest of the working class remained particularly pervasive.[5] Starting with the mid-1980s official misgivings about the viability of Marxism-Leninism had appeared frequently in the media.

Kadar's regime showed relative restraint towards 'those who thought otherwise'. The limits of the Party's patience were understood by most people. Whereas criticism of domestic (particularly economic) shortcomings was acceptable and at times even encouraged, any sort of propaganda against the Soviet Union, Hungary's socialist neighbors, and the viability of the regime itself remained out of bounds.[6] In the early 1980s an increasingly vocal group of dissidents emerged that began to publish *samizdat* journals and books. It seemed that as long as the democratic opposition was not working overtly at overthrowing the regime, it would be left essentially unharmed.[7] By 1988, several semi-legal political organizations emerged some of which were to play decisive roles in the political transition of 1989–90.

In the 1980s the regime made half-hearted attempts to introduce political reforms, particularly in the electoral, legislative and constitutional areas. All of them attempted to appease the population while making sure that the political monopoly of the HSWP would remain intact. Consequently, the results were less than spectacular. Although the HSWP evidently recognized the popular need for democratization, its efforts could not satisfy the people.[8] The fundamental problem of genuine political participation could not be resolved as long as the party was clinging onto its all-encompassing political power. As Zbigniew Brzezinski noted, 'genuine participation is incompatible with the rule of a Leninist-type party'. The system's 'fatal flaw', then, remained the party.[9]

At the HSWP's 12th Congress (1980) the return of the reformist policies was underscored by the dismissal of some of its most ardent opponents. Several speakers at the Party's 13th Congress (1985) criticized the shortcomings, and even the general decline of party life on all levels. By the late 1980s the more realistic Party leaders, such as Patriotic Peoples' Front (PPF) leader Imre Pozsgay, had realized that 'ours is no longer a mere economic crisis, but the political crisis of a system that must regain credibility'.[10] Kadar's reluctance to deal with Hungary's mounting economic difficulties had been recognized not only by the population but by the HSWP's membership as well. In 1987–88 alone, 73,000 people, or 8.3 percent of the membership, left the Party,[11] and according to a young party functionary 'new party members could not be drawn into the Party even with a lasso'.[12]

In May 1988 the HSWP held a National Conference to discuss the pervasive economic problems. A large majority of delegates voted to replace Kadar (he was given the ceremonial post of party president) with Prime Minister Karoly Grosz. Kadar, along with his staunch allies, lost his membership in the Politburo as well. After 16 years Rezso Nyers regained his seat in the Politburo. Another welcome addition to the ruling body was Pozsgay, a strong supporter of economic and political reforms.

B. Hungary and Gorbachev (1985–88)

Initially, the ascent of Mikhail S. Gorbachev to the top position of the CPSU signalled little change for the Hungarian leaders, who had to wait for the Soviet approval of the NEM until the General Secretary's June 1986 visit to Budapest. The evolution of Gorbachev's East European policy can be divided to three distinct stages.[13] In the first stage (1985–86) it appeared that he would attempt to 're-establish order' but it was also clear that Gorbachev had no plans to further his own domestic economic program by 'squeezing' Eastern Europe. During this period several articles appeared in the Soviet press warning Hungary about the dangers of too close economic cooperation with Western states.[14]

In the second stage (1986–87) Gorbachev was more sympathetic to manifestations of limited independence within the region. In the summer of 1986, roughly corresponding with his celebrated visit to Budapest, a number of Soviet newspapers and magazines (e.g., *Ekonomicheskoe Sotrudnichestvo, Literaturnaya Gazeta, Novoe Vremya*) began to pay close attention to Hungary and its economic reforms. A series of *Pravda* articles depicted the country's reform efforts positively.[15] The communique issued after the Gorbachev–Kadar meeting reflected a 'full identity of views on economic issues'.[16]

During the third stage (1987–89), the Soviet leader stressed the need for the reform of intra-bloc relations while remaining tolerant of unorthodox behavior in the bloc. As far as Soviet–Hungarian relations are concerned, Moscow expressed not only its approval but also its interest in Budapest's economic reforms.[17] In early 1987 a top Gorbachev adviser, Academician Oleg Bogomolov, admitted that the Hungarian experience was helping the Soviet Union in its own reform efforts and contended that many elements of the Hungarian NEM could be used by the USSR.[18] Within a year, CPSU Politburo member Yegor Ligachev, Foreign Minister Eduard Shevardnadze, Defense Minister Sergei Sokolov, and Prime Minister Nikolai Ryzhkov also paid visits to Budapest. All applauded the Hungarian reforms and called for increased cooperation within the CMEA.[19] Notwithstanding Moscow's interest, the NEM that Soviet experts had studied so intently was a failure. The economy did not function efficiently and the gains in living standards were financed to a large extent by Western credits.

By late 1987, Kadar was clearly out of sync with Moscow. At the 70th anniversary of the October Revolution the reception extended to Kadar was less friendly than usual and the press release following his unusually short private meeting with Gorbachev suggested Moscow's disenchantment with him.[20] In February 1988, Supreme Soviet President Andrei Gromyko visited Hungary on his first trip abroad since 1985. Ostensibly, one of Gromyko's tasks was to patch up political differences between Kadar and Prime Minister Grosz, himself a belated convert to reformism.[21] Moscow wasted few tears on Kadar following his replacement at the helm of the HSWP. For Gorbachev, Grosz was the epitome of the new, more youthful brand of leader he was impatient to see take over in the region.[22]

It is important to see that Hungary gained little from either *perestroika* or *glasnost'* aside from the obvious benefit of the more favorable Soviet political climate. As Timothy Garton Ash observed, 'To describe the Hungarian economic reforms as *perestroika* is also close to an insult. The Hungarians have been working at it for more than 20 years; they have gone farther in deeds than the Russians have in words; they now face problems of which the Soviets can only dream.'[23]

C. Hungary and the West

The beginning of Hungary's active courting of the West coincided approximately with the retrenchment in the reform movement. As François Mitterrand put it in 1976: 'Talking to the Hungarian leaders . . . I met realists who . . . are naturally loyal to their ideology but show interest in foreign experience at the same time . . . The country is part of the

European mainstream.'[24] By the mid-1970s, and particularly after the 1975 Helsinki Conference, Hungary began to look for answers for its worsening economic problems in the West. In the years to follow, Kadar visited most West European states and Budapest played host to scores of Western leaders. Kadar's reception in the West European capitals was invariably warm, reflecting his regime's growing reputation as the most liberal in the region.[25] The tangible benefits of Hungary's Western policy included the return of St. Stephen's crown by U.S. Secretary of State Cyrus Vance in 1978, as well as membership in the IMF, GATT, and other international organizations. In 1978 Hungary also gained 'Most Favored Nation' (MFN) status from the United States.

Although for thirty years Budapest followed the Soviet foreign policy line religiously, starting with the 1980s Hungary's external relations began to be dictated more and more by domestic desiderata. Although Hungary failed to express any enthusiasm about the Soviet invasion of Afghanistan it supported the Soviet stance in the United Nations. While verbally backing Moscow's actions, Hungarian leaders pledged to do their 'utmost to protect the fruits of detente and promote its continuity'.[26] In 1985, evaluating the dissimilarities of Hungarian foreign policy to those of other WTO states, Deputy Minister of Foreign Affairs Istvan Roska said that 'if one stands on the ground of reality, one has to accept our different ways and not consider them aberrations'.[27]

D.   The Economy: Reform and Retrenchment

Kadar's regime was well aware that the HSWP's track record would be measured by its economic achievements. In a 1974 article he wrote that 'a large segment of the working class does not evaluate the Party's activities on the basis of ideological accuracy but by their living standards'.[28] The NEM created a second economy and a second society, allowed the restrictions caused by central planning to be reduced, fiddled with the market, and introduced a comprehensive price reform that substantially cut subsidies, particularly on luxury items.

By the late 1970s it became apparent that the retrenchment made the economy's problems worse instead of solving them.[29] The leadership, now with Moscow's tacit approval, set out once again on the reform path. Timing, however, was less favorable than in 1968 particularly due to the unfavorable external environment. Consequently, results proved to be less than sensational. Renewed emphasis on intensive development by 1980 bore fruit and favored progress but could not reverse the deterioration of the economy. Hungary needed hard currency income; its products, however, became less and less competitive in quality and price on the world market, especially when stacked up against the wares of the newly industrializing Southeast Asian states. In addition, inflation and accumulating foreign debts represented serious problems.[30] Low labor discipline and popular frustration with the economy reflected the deterioration of living standards. Furthermore, the government had run up a considerable budget deficit in every year starting with 1985. In 1988, for the first time in a socialist state, income tax and value added tax were introduced. The Grosz government implemented steep price increases and other austerity measures but no tangible progress was achieved.

Throughout the period Budapest was clearly dissatisfied with the CMEA whose obsolete structure and trade mechanism hindered Hungarian economic reforms. Within the CMEA there were conflicting conceptions of integration: the USSR stressed specialization and expanded cooperation while Hungary desired expanding trade with the West to support technological development and improvement in living standards. Until 1974 Hungary had a positive trade balance with the CMEA but this trend was reversed in the 1974–81 period when increased fuel and raw material prices turned to favor the Soviet Union.[31] The 1975 introduction of the 'sliding scale' of energy prices in the CMEA hurt Hungary especially severely because of its poor endowment in natural resources and its need for increasing amounts of fuels.

E. Pervasive Social Malaise

The 1968–88 period may be conveniently divided into two one-decade subsets.[32] Until the late 1970s many Hungarians experienced substantial improvements in their living conditions as a result of the regime's economic policies aiming at popular satisfaction. By the early 1980s, however, this favorable trend reversed and social problems began to surface rapidly. By the end of the decade there were few diseases that had not yet infected Hungarian society. Perhaps the most severe of these ills was the general pessimism and apathy that characterized the population's attitude regarding the future.[33]

The Party and the government were unable to come up with a comprehensive youth policy that could reverse the tendency of the alienation and growing pessimism of young people. The government was also unable to find a remedy to the country's notorious housing problem. The lack of affordable housing, in turn, was one of the main causes for the serious demographic problems. Between 1980 and 1988 Hungary's population decreased by almost 90,000 (close to one percent); the number of those aged under 30 by 360,000. At the same time, the number of divorces rapidly increased while the number of marriages showed a negative trend. Social scientists had long warned that as economic difficulties became more severe, aggression and the need to find scapegoats would become more prevalent. Anti-Semitism, gypsy bashing, and violent attacks against foreign students had become the trade marks of underground youth gangs (calling themselves 'skinheads'). Statistics also suggested drastic increases in all types of violent crime.[34]

The system of Hungarian health care was also plagued by fundamental problems as a result of the economic situation. Economic decline forced a large proportion of the adult population to hold down two jobs in order to make ends meet. This stress on working people, in turn, put increased burden on the health-care system. Between 1970 and 1985 the average lifespan of Hungarian men had fallen from 66.8 years to 65.6.[35] Moreover, Hungary had the highest per capita suicide rate in the world. This tragic problem – termed *morbus hungaricus* by the eminent writer, Gyula Illyes – had become even more serious by the late 1980s.[36] Hungary was also a world leader in alcoholism.[37] Amidst these conditions the spread of poverty was hardly surprising. According to government figures, the number of 'needy persons' had doubled in the late 1980s.[38] Data published by the Central Statistical Office showed that in 1987 660,000 people (i.e., over 6 per cent of the population) lived below the officially set subsistence level.[39] During the 1980s a permanent underclass had formed that could harbor little hope to shake off its predicament.

Part II   Civil–Military Relations

In 1968–88 developments in civil–military relations and in the Hungarian military establishment reflected those in the country's political, economic, and social affairs. There were several important differences, however. The HPA was a great deal slower to react to the incremental changes in the political atmosphere than other social strata. The main reason for this phenomenon lay with the fact that no societal organization was more profoundly penetrated and controlled by the HSWP than the armed forces. Nonetheless, by the late 1980s the HPA also acquired some distinctive new characteristics that made it dissimilar to the other armies of the Warsaw Pact. Although some of these changes were quite subtle they were unmistakable signals of a discreet shift from uniformity to national orientation.

A.   The HPA's Internal Missions

According to A. A. Timorin, a Soviet military tactical specialist, there are three internal functions of all socialist armies: they act (1) as a psychological deterrent against anti-socialist forces; (2) as a reserve of manpower and equipment for the internal security forces; and (3) as a 'combat force in cases when the opposition of the enemies of socialism acquire significant scale, intensity, duration, and sharpness (a counter-revolutionary uprising, mutiny, banditry, the unleashing of civil war)'.[40] Soviet sources often add that no WTO army would have to rely entirely on its own resources, since 'fraternal help' from other Pact armies would be rendered as a matter of course.[41]

The Hungarian regime did not shy away from admitting that one of the HPA's functions was to resist internal strife. At a 1970 Politburo meeting Kadar asserted that it was the HPA's task to defend the regime from internal opposition. 'It would be untenable that a ruling class could let power slip out of its hands when its armed forces sit still in their barracks,' he said.[42] The 1976 Defense Law regulated the army's internal missions as follows: cooperation in the protection of national security and domestic order; participation in the national economy and in the education and training of youth; and rendering assistance at times of natural disasters.[43] Nonetheless, official publications by the early 1980s conceded that the internal-repressive functions of the HPA had diminished as a result of political consolidation.

Aside from the HPA, two organizations were charged with the responsibility to defend the regime in domestic contingencies. In Hungary, unlike in the other socialist states of the region, the uniformed security police was abolished in 1956. The Ministry of Interior (MOI) controlled the activities of both the state's conventional police forces and the Border Guards (*Hatarorseg*, BG). Supervised by the MOI and operating according to unified WTO regulation, the BG consisted of 16,000 men, of whom 11,000 were draftees.[44] In addition to the MOI, the BG was also controlled by the MOI's Party Political Committee, its own CiC, and the HSWP Central Committee Secretariat's Administrative Department. Party membership was a prerequisite for professional service in the BG and both HSWP and CYL membership rates were higher there than in the HPA.[45] Consequently, the BG would probably have been more reliable than the army as a whole in an internal emergency, although the high ratio of conscripts (69 percent in the BG versus 55 percent in the HPA) might have been a source of problems.

Theoretically, the function of the 60,000-strong Workers' Guards (WG) was similar to that of any national guard, but in practice it was only equipped with small arms and in the event of internal disturbances its activities would have been limited to maintaining general control over the population.[46] Party membership in the WG was relatively high: 82 percent in 1980.[47] Although in a domestic crisis BG and the WG units could have been utilized, in a larger than merely local conflict – because of the absence of specialized MOI details, similar to the Polish 'ZOMO' and the Romanian 'Securitate' – re-establishing order would have been the HPA's task.

B.   The Party, the State, and the Armed Forces

Although some aspects of civil–military relations had changed in the 1968–88 period, the major contentions of the models examined in Chapter 1 pertaining to the Party's domination of the armed forces continued to hold true. The HSWP's rule over the HPA had become somewhat more indirect by the late 1980s, however. This shift was far more subtle and less perceptible than the changes witnessed in the political domain.

The HSWP exerted its control over the HPA through the closely integrated work of the HSWP Central Committee and its Administrative Department, and through the 'direct subordination of the armed forces to the Party's policies'.[48] Working together with the MPA – whose head reported directly to both the MOD *and* to the Secretary in charge of the Administrative Department – were the political department heads at the division level, and the political officers in place all the way to the battalion level. Yet another channel of the HSWP's control of the armed forces was the Party Committee of the HPA, a party organization that enjoyed equal status with the county HSWP committees.[49]

Furthermore, the HSWP also employed another body, the Army Committee of the Central Committee, to evaluate the army's political work.[50] This organization was unique within the Warsaw Pact and its existence seemed to indicate the Party's concern about the supervisory work over the army, justified by reports of relaxed 'ideological awareness.' Political control over the army was also exercised – albeit largely theoretically – by the National Defense Committee of the National Assembly (parliament). Invariably, the Chairman of the Defense Committee was a member of the HSWP Central Committee as well. All of these organs were utilized to exercise political supervision, both through the selection of trusted party members for command positions, and through the supervision of the HPA's party organizations.

The HSWP's control of the military was not codified in any way. The

1972 Constitution merely pointed to the Party's 'guiding role' in society in accord with other Soviet-type constitutions. The Party's role in the 1976 Defense Law was left similarly unspecified. The paragraph on the 'general guiding principles' of the armed forces, however, stated unambiguously that 'the basis of the armed forces' direction and the definition of its tasks is the defense policy of the *Hungarian People's Republic*' (that is, the state and *not* the party).[51] A theoretical article on 'Our Party's Defense Policy' explained that the 'most significant political axiom of our defense is . . . the consistent enforcement of the party's guidance and control'.[52] Important resolutions concerning the HPA were made either at the quinquennial HSWP's congresses or, much less frequently (e.g., only once in the 1970s) at CC or PB sessions when the army was on the agenda.[53]

An effective tool of the Party's control over the armed forces was the so-called 'lists of sensitive positions' or 'cadre lists' (*hataskori listak*). These were classified registers of positions the appointment to which was exercised exclusively by the HSWP CC. Between 1968 and 1985 seven such lists were prepared, each updating the preceding one.[54] The document reproduced below dates from 1971 and specifies the HSWP body with which the appointing authority rested and the pertinent positions.[55] The list demonstrates lucidly the extent of direct control the HSWP's various organs exercised over the HPA.

The HSWP Central Committee:
– President, Vice Presidents, and members of the Council of Ministers (i.e.,
    including the Minister of Defense).

The HSWP Politburo:
– State Secretaries;
– First Deputy Ministers;
– Chief of the MPA;
– Hungarian deputies of the CiC, Chief-of-Staff, and Chief of the Technical
    Committee[56] of the WTO's United Armed Forces (UAF);
– promotions to the rank of general and in the corps of generals.

The HSWP Central Committee's Secretariat:
– deputy ministers of defense and others holding the same rank (e.g., the
    Secretary of the National Assembly's Defense Committee);
– General Secretary of the Hungarian Defense Association (HDA – *Magyar
    Honvedelmi Szovetseg*);
– army and brigade commanders;
– Commander of Civil Defense;

– Commander of National Air Defense;
– Attorney General of the Supreme Military Court.

The HSWP Central Committee's Administrative Secretariat must also endorse the appointment of:

A. military positions:
– chiefs of the technical, infantry, and tank corps of the HPA;
– First Deputy of the Chief-of-Staff of the HPA;
– MOD Department Chiefs and their deputies;
– Commander of the Miklos Zrinyi Military Academy;
– division and special troops commanders;
– Chief-of-Staff of the Commander of Civil Defense
– candidates for study at the Staff Academy of the Soviet Union (Voroshilov).

B. party positions within the HPA:
– first secretaries of the HPA, divisions, (national) Civil Defense, and (national) Air Defense party organizations.

The HSWP Central Committee's Agitational and Propaganda Department:
– chief editors of *Nephadsereg* and *Lobogo* (the HPA's weekly and monthly publications, respectively).

The HSWP Central Committee's Administrative Department:
– Department Chiefs of the HPA's MPA;
– commanders of the military colleges;
– deputies, political deputies, and chiefs-of-staff of the HPA, Air Defense, division, and Civil Defense commanders;
– promotions to the rank of colonel.

As in the 1948–68 period, the Party continued to coopt members of the high military leadership. Several HPA leaders retained or gained seats in the CC although none was appointed to the PB. Military representation in this body averaged approximately 3 percent during this period.[57] In addition, HPA leaders also received positions in the state hierarchy. Many officers were members of local administrative bodies (e.g., city or town councils,) and some were 'elected' to the National Assembly.[58] As a general rule, only high-ranking military/political officers acquired seats in the national legislature.[59] The ranks of parliamentary deputies almost invariably included the Minister of Defense, his Chief-of-Staff, and the Chief of the MPA.

The CYL's work in the armed forces was supervised by the HSWP's

Youth Committee, the Administrative Department of the HSWP Central Committee, and the HPA Committee of the CYL. In addition, CYL activities were also overseen by the HPA Executive Committee and by the Youth Division of the MOD's MPA.[60] On every level, the CYL was subordinated to the parallel party organization. The CYL was primarily responsible for the political and ideological education of draftees as the majority of professional cadres were members of the HSWP.

Despite the intricate mechanism of Party domination, in 1968–88 – and particularly starting with the 1980s – the army and the general press featured innumerable articles criticizing party–ideological work and discipline in the HPA. At the root of these shortcomings were the general political apathy of armed forces personnel and their lack of interest in ideological matters. According to an official history of the HPA, one of the main tasks of the armed forces in the 1960s was to 'develop the socialist aspects of the army's internal life', while in the 1970s 'to consolidate and intensify its overall socialist character'. The achievements, lamented the authors, poorly reflected the possibilities for improvement.[61] The HSWP's 11th Congress (1975) again designated raising the level of morale and political work as the HPA's most important task for the following five-year period.[62] Although the army's low 'political consciousness' was often reproached, HPA leaders generally praised the firmness of ideological commitment in the forces.[63]

C.   The MPA and Party Life in the Military

The MPA maintained a large organization and greatly contributed to the bureaucratization of the armed forces.[64] The MPA had no utility for the armed forces *per se*, indeed, some observers noted that had it been abolished from one day to the next, no one would have noticed.[65] In the early 1970s the MPA created a new body, the Pedagogical and Methodological Center, to improve political work and to offer advanced training for political officers. The Center's activities notwithstanding, the quality of political guidance and the professional standards of supporting materials issued by the MPA to political officers remained 'unqualifiably low'.[66]

The secretaries and functionaries of the HPA's party organizations were selected by the 'higher organs' and elections to these posts lacked any pretense of spontaneity.[67] At the same time, party functionaries and political officers continued to possess the ability to influence military-professional issues even though they were rarely experts in military matters.[68] The input of these cadres was instrumental in decisions pertaining to questions of personnel, discipline, and organization.

Although challenging orders was prohibited, the regulations of the HPA allowed discussion and the forwarding of proposals on different fora. These outlets, however, were essentially restricted to debates at party and CYL meetings and severely limited the participation of non-members. It appears from the literature that those who failed to take part in these gatherings missed little. Many an article castigated the dullness of party and CYL meetings, the tediousness of their format and conduct, and the monotony of general party life in the HPA.[69] Party and CYL membership among professional soldiers continued to be the norm. Around 90 percent of the officers were members of the HSWP, 10 percent of the CYL.[70] Party and CYL affiliation among NCOs was somewhat lower while approximately 60 percent of conscripted soldiers held membership in the CYL.[71] The HPA's party organizations accepted 2,000–2,100 new members annually.[72] A telling statistic that commended the work of political officers is that about 20 percent of conscripts joined the CYL during their military service.[73]

At the same time, many CYL-affiliated draftees failed to measure up to the expectations of their organization. In 1986, for instance, 38 percent of CYL members in the HPA were subjected to some sort of disciplinary action.[74] In spite of enormous resources expended on socialization within the military, the soldiers' response to the regime's messages did not meet the political leadership's expectations. The high level of party and CYL membership in the armed forces should not be taken to indicate genuine loyalties. Most officers who joined the HSWP did so because of the obvious payoffs of party membership in career advancement.[75] Being a party member was simply a 'part of the job' for most professional military officers.

The lack of desired results in the politico-ideological training of conscripts was indicated by the 1982 introduction of 'company trustees', a 'new breed of political commissars' in the military.[76] Trustee candidates (70 percent were HSWP members), recommended by their local HSWP and CYL organizations, were selected from soldiers who had already completed basic training.[77] The first political trustee training course – specializing in party politics and general political and military studies, and lasting for four months – started in August 1981. The graduates of the course received NCO ranks. Their functions were twofold: first, to improve discipline and morale in the units (companies) assigned to them and second, to inform the conscripts about significant political events, and to lead various political activities, such as discussions relating to ideological and political issues, viewing films on relevant topics, etc.[78]

By 1987 the trustee system was subjected to a great deal of criticism. Soldiers saw yet another taskmaster in the 'trustees' and were generally wary of them. Angered by their quick advancement in rank even though they were non-professional soldiers, NCOs had also been unable to develop good working relations with the trustees.[79] In retrospect, it appears that the trustee system – unceremoniously abolished in 1989 – was a political blunder as it was incapable of achieving the desired results yet it unnecessarily antagonized both draftees and NCOs.

A small segment of draftees the HPA could scarcely even hope to indoctrinate: conscientious objectors to military service and prospective students of theological seminaries.[80] Beginning with 1966, those accepted to theological schools had undergone the same training as their more secular cohorts with a few modifications: they were permitted to keep Bibles in their lockers, to attend religious services in civilian clothing on their leave, and to consult with their church superiors. They too were obliged to participate in all military and political activities.[81] For those whose religion prohibited bearing arms the HPA offered the possibility of military service without weapons starting in 1976. Only two such denominations existed in Hungary, both of them very small: the Church of Nazarene and the Jehovah's Witnesses (the latter was illegal until the late 1980s). During the late 1980s approximately 60–70 draftees selected the non-armed service option annually.[82] Those few who objected to military service for political reasons, did so on the grounds that the regime was illegitimate and undemocratic.[83] If they remained resolute in spite of the dissuasion of HPA authorities, they were brought to trial and sentenced to a few years (the maximum five-year punishment was never imposed) in prison.

D.   Democratization and the Surfacing of National Attributes

Some of the most important developments in this period were the HSWP and the HPA leaderships' efforts to democratize the armed forces along with the emergence of some national (as opposed to 'socialist international') attributes in the army. These phenomena were the results of conscious policy decisions – aiming to elicit social support for and recognition of the military.

In 1970 the HPA introduced the position of 'ombudsman' officer whose responsibility was to assist in safeguarding the interests of professional and reserve military cadres. The 1975 Service Code (*Szolgalati Szabalyzat*) delineated the rights and responsibilities of soldiers, thereby seeking to prevent potential abuses of power. The 1976 Defense Law also featured several aspects that intended to democratize the armed forces. Particularly noteworthy were measures that altered the situation of draftees – the representatives of the 'civilian society'. For the first time, the rights of soldiers were protected by special provisions, and lines of complaint against professional cadres were clearly defined.[84]

The new 1988 Service Code abolished several unnecessary regulations that made the draftees' service time more difficult. For instance, conscripts were allowed to keep civilian clothes in the barracks and to wear them on leave. Furthermore, the Code permitted draftees to hitch-hike and codified their right to fifteen days of leave per annum. Even more significantly, the document attempted to put a stop to the traditional mistreatment of soldiers just entering the service by their peers who had already served some time, by stating that the latter enjoyed no privilege over the former if ranks were the same.[85]

National characteristics emerged primarily in the context of Hungary's relations with the WTO. Nevertheless, there were several signs of this phenomenon in the purely domestic military context as well. For the first time since 1948, the 1975 Service Code emphasized not only the values of 'internationalism' but also called for soldiers to uphold *national* military traditions.[86] Starting with the late 1970s the HPA acquired more and more national features. In 1978, for instance, the entire system of the HPA's supply services was reorganized. The goal of this project was to make the services more efficient and the result was an organization fundamentally different from its Warsaw Pact counterparts. After 1985, the HPA's shift toward national values further accelerated.[87] The relatively liberal treatment of conscripts, the reduction of the length of their service time, the apparent reluctance to keep up with the Soviet-dictated growth in military spending, and proliferating contacts with Western armies suggested an increasingly unambiguous departure from the Warsaw Pact line.

To be sure, these factors should not be overestimated and construed as an outright opposition to the Pact, much less equated with Romania's relatively independent stance *vis-à-vis* the WTO. Nevertheless, one must see an intelligible trend toward more willingness to counter Pact policies that adversely affected Hungarian interests. The fundamental objective of this policy was to forestall the long-term subordination of Hungary's national interests to that of the Warsaw Pact (and, what may be tantamount to it, to that of the Soviet Union). In the next chapter we will see this trend to its logical conclusion.

E. Social and Disciplinary Problems

As any draft-based army, the HPA, too, was a microcosm of societal attitudes and behavioral norms. As we have seen, in the 1970s and 1980s

Hungarian society became affected by a plethora of social ills. Since the army enlisted young males, a cross-section of society most open to harmful social influences, its problems were more serious than those of society at large.

The general health and fitness conditions of many young men who appeared before the army medical examiners' board was so low that they either could not be conscripted, or had to be exempted from more rigorous training. In 1980, for example, 10–11 percent of draft-age youngsters were unfit for military service and a further 4–5 percent could only be drafted with limitations imposed on their training.[88] The number of suicides and self-mutilation in the HPA was fivefold of that in the general population.[89] Crime – for the most part, petty theft, larceny, and traffic violations – was rampant and became the topic of a great many books and articles. Starting with the early 1980s drug abuse exacerbated difficulties epitomized by the army's long-standing alcoholism problem.[90]

Partly as a result of these shortcomings, serious breaches of discipline – e.g., AWOL – occurred frequently. Disciplinary foibles were aggravated by commanders unwilling to report them to their superiors.[91] (The officer informing his superior of these shortcomings could expect to be reprimanded and held responsible.) Harassment and physical violence directed against new draftees by their more experienced peers often caused severe psychological problems and drove some to suicide.[92] By the mid-1980s the number of conscripts with some criminal past reached record proportions (fifteen percent of those coming from Budapest).[93] In the early 1970s, the MPA's remedy for the disciplinary problems was to demand from commanders to maintain 'iron discipline' and to utilize punitive sanctions to the fullest.[94] In the 1980s, as a result of the democratization process in the military, the HPA's attitude towards disciplinary problems had softened.

F.   The Military Elite

Similarly to some other Hungarian administrative and governmental hierarchies, the HPA leadership became infamous for its widespread corruption, mismanagement of funds, and lack of professionalism. Until late 1984 the composition of the military elite remained essentially unaltered. The only major change occurred in 1973 when Chief-of-Staff Lieutenant General Karoly Csemi was replaced by Major General Istvan Olah. Defense Minister Colonel (and later Army) General Lajos Czinege epitomized everything that was wrong with the military leadership. Czinege's ministerial tenure lasted for a quarter century (1960–84), he was a HSWP CC member for 30 years, served as a deputy in the National Assembly, and chaired or participated in countless committees. Reports of his indecorous private and professional conduct (he squandered millions for his own luxuries, physically insulted his subordinates, etc.) already reached the Party leadership in the early 1960s but the Defense Minister held on to his position and to his virtually unbridled power in his bailiwick.[95]

What reportedly saved Czinege from the humiliation of dismissal were his excellent contacts with not only the Hungarian but also with other East European and Soviet party and military leaders. According to some accounts, the Defense Minister was Kadar's favorite lieutenant which is difficult to see given their diametrically opposed personalities and conduct.[96] In 1984, the same year he was awarded the USSR's prestigious Lenin Prize, Czinege was replaced as Minister of Defense and appointed Deputy Prime Minister. How could this happen to someone with a sixth-grade education in the mid-1980s was an enigma that puzzled Czinege himself. In all probability, he was promoted in order to prevent rumors of his dismissal.

Czinege's replacement in the MOD was General Istvan Olah, the former Chief-of-Staff and a well-trained professional officer. Olah, a soldier-politician with profound patriotic feelings, shared his thoughts on military reform only with his deputy, MPA Chief Ferenc Karpati. Olah unexpectedly died in December 1985 and was succeeded by his confidante. Although Karpati's appointment was quietly criticized in the HPA – mainly because he made his career in the army's political apparatus – he was not an unwise choice as he could be expected to promote his predecessor's ideas.[97] An early critic of Czinege's conduct, Karpati attempted to introduce some reforms, but his initiatives were all too often stonewalled by his subordinates. He made an effort to raise the living standards of career soldiers and to elevate the prestige of the profession. Karpati's labor in this area achieved some successes but could not radically alter the situation.[98]

Karpati was capable of halting some of the most troublesome tendencies in the military leadership, relating to professional conduct and discipline. Under Czinege, MOD bureaucrats were notorious for blatantly neglecting their duties. Superintendents of the HPA, for instance, routinely failed to visit the units assigned to them for years at a time; in one case, the Zrinyi Military Academy was not called on by its MOD overseers for 20 years.[99] The conduct of army leaders at HPA and WTO military exercises also left a great deal to be desired. Evaluations of maneuvers were often falsified, offering far better reports than merited. As long as supervisors dispatched from the MOD were wined and dined in suitable fashion, commanders of the performing units could be certain of favorable assessments. Military leaders had been frequently seen by their soldiers and colleagues in compromising situations. Colonel Imre Bokor, whose book on the military published in late 1989 shocked not only the HPA but also the general population, specifically mentioned a rocket-forces exercise held in the Soviet Union where Hungarian generals distinguished themselves only by the amount of food and alcohol they consumed:

> [During the exercise] the supervising generals *had been eating, drinking, and hunting,* to pass the time somehow. Sandor Mate, Chief-of-Staff of the Directorate of Rocket-Artillery had been drunk *practically all the time.* Major General Gyula Simonyi had also been under the influence of alcohol *throughout.* Major General Miklos Varadi dumbfounded those Hungarian and foreign commanders present by *dancing on top of the table* without falling off even once, which was a *respectable achievement* considering the amount of alcohol he had previously consumed.[100]

Mismanagement of cadre policy in the MOD was also pervasive and resulted in an astounding waste of human resources. Well-trained officers often filled positions not related to their expertise while the positions they were suited for were occupied by incompetent cadres.

Part III   Political and Military Training

The system of military training also demonstrates the HPA's cautious and gradual departure from the orthodox WTO line. Two such factors should be stressed: first, the move from emphasizing 'international' toward 'national' values in order promote Hungary's national interests and to elicit more loyalty from officers and soldiers and more respect from the public; and second, the easing of requirements in military education at all levels to alleviate the chronic recruitment problems. Needless to say, neither phenomenon pleased Hungary's Warsaw Pact partners.

A.   Military Education in the School System

Military education had been a compulsory school subject in Hungary since the mid-1960s. The total annual instruction time officially devoted to military education was regulated by the 1976 Defense Law as six hours in primary schools (grades seven and eight), and 20 hours in secondary and vocational schools.[101] In 1981–82 the system of military education was significantly altered by the introduction of separate instruction for boys (focusing on their future military training) and girls (stressing civil defense duties).[102]

The severity of problems in military education were demonstrated by their extensive discussion in the press and by the frequent changes of curricula. Until the early 1980s, military education in primary schools emphasized concepts such as the homeland, socialist construction, and friendship with the USSR and other socialist states.[103] The 1981–82 changes in the military education system featured a subtle but unmistakable shift towards the inculcation of national values, patriotism and stress on Hungarian military traditions.[104] Military education was also a subject in the curricula of all first-year university and college students, despite the fact that most males had already served a year in the army as pre-admission students. Students were at times required to retake the course in their sophomore years because of their abysmal attendance record.[105] In spite of official optimism, problems in military education persisted until its eventual abolition in the late 1980s.

A new and fundamentally different agent of defense education was the institution of military boarding schools at the secondary level, introduced in 1974 for the 14–18 age group. The creation of these schools was necessitated by the regime's inability to attract sufficient number of qualified youths to professional military service. Those who graduated from the schools were accepted *automatically* at military colleges.[106] By the late 1980s, there were approximately a dozen such institutions, all but one located in provincial cities. Students received free room and board, clothing, and even a modest allowance. Not surprisingly, the boarding schools had no recruitment problems.[107]

A channel of indirect political–military indoctrination was the HDA, the equivalents of which could be found in all WTO states. The HDA was a large organization maintaining 4,594 local branches with more than 150,000 members in the late 1970s.[108] HDA clubs trained thousands of motor vehicle drivers, signal experts, model builders, etc. The knowledge of HDA members was utilized by the army during their service time. As a general rule, HDA activities were supervised by active and retired HPA officers who attempted to inculcate in their charges the politico-military values of the regime.[109]

B. Officer Training

In 1968–88 few changes were implemented in officer education. The most important of these was the 1985 reform. Effective with the 1987–88 academic year, the length of academic programs at military colleges was reduced from four to three years. This measure was necessitated by two factors. First, the HPA had been facing severe recruitment problems and planners thought that the shorter period of study would seem more appealing to some candidates. Second, the demographic situation also favored an abbreviated training period: a significant proportion of professional military personnel had reached retirement age and replacement was an urgent task.

Other regulations of the reform allowed officer candidates to store civilian clothing in their dormitory quarters and did not require them to wear their uniforms.[110] Furthermore, in their third year, students were classified as 'professional military personnel', received salary and benefits commensurate with that designation, and were relieved of various maintenance duties not directly related to their training. Furthermore, the base allowance of military college students was doubled in January 1986. At the same time, a so-called achievement bonus (*tanulmanyi potlek*) was introduced to stimulate academic performance.

The military press repeatedly emphasized, presumably to alleviate domestic and WTO misgivings, that despite the shortening of the training period educational requirements would remain the same.[111] According to army literature, this was to be achieved by a reorganization of curricula and more efficient use of time. Prior to 1987 the methods of instruction were also updated periodically to 'create a higher level of educational integration'.[112] Under the 1985 reforms officer candidates were expected to combine mastery of military subjects with the additional requirement of 'developing socialist human and comradely behavior and strict self-discipline'.[113] The political commitments of future officers to the HSWP, and, ultimately, to the Soviet Union was still considered one of the fundamental ingredients of their military higher education.[114]

A small number of Hungarian officers continued to receive their undergraduate and advanced training in the Soviet Union, Poland, and, more recently, Czechoslovakia.[115] At the undergraduate level, a degree from a foreign institution did not, in itself, confer privileged status on its recipient since training abroad was necessitated by the fact that in some specialties it was unavailable in Hungary. Aspiring fighter pilots and flight engineers, for instance, were trained exclusively in the USSR. To promote integration between the 'fraternal' armed forces, foreign undergraduate students in Soviet training schools were mixed with their Soviet colleagues.[116] It appears that requirements were higher in Soviet schools than in similar Hungarian institutions.[117] The official image of Russian military educators continued to portray them as patient and devoted teachers in both undergraduate colleges and graduate schools. Graduates of Soviet institutions recalled that their instructors 'simply would not give up on anyone' and 'could teach even a bear to fly a plane'.[118]

Graduate military training was desired by a significant proportion of HPA officers. Most of them, however, preferred to receive that training in Hungary. A survey taken in 1978 indicated that only three percent of those who wished to take subsequent staff training courses wanted to attend Soviet military academies.[119] The fact that a considerably larger proportion of students did study in the Soviet Union suggests that officers who sought advancement in their professional careers recognized the necessity of studying in the USSR and did so only reluctantly. The unfamiliar environment, the lack of Russian language facility and the protracted separation from family were certainly some of the reasons for this aversion.

C. Problems of Recruitment and Prestige

Even though entry requirements to military colleges were kept almost ridiculously low, there were still major shortages of *qualified* applicants. (One exception was the Kilian Air Force College that could ordinarily select from a large pool of first-rate candidates.)[120] Military colleges placed a strong emphasis on ideological conformity, but academic requirements tended to be light. Furthermore, the HPA leadership even offered an alternate route for those failing to meet even minimal requirements, such as a high school diploma.

In addition to the poor academic credentials of applicants, particularly when contrasted with those of candidates to civilian institutions, questions regarding the career motivation of prospective officer candidates also persisted. A survey examining their incentive to apply to military colleges revealed that 27 percent were inspired by the handsome uniforms and material advantages rather than by professional or ideological reasons.[121] Individuals of worker or peasant backgrounds coming from rural areas made up the majority of students in military colleges; their proportion remained much lower in civilian institutions of higher learning.[122] The high percentage of working-class students was partially by design, since military colleges – concerned with potential problems of political reliability – preferred them to those with roots in the intelligentsia.[123] Another reason was that, compared with their working-class peers, youngsters from the latter group generally considered the military career an appalling career choice.[124] Many of those admitted to military colleges did not finish their studies as a result of their poor academic performance, illness, or lack of motivation.

The low prestige of the military profession was perhaps the most important reason for the aforementioned recruitment and replacement problems. Making a joke out of the army became a favorite pastime of comedians, writers, and playwrights. As a result of the open ridicule, at the 13th HSWP Congress Defense Minister Olah called for the Party to pay 'greater attention and responsibility toward negative, cynical, and derogatory expressions directed at the activities of soldiers'.[125] The obsolescence of the HPA's arsenal conveyed the message to many technically oriented youths that equipment modernization was not a priority on the political leadership's agenda. Moreover, during the 1970s and 1980s the military career lost its financial appeal. Contrary to popular belief, the remuneration of the military profession had been surpassed by that of many other occupational strata.[126] To make matters worse, military personnel were denied the opportunity to take part in Hungary's extensive 'second economy'. To appreciate this disadvantage, one should note that two out of three Hungarian workers supplemented their incomes significantly from this source.

On the positive side, the military profession maintained some of its advantages. Retirement age, for instance, continued to be set at 55. The pay of young officers was relatively good, especially when compared with that of other newly graduated professionals.[127] Furthermore, the military profession retained one considerable advantage over civilian occupations: no one employed by the HPA needed to fear unemployment. Given the emerging trend toward 'acceptable levels of unemployment' by the late 1980s in the civilian sector, job security became an attractive feature of the military career.

Part IV   The HPA, the Warsaw Pact, and the West

The years 1968 and 1969 were turbulent in the Warsaw Pact. Romania's and Albania's stance against the invasion was unambiguous, Hungary's reluctance to participate was also hard to ignore. A few weeks after the invasion a *Pravda* article put forth the concept of limited sovereignty in the socialist bloc.[128] The article, which became the theoretical foundation of the Brezhnev Doctrine, argued that sovereignty must not be interpreted abstractly among the socialist states, for the laws of the individual countries must be subordinated to the rules of the international Communist movement. Moscow reserved the right to intervene militarily or otherwise in the Pact states' domestic emergencies along with the prerogative to decide when such intervention was called for. The Brezhnev Doctrine was incompatible with the Warsaw Pact guarantees of independence and national sovereignty. In a sense, however, there was nothing really new about the Brezhnev Doctrine since sovereignty in the Soviet bloc was limited from the very beginning.[129]

Hungary's membership in the Warsaw Pact had serious implications on civil–military relations. The invasion of Czechoslovakia served as a reminder for military personnel that the HSWP was not the only important master of the HPA, and, moreover, not even *the* most important one. The invasion and the Brezhnev Doctrine also cautioned any potential Hungarian (or East European) attempts of gaining a more independent role within – let alone outside – the Pact. By the end of the 1980s, however, the contention of Alexiev's model (positing divergent perceptions of national versus ideological desiderata) did apply to the Hungarian case as a result of the gradual acquisition of more national characteristics of the HPA.

A. Unity and Conflict in the Pact

The main business of the March 1969 meeting of the PCC was the reorganization of the Warsaw Pact's organizational structure.[130] The underlying reason for the alteration of the Pact's design was the Soviet desire 'to bring the East Europeans more directly into the working of the Pact without lessening essential Soviet control over all its activities'.[131] In other words, the aim of the reform of the WTO's structure was to improve the access and *actual* participation of NSWP states in decision-making and to refine and rationalize the division of labor. At the same time, as Jeffrey Simon has argued, the reorganization of the Pact was not the result of a crash effort but originated in post-1965 NSWP pressures to gain at least a consultative voice in military matters.[132] As a result, the representatives of NSWP states participated in all of the newly created bodies.

Under the terms of the reorganization, two new multinational bodies were set up to aid the Soviet CiC. The Committee of Defense Ministers was to meet irregularly to review and approve the decisions of the more substantive of the two bodies, the Military Council. The third important new organization was the WTO Technical Committee, which was charged with the standardization and integration of weapon systems into the member armies' arsenals. At the 1976 Bucharest meeting of the PCC, the military–administrative structure of the Warsaw Pact was further modified by the establishment of the Council of Foreign Ministers and the re-creation of the Joint Secretariat. The former met frequently on an *ad*

hoc basis to discuss the international political situation and to synchronize
the positions of Warsaw Pact states.[133] The latter, created in 1956, had
subsequently lapsed into desuetude, but was resuscitated to coordinate
WTO foreign policies between PCC sessions.[134]

In spite of the underlying purpose of the structural reorganization to give
the Pact an appearance of equality, most Western observers agreed that the
changes were merely cosmetic and did not threaten Moscow's domineering
position and virtually unbridled decision-making power.[135] Throughout the
1968–88 period the Soviets maintained their monopoly over the WTO's
command positions. In its 35-year history, no East European officer was
ever entrusted with an operationally significant position in the WTO. It
is difficult not to recognize that a major function of the Warsaw Pact was
to police the East European regimes. The NSWP states never acquired the
role of the active and influential junior partner they hoped for. The Kremlin
continued to make all important military/strategic decisions pertaining to
the region. Furthermore, Moscow also retained its control over intra-Pact
communication.[136]

Although there was no open admission of the problem in the Warsaw
Pact in 1968–88, the cohesion of the organization was rather shaky and
the reliability of the NSWP states continued to pose a sensitive question.[137]
There were several indications of the deficiencies in the NSWP armies'
commitment level. Soviet leaders from Khrushchev on pressed for greater
integration in the bloc – even Brezhnev shared his predecessor's view that
integration did not have to mean uniformity – and accepted some measure
of unorthodox domestic behavior among the NSWP states. Through the
years the level of Soviet patience fluctuated widely and was dependent on
a number of criteria, such as Soviet perception of the international situation,
the balance of power in the Kremlin, etc. Relative Soviet permissiveness
manifested itself mainly in areas such as economic and cultural policy, and
did not extend to the military arena.

The inability and occasional reluctance of NSWP states to increase
their military outlays adversely affected strategic planning in three crucial
areas.[138] First, the obsolescence of much of the NSWP armies' equipment
posed questions about their ability to keep up with the Soviet army in the
event of a conflict. Second, technical disparities between Soviet and NSWP
arsenals exacerbated problems of inoperability. And third, the firepower of
NSWP divisions was considerably less than that of their Soviet counterparts
as a result of the former's quantitative and qualitative inferiority. For these
reasons, Moscow continued to demand more NSWP military expenditure
but its requests often remained – certainly in the case of Hungary –
unfulfilled.

In this period unmistakable signs of opposition surfaced within the Warsaw Pact. The NSWP states expressed neither willingness to support the USSR in the 1969 Ussuri crisis nor enthusiasm about the Soviet adventure in Afghanistan a decade later. (In fact, in both cases Eastern European spokesmen went out of their way to declare that their obligations did not apply in these conflicts.)[139] NSWP states were clearly not happy with the Soviet decision to deploy SS-20 'operational-tactical' missiles in Czechoslovakia and in the GDR.[140] Romania's role in the Pact continued to be at least an irritant for the other member states.

According to Czinege, animosities within the Pact flared up during the Polish crisis of 1980–81. He recently described that at the December 1980 Moscow meeting of the Council of Defence Ministers the Soviet minister, Marshal Dimitri Ustinov, implied that the Polish situation might necessitate joint WTO military effort. The meeting, according to Czinege, degenerated into a verbal duel between Ustinov and Marshal Ogarkov on the one hand, and the East Europeans desperate to avoid military confrontation, on the other.[141] During the meeting Czinege made repeated phone calls to Budapest, where party and government leaders supported his position. Some observers question Czinege's account or at least the genuineness of Ustinov's outbursts.[142] In any event, the invasion of Poland was not, in all probability, seriously considered.

During the short tenure of Andropov, military thinking within the Pact was perceptibly liberalized, sessions of the Military Council, for instance, became more relaxed. His more flexible attitude toward the NSWP states apparently left a favorable impression on East European military leaders.[143] NSWP opposition to Soviet policy took on new life in 1984 when the GDR, Hungary, and Romania expressed their displeasure with the Soviet view of East–West relations at the Council of Foreign Ministers' meeting in late April.[144]

Some NSWP states – notably Hungary and Poland – utilized international arms reduction talks (Conference of Security and Cooperation in Europe [CSCE], Mutual Balanced Force Reductions [MBFR]) to discreetly put distance between their own views and those of Moscow.[145] In 1985, the prolongation of the WTO for a further 20 years stirred discussion in the NSWP states, particularly in Romania.[146] Although Bucharest was the first to agree in principle to the renewal of the Pact, the Romanians let it be known that they were lobbying hard for an extension of only ten or even five years. According to some reports, they received muted support from Hungary and East Germany.[147] Eventually, however, the 20-year extension was signed by all member states.

B. Hungary and the Warsaw Pact

Particularly since the 1970s Hungary had participated in a great number of joint exercises with the Pact's northern tier states (Czechoslovakia, GDR, Poland). Its most frequent partners were the Czechoslovak and the Soviet armies, no doubt at least in part for reasons of geographical proximity. It was the most active among the southern tier armies (Bulgaria, Hungary, Romania) although it took part in far fewer joint maneuvers than its northern tier counterparts. No large-scale joint exercise was held in Hungary until the 1979 Shield maneuvers, commanded for the first time in the WTO's history, by a Hungarian (Defense Minister Czinege).[148] To ensure reliability, Hungarian units, along with those of other NSWP states, were treated as a part of the Soviet Army and were 'sandwiched' between Soviet troops.[149]

Predictably, the HPA earned high marks for its performance in the joint exercises. (Then again, to my knowledge, no WTO press organ published as much as a mild criticism of the accomplishments of a member state's army in the maneuvers.) Following the Shield-79 exercise, for instance, the Commander of the United Armed Forces, Marshal Kulikov said that 'HPA units proved their preparedness, their ability to take part in combined actions, taking responsibility for the execution of the lion's share of practical tasks'.[150] The few meaningful points that can be deduced from a plethora of similar platitudes indicate the HPA's adeptness in military engineering, particularly bridge-building, and communications.[151]

One important function of the joint exercises was to strengthen fraternal feelings between the 'brothers in arms'. The number of articles describing cases of 'comradely behavior', the 'flowering of true friendships', and 'unselfish assistance' between soldiers of the WTO armies is virtually endless and often portray improbably idyllic relations with the civilian population as well. An example from the October 1970 'Comrades in Arms' exercise held in the GDR:

> Our boys prepare for the exercise in an atmosphere of true friendship and brotherhood. They received the kindest gift from an eight-year-old blonde girl who, upon seeing the Hungarian armored vehicle column, ran out to the street in her nightie and gave her most treasured possession, a doll, to the commander.[152]

In addition, by the early 1980s Hungarian press reports of the joint exercises began to emphasize not only the incredibly rapid development of life-long friendships between HPA soldiers and their Czech and Russian counterparts[153] but also their concern for the environment and their supposedly heroic efforts to save money. ('You should have seen, dear readers, the helicopter's pilot maneuvering to land without destroying as much as a single wheat-stalk.')[154]

Although we have seen the many aspects of Hungarian dissent in this period, it is important to note that official Budapest never questioned Hungarian membership in the Pact. HSWP leaders occasionally disagreed with the foreign and military policies of the WTO but never failed to consider Hungary a solid part of the alliance. According to a 1971 article:

> Our membership in the WTO enabled us 'A) to develop the components of our forces most important to *us* . . . ; B) to acquire our armaments from the brotherly countries, especially from the Soviet Union; C) to rely on the rich experiences of the brotherly countries gained in improving their armed forces'.[155]

Such confirmations of Hungarian allegiance notwithstanding, the most important development of the HPA and its relations with the USSR and the NSWP states was the clear emergence of its national characteristics. Christopher Jones correctly pointed out that one function of the joint WTO exercises was to deny the national traits of NSWP forces.[156] Starting with the mid-1980s, however, Hungarian generals attempted to obstruct this Soviet effort.

The HPA followed the structural set-up of the Soviet Army in virtually every detail from its inception. By the mid-1980s, however, Hungarian military leaders realized that such a structure did not favor the HPA and commenced the reorganization of the army replacing the Soviet-type system based on divisions with a scheme of which the core were brigades. This organizational structure – substituting brigades for regiments and divisions – HPA leaders explained, was less costly, more mobile, and more adaptable for Hungary's geographical conditions.[157] Apparently the High Command of the WTO did not take kindly to the Hungarian upsetting of the long-standing organizational stability of the Pact forces. Nonetheless, Czinege – and later Olah and Karpati – were capable of convincing Pact leaders that the new scheme, completed in 1987, would not detract from the HPA's contribution to the Pact.[158]

Three examples should be mentioned here insofar as they illustrate the Hungarian shift toward a national orientation of the HPA.[159] First, in 1986 top HPA officers – led by Chief-of-Staff General Pacsek – refused to collaborate with their Soviet colleagues on a book on Warsaw Pact policy that ignored the HPA's national traits. Second, at a 1984 staff exercise (with Czechoslovak, Hungarian, Polish, and Soviet units in participating) the task of Hungarian troops was to destroy railway lines in Czechoslovak territory. The Hungarian officer in charge opposed the HPA's participation in this part of the maneuvers because of the troublesome implications of 1968. The WTO leaders concurred. Third, at a 1987 joint exercise held in Hungary and commanded by Marshal Kulikov, the standard 40-kilometer (25 miles) security belt was assigned to HPA troops. Hungarian State Secretary for Defense Morocz objected to such a wide zone positing that in the Hungarian context it could include two counties and therefore a large inhabited area. Morocz further argued that participating young HPA officers should not be taught to adhere to such irrational rules. Again, following a few minutes of reasoning the Soviet commander conceded the Hungarian the point and agreed to a much smaller, 10–15 km security zone.

While the alliance was accepted by the Hungarian elites as a given, there was a far weaker sense of integration with the Pact as a whole in Hungary, than, for instance, in Bulgaria, Czechoslovakia, or East Germany. The reliability of the HPA – and that of its NSWP partners – is a complex issue that one could only speculate about. I would agree with Ivan Volgyes who concluded that while the HPA could be relied on in an external-defensive scenario and could probably be counted on to remain at least neutral – if not to defend the regime – in an internal-defensive contingency.[160] I also share his skepticism regarding the HPA's participation in an external-offensive scenario, particularly in the case of a WTO attack on NATO. In my view, the HPA would have been dependable in a conflict with Romania, and would probably have performed well against Czechoslovakia had the perceived objective been the repossession of historical Hungarian territories.[161] Obviously the reliability of NSWP armies could only be considered in the given political and military context (e.g., the duration of hostilities, domestic political and socioeconomic conditions, military preparedness, etc.) for which Daniel Nelson elaborated a useful framework.[162] These less than complimentary views on the reliability of the HPA – and its NSWP partners – were also generally confirmed by emigre WTO officers.[163]

C.   The Hungarian Military's Western Contacts

Another development suggesting increased attention paid to national interest in this period was the origination of contacts between the HPA and non-Warsaw Pact states. These gestures marked the first cautious steps toward the Hungarian armed forces' unambiguous move away from the

WTO that culminated in the 1988–90 period. HPA leaders visited neutral countries on several occasions in the 1970s and 1980s. As early as 1972, Deputy Minister and Chief-of-Staff Karoly Csemi made an 'official and friendly visit to Finland'.[164] Hungary's particularly good political relations with Austria were also duplicated in the military sphere. The two defense ministers met a number of times. In addition, Hungarian soldiers participated in Alpine training courses in Austria, hosted by the Austrian armed forces.[165]

From the early 1980s Hungary was an active participant in international conferences on various aspects of military affairs, such as in the Geneva disarmament talks beginning in 1983. Some HPA officers spent considerable time at the Geneva conference and at other international meetings and established contacts with their colleagues serving in NATO forces. High-level official visits, particularly with the representatives of neutral countries, continued through the 1980s. Colonel Laszlo Szegedi, the head of MOD's Foreign Affairs Department, said that in 1986–88 alone the HPA had welcomed delegations from the USA, Canada, the United Kingdom, Switzerland, Thailand, Austria, and Argentina.[166] The 'Generals for Peace and Disarmament', an international organization founded in 1981 by 16 retired NATO generals, welcomed several Hungarian members. In fact, Ret. General Csemi became the co-chairman of the WTO's contingent in the organization. Csemi even admitted that NATO generals were more tireless in their peace movement activities and in their home countries than their Warsaw Pact counterparts.[167]

Apparently not all of the communication between HPA officers and their Western colleagues was authorized, much less approved, by Moscow. For instance in 1984, coinciding with Soviet deployment of SS-20 missiles in Czechoslovakia and the GDR, Hungarian officials privately informed Westerners that they did not want any Soviet SS-20 missiles on Hungarian territory and disapproved of Soviet arms control policy.[168] From 1987, on the basis of the 1986 Stockholm agreement, the HPA conscientiously informed NATO of exercises held in Hungary, even of those that it had no obligation to report.

Summary

As noted in Chapter 1, an essential attribute of East European civil–military relations was the notion that aside from the Party and the army a third actor – the Soviet Union (and the Moscow-dominated Warsaw Pact) – also impinged on this relationship. One of the main themes of this chapter was the examination of a trend that resulted in a more autonomous Hungarian polity and, to a lesser extent, armed forces. This process of acquiring more and more national characteristics was certainly favored by the population and put the armed forces in a more favorable light. This development, as noted above, corresponds with Alexiev's model.

None of the models, however, considered the possibility that the party's control over and indoctrination of the armed forces may not be sufficient to affect the soldiers's attitudes. As we have seen, the HPA had faced serious problems of discipline and political 'awareness'. The relative tolerance toward dissent in the late Kadar era did not leave the military unaffected and encouraged 'relaxed attitudes' toward matters of ideology and *partiinost'*. As the work of Herspring and Volgyes suggested, the decreased political dynamism of the professional cadres may have been a consequence of the parallel phenomenon of increased professional specialization.

At the same time, the Party attempted to maintain its close control over the armed forces to the smallest details. It sought to combat political problems by introducing a 'second generation' of political officers ('trustees') and refused to waive military service for conscientious objectors. The military did not play a role in political decision-making. The Hungarian case appears to support Odom's model of 'institutional congruence' as the army leadership neither assumed the role of an interest group, nor did it participate in policy-making.

I have also tried to stress the decreasing social esteem of the military. As noted in Chapter 2, the military profession was surrounded by an aura of respect and even romanticism in Hungarian culture before 1945. This prestige had totally evaporated in the Communist period. There were many reasons for this notion. The HPA leadership was uneducated, corrupt, and displayed no characteristics of the gentleman soldier of times bygone. The remuneration of the profession, especially in contrast to that of the emerging entrepreneurial stratum in the 1980s, was poor. But even more importantly, the public considered the HPA the defender of an illegitimate regime. The primary result of this notion was the difficulty encountered in recruiting qualified officer candidates.

Some of the most important developments in this period were the limited democratization of the armed forces and the occasional manifestations of the HPA's unwillingness to subordinate itself to the USSR and the WTO. The next chapter will examine these phenomena in the 1988–90 period.

5 The Second Transition: Democratization (1988–90)

The preceding three chapters analyzed civil–military relations in Hungary from 1945 to 1988. We have seen that although the HPA was robbed of virtually all of its national characteristics during the period of 'sovietization', following the 1956 Revolution a very slow process of 'nativization' commenced, marked by such factors as the renewed emphasis on Hungarian military traditions in education and training and the restructuring of the HPA's organization. Although the basic patterns of civil–military relations showed few signs of change, the steady albeit slow movement toward the 'nationalization' and democratization of the military establishment began. By the mid-1980s, Hungary's reluctance to follow unconditionally Soviet directions became evident.

This chapter examines the period extending from the May 1988 Conference of the Hungarian Socialist Workers' Party until the end of 1990. In two and a half years Hungary's political and military structures were drastically transformed. The political transformation from a single-party paternalistic dictatorship to a multi-party democracy was concomitant with the metamorphosis of civil–military relations as well. During this period the essential role of the Hungarian armed forces underwent a complete change. One of the main functions of the HPA under four decades of Communism was the defense of the Party's political monopoly from its internal enemies; the collapse of the regime made this function irrelevant.

In some areas, such as Hungary's economic situation or the arsenal of the HPA, either very little change occurred in 1988–90, or change occurred that does not warrant extensive analysis here. Therefore, this chapter concentrates on the elements of defense policy and military affairs where reforms and processes of transformation were most significant. Part I offers a brief summary of Hungary's political transformation in 1988–90. Part II analyzes the shift in civil–military relations; Part III focuses on the subsequent democratization and reorganization of the armed forces. Part IV deals with the international relations of the Hungarian armed forces.

Part I   Political Background: From Communism to Democracy

A.   Domestic Politics

Karoly Grosz's emergence as HSWP leader at the May 1988 HSWP Conference was welcomed by large segments of the party membership and even the population because it promised a change from Kadar's reluctance to deal with Hungary's mounting political and economic problems. The new HSWP Politburo remained divided between hardliners led by Grosz and reform-minded politicians such as Imre Pozsgay and Rezso Nyers. In November 1988 Grosz relinquished the premiership to Miklos Nemeth, a young and capable HSWP politician. It soon became apparent that Nemeth would strengthen the ranks of reform-Communists.

The measure of public support Grosz enjoyed after May 1988 had considerably eroded by the end of the year following police brutality used against demonstrators in June, and his ill-fated meeting with Romanian President Ceauşescu in August.[1] Moreover, the fragile balance of power in the Politburo suffered severe blows due to the independent stances of some of its members. In October 1988 Pozsgay implicitly supported the emergence of an alternative movement, the Hungarian Democratic Forum (HDF) by his participation in its founding meeting. Antagonism deepened between the popular Pozsgay and his foes in the Politburo after the former declared that the 1956 Revolution, officially still tagged as a 'counter-revolution', was a 'popular uprising', apparently without consulting Grosz.

In the meantime, the HSWP's membership declined precipitously. The evolving crisis of Hungarian socialism was to a large degree due to the HSWP leaders' apparent perplexity regarding the changing role and function of ideology. The Central Committee, as Grosz openly admitted, lacked unity of opinion and was beleaguered by 'debates about questions of tactics, methodology, and working style'.[2] By March 1989 there were, in fact, three separate parties within the HSWP representing 'conservative order', 'moderate order', and 'socialist reform'.[3] The leadership seemed to have realized that some form of democracy within the party was an essential condition for regaining the membership's support. The limited party reforms introduced in 1989, however, could not alter the overall disenchantment of the rank and file membership.

The government and party leadership also tried to introduce broad political reforms, but was unable or unwilling to realize that the time when 'fine tuning' and 'quasi reforms' could appease the population had passed; now systemic changes were necessary.[4] The leadership attempted to initiate or at least study the possibility of reform in several areas of politics – particularly electoral, parliamentary, constitutional, and trade union politics. Nonetheless, most of the grandiose intentions quickly degenerated into piecemeal reforms. Furthermore, the measures designed to modernize the country's legislative system 'were not really necessary and some were downright regressive'.[5] The leaders' position on the issue of political pluralism had gone through a remarkably rapid transformation. As late as July 1988, Grosz firmly rejected the idea of a multi-party system.[6] Even Pozsgay, the most liberal member of the leadership, remarked at the time that if a multi-party regime were to be established, it would result in a comedy of 'partner parties' for the HSWP, and the situation would be 'even more ridiculous than it is today'.[7] Nonetheless, in November 1988 the government permitted the establishment of political parties and pertinent laws were enacted in a few months.

Taking advantage of the fluid political situation and the relative tolerance of party and government leaders, a large number of democratic political organizations quickly emerged and began to establish themselves as parties.[8] Some of these, such as the Social Democratic Party (SDP) and the Independent Smallholders' Party (ISP) already existed prior to the elimination of non-Communist political organizations in 1948. Others, such as the HDF, the Association of Free Democrats (AFD), or the Association of Young Democrats (AYD) were newly created.

A further milestone in Hungarian politics was the reburial of Imre Nagy. The opposition had long demanded an appropriate funeral for Nagy and his associates executed in 1958. In October 1988 Janos Berecz, the HSWP CC's secretary in charge of ideology, announced that Nagy would soon receive a 'proper tomb', signalling the leadership's weakening resolve.[9] The reburial that took place on the 31st anniversary of the execution (June 1989) attracted tens of thousands and offered an opportunity to opposition politicians to gain public recognition.

The June 1989 Polish elections provided additional momentum to the HSWP's reformist wing. In April, an agreement was reached between the Polish United Workers' Party and the Solidarity-led opposition which led to the holding of partially free elections. The results astonished not only foreign observers, but even the most optimist members of the Polish opposition: they won 260 of the 261 Sejm seats open for competition and all but one of the Senate seats.[10] Mikhail Gorbachev's explicit rejection of the Brezhnev Doctrine in his July 1989 speech to the Council of Europe offered an additional boost to Hungary's reform-Communists.

Between June and September 1989 so-called round-table negotiations were held between the HSWP and the opposition. The round table, aside from its significance as a new form of dialogue between the rulers and the opposition, served as a forum for the opposition parties to familiarize the HSWP, the other parties, and most important of all, the general public with their views and programs. Agreement about the new electoral law was reached in early September. A national referendum held in November decided that Hungary's president would be elected following the March–April parliamentary elections.

In the meantime, the HSWP had continued to lose support and faced internal crises. In late June 1989, the top ranks of the party were reorganized. The party leadership elected Nyers as Chairman and as a member of a four-man Presidium also including Pozsgay, Grosz, and Nemeth. The October 1989 HSWP congress resulted in the creation of a new, reform-minded socialist party (Hungarian Socialist Party [HSP] – *Magyar Szocialista Part*) led by the erstwhile reform-Communists of the HSWP: Nemeth, Nyers, Pozsgay, and Foreign Minister Gyula Horn. The HSWP, reduced to its hard-line elements, continued to operate.

On October 23, 1989, the 33rd anniversary of the 1956 Revolution, Matyas Szuros, the Chairman of the National Assembly proclaimed the Republic of Hungary (in place of the People's Republic). The day before parliament decided to abolish the HSWP's private army, the 60,000-strong Workers' Guard. The winter of 1989–90 was an eventful political period the likes of which the country had not seen for decades. Newly formed parties were recruiting members and campaigning before the upcoming elections. The HSP, inheriting its governing position from the HSWP, attempted to distance itself from the 'mistakes of the past' and followed a liberal course. Nonetheless, the election results demonstrated that Hungarians embraced the opportunity of real choice and turned their backs upon the country's rulers.[11]

The elections were won handily by the right-of-center HDF (42.5 percent), followed by the left-of-center AFD (23.8 percent), and the pre-1948 favorite ISP (11.4 percent). The HSP only secured 8.5 percent of the votes while the HSWP was unable to reach the 4 percent level necessary for parliamentary representation.[12] In early May the new governing coalition, composed of the Hungarian Democratic Forum, the Independent Smallholders' Party, and the Christian Democratic People's Party (CDPP) began work under the premiership of Jozsef Antall (HDF). In August the legislature elected Arpad Goncz (AFD) as President of the Republic of Hungary.

Since the Antall government took office, it has had to face a multitude of political, economic, and social problems. The government and legislature have made a concerted effort to drastically restructure the political and economic system guiding Hungary's return to political pluralism and a market-oriented economy. The government's major problem continued to be the country's disastrous overall economic situation – high inflation, low productivity, large foreign debt, to mention just a few problems – for which no easy medicine could be found. The Antall government encountered several widespread strikes of which the most memorable was the taxi drivers' walkout in October 1990 that paralyzed ground transportation throughout the country for days. In December, opposition criticism, disagreements within the governing coalition, and the incompetence of some ministers forced a limited reorganization of the government. In spite of these problems and although Hungary shared the socioeconomic predicament of underdeveloped countries, transformation to a Hungarian democracy was well on the way by the end of 1990.

B. Foreign Policy

Since the early 1980s foreign policy was one of the few areas that Hungary's Communist leaders could call a success. During the 1988–90 period this trend continued, even under the short tenures of the Grosz and Nemeth governments. Within the Soviet bloc Hungary's affairs were generally well-managed with a few exceptions. Ceauşescu's plan to erase thousands of villages – most of which happened to be populated by Hungarians – incited the anger of Hungarian citizens. The Hungarian leadership made several unsuccessful attempts to iron out differences with Romania. Another contentious issue that also exacerbated the Grosz government's crisis of legitimacy concerned a joint hydroelectric project with Czechoslovakia which the Hungarian opposition fiercely contested due to its potentially harmful economic and environmental effects. Eventually the project was unilaterally broken off by the Hungarian government thereby causing tension with the Prague leadership.

In spite of the dramatic transformation of Hungarian politics from post-Communism to a multiparty democracy, Budapest's relationship with Moscow was relatively undisturbed. First, by 1988 Gorbachev apparently had decided not to interfere with the developments in Eastern Europe. The Soviet leadership recognized diversity in the bloc and appeared committed to consultation with, rather than issuing directives to, the region. Moscow's first priority was taking care of its own economic and political problems. Even political – let alone military – intervention would have undercut Gorbachev's efforts to divert resources away from the military to domestic needs and to gain Western assistance in doing so. The Soviet Union played the role of an interested but not terribly concerned bystander throughout the East European transformation. Political developments in Hungary, for instance, were generally reported objectively and without scathing criticism in the USSR.[13] Second, Hungarian politicians were continuously reassuring Moscow about their sensitivity to Soviet interests and their actions reflected awareness of the geopolitical realities. Nonetheless, Moscow and Budapest disagreed on several issues. One of these had centered around the utility of the CMEA until it was disbanded in January 1991.[14]

Hungary did face short-term conflicts with Czechoslovakia and East Germany following the Nemeth government's decision to dismantle the 'iron curtain' on Hungary's border with Austria. Berlin and Prague condemned the Hungarian decision. Later the GDR and Czechoslovakia fiercely protested Budapest's refusal to return East German refugees to their homeland, but the rapid collapse of these regimes prevented the development of serious crises. In fact, the decision yielded Hungary considerable political capital in the West, and particularly in West Germany. Although the Nemeth and Antall governments continued to make gestures toward post-Ceauşescu Romania, tensions between the two countries did not ease perceptibly. Hungary offered medical and humanitarian aid to Romania following the December 1989 Revolution, indeed, Foreign Minister Gyula Horn was the first foreign statesman to offer aid and visit the country. Hungary achieved its greatest foreign policy successes with the industrialized West.[15] In 1988–90 Hungarian leaders met virtually all of their Western counterparts a number of times. For example, Hungarian leaders met their American colleagues on several occasions. Grosz visited the U.S. in 1988 and met President Reagan; then in the following year Nemeth hosted President Bush in Budapest, while in the fall of 1990 both President Goncz and Prime Minister Antall were welcomed in the White House. The Antall government intends to build on the successful foreign policy of the reform-Communist Foreign Minister Gyula Horn, whose name has become synonymous with the aggressive Hungarian opening towards the West.

In its economic predicament Hungary is in dire need of Western goodwill and economic aid. One of the main themes of the present government is the 'return to Europe', that is to say, Western Europe. Some successes were already achieved in 1988–90. In November 1990 Hungary became the first East European state to be admitted into the Council of Europe. A year later the European Community extended associate membership to Hungary, as well as to Czechoslovakia and Poland. Although full membership in the European Community remains a faraway prospect, Budapest seems determined to achieve that objective in the 1990s. In spite of its crisis-ridden economy, the country has been able to secure loans and sympathetic treatment from Western creditors.

Part II   The Transformation of Civil–Military Relations

The political transformation of 1988–90 resulted in equally significant changes in civil–military relations. By the end of 1990 the political structure of the Hungarian armed forces was completely reorganized and the military brought under the *de jure* control of the democratically elected parliament and its President. In June 1989 the National Assembly approved the text of the new military oath that obliged soldiers (along with civil servants and policemen) to serve the Republic of Hungary and its Constitution. The new pledge expresses the independence of the HPA from party politics and ideology, the end of party control, and the allegiance of its signers to Hungary's post-communist constitutional order and national sovereignty.[16] In November the new oath was signed by over 99 percent of the HPA's professional (officer and NCO) corps.[17]

Not surprisingly, none of the existing models of communist party–army dynamics considered the possibility of such a drastic transformation of civil–military relations. Models pertaining to the Soviet Union have examined the subject matter as an essentially static phenomenon and ignored the possibility of change in the relationship. The three theoretical constructs concerning Eastern Europe do contemplate the dynamics of evolution but none discuss the possibility of transformation of civil–military relations from a Communist to a democratic political system.

A.   Depoliticization: The End of Party Control

The changes in the political life of the armed forces were very rapid. One of the main avenues of the Communist party's control over the military was the extensive system of party organizations in the armed forces; their gradual elimination and the subsequent prohibition of any party activity in the army was the most important aspect of depoliticization.

If one is to believe General Szombathelyi, Grosz's military adviser, the party had relinquished its control over the HPA and 'did not demand any privileges in the armed forces' following the May 1988 HSWP Conference.[18] In late 1988, the HSWP CC's Administrative Department, the CC organization responsible for the armed forces, was abolished within the framework of an organizational reshuffling. This did not yet mean, however, that the HPA ceased to be the HSWP's army. For all practical purposes, the army's Supreme Commander remained HSWP chief Grosz and the political allegiances of the HPA continued to be unambiguous. Neither the HPA's internal regulations nor the Constitution prescribed who possessed the ultimate authority over the military. Hungary's Prime Minister, Miklos Nemeth, inadvertently provided a good illustration of this problem. When asked in July 1989 who was the Commander-in-Chief of the armed forces, the Prime Minister answered that 'it is not possible at present to give an unequivocal reply to this'.[19] The National Assembly simply did not have the authority to deny the HSWP an outright takeover of the armed forces since the HPA was under party not state or government control.[20] The law permitting HPA personnel to join political parties other than the HSWP was approved by parliament, against the opposition of the army leadership, only in late June 1989. In reality, the HSWP maintained direct control over the HPA until late summer 1989.[21]

Throughout the first half of 1989, the military press published a large number of articles examining the politico-ideological decay within the armed forces. Most of these studies, however, did not see – or did not want to overtly acknowledge – the hopeless disintegration of the HSWP and its youth organization (CYL) within the HPA. Instead, they sought to remedy the ills of the army's HSWP organizations by prescribing 'enhanced party discipline' and, especially, 'renewal'.[22] The criticisms targeted the 'work style' and 'authoritative atmosphere' of seemingly endless party meetings as well as the disenchantment of the party members who frequently failed to attend.[23] This is, of course, not to say that the majority of the army's professional cadres shared these views; rather it signifies that as late as spring 1989 only these opinions could be published in the military press. It is clear, however, that as a general rule, the older generation in the HPA was reluctant to embrace the political transformation taking place in Hungary.

The generals, connected by a myriad ties to the HSWP, would have preferred even the admission of new parties in the military to the abolition of the HPA's HSWP organizations, according to Defense Minister Karpati.[24] The army leadership repeatedly stressed the professional corps' 'commitment to socialism' and that the HSWP's 'influence' in the armed forces was justified as long as its program was acceptable for the population.[25] They conveniently ignored the fact that Hungarians were never asked whether or not they 'accepted' the Communist party's program. In May, General Szombathelyi still insisted that there was nothing objectionable in a politicized army as most militaries did play a political role. He added that direct HSWP control over the HPA ceased in early 1989 although the party did not wish to give up its influence (i.e., organizations) in the armed forces.[26] In September the Code of Service was modified in to allow HPA personnel to join other political parties and to participate in religious services in uniform.[27]

A few months and a hot political summer later, speakers at the HPA's Party Conference conceded that the 'membership had been turning away from the HSWP and was declining'; that although approximately 82 percent of professional soldiers retained their party cards the 'signs of social crisis did not leave the HPA unaffected'.[28] Even though at the September 1989 meeting of the HPA's HSWP Committee the existence of 'reform committees' within the organization was denied, the reform committees held an important meeting in mid-September at which several reform proposals concerning the military's depoliticization were heard. The participants agreed that the army could not be used to promote political interests and voiced their intention to bar all parties (including the HSWP) from the armed forces.[29]

At this point, however, there was no consensus within the military – or more precisely, between most of the army leaders and the officer corps – regarding the future political position of the HPA. At the September HPA Party conference General Bela Gyorgyi, First Secretary of the HSWP in the armed forces, acknowledged that the demand for the military's depoliticization aroused 'uncertainty' in the army. Nonetheless, the delegates agreed that HSWP organizations should leave the armed forces (the MOD by the end of 1989, other HPA bodies by late 1990).[30] Some participants called for an acceleration of this schedule; they got their wish since by early 1990 there were no active party organizations in the military.

It is important to note that while senior army leaders were reluctant to embrace the political transformation, throughout the process they continued to reassure the population that the HPA would remain calm and had no intention in getting involved in politics.[31] Although few Hungarians believed in such an eventuality, taking such an unambiguous stance certainly earned points for the armed forces. The fact that some generals were less than happy at seeing the unfolding political events is entirely understandable in view of the privileges and high party contacts they stood to lose.

By February 1990, the Nemeth government's Deputy Defense Minister Szombathelyi announced that the depoliticization of the army was completed.[32] For four decades, the Communist propaganda machine had made an immense effort to socialize the armed forces, but in the end it turned out to be ineffectual. What were the reasons for this failure? First of all, as the models of Herspring and Volgyes on the one hand, and of Alexiev on the other pointed out, the 'socialist value system' with its heavy emphasis on 'international' values had never replaced national allegiances in the armed forces. Second, many members of the professional officer corps, let alone the draftees, resented the Soviet domination over Hungary in general, and over the HPA in particular. Third, professional personnel had been annoyed by the large amount of time spent with political-ideological training at the expense of the improvement of professional skills. Fourth, the deterioration of the living standards of professional cadres adversely affected their morale. Finally, owing to all of these factors, the prestige of the military had decreased; as a result, fewer qualified candidates were applying to military educational institutions thus the HPA had faced persistent recruitment problems.

The majority of professional cadres, then, welcomed 'the end of ideology' and the opportunity to concentrate on military rather than political matters.[33] In September 1989 the participants of the HSWP and opposition round-table negotiations agreed to set up a Defense Council following the general elections. The President of the Republic, the Chairman of Parliament, the Prime Minister, the members of the government, one representative of each party in parliament, and the Chief-of-Staff of the armed forces would constitute this Council which would exercise the powers of the President and the government in cases of emergency.[34]

In early 1990 the Defense Law was modified, according to the recommendations of the round-table, so as to revoke the license of the armed forces to interfere in domestic political processes.[35] This event drastically changed the character of the Hungarian army, for it freed the military from one of its most important function under Communism: the defense of the regime from its internal foes. In March 1990 parliament agreed to change the name of the armed forces from Hungarian People's Army (*Magyar Nephadsereg*) to Hungarian Army (*Magyar Honvedseg* – HA).

The new Hungarian parliament included only two deputies with extensive military affiliations, both long retired and imprisoned by the Communists. Kalman Keri (born in 1901) had been a high-ranking officer in Horthy's army and subsequently the 'tenant of several Soviet and Hungarian penal camps and prisons'.[36] The other was General Bela Kiraly (born in 1912) who returned after a 33-year stay in the United States. Both former officers – along with other martyrs of the Hungarian armed forces persecuted by the Communist regime – were rehabilitated.

B. Political Officers, Military Training, and Prestige

In December 1989 Prime Minister Nemeth announced that the HPA's Main Political Administration was abolished since it was 'no longer needed'.[37] The MOD had already reclassified political officers as 'educational, social, and political' officers in September 1989. Their new job description was to offer patriotic training, as well as cultural and political enlightenment to conscripts although one might suspect that such an abrupt decision resulted in little more than a change of labels.[38] The Antall government's Defense Minister, Lajos Fur, then decided that these functions ought to be carried out by unit commanders and their subordinates as in most democratic armies (or, as it were, in the pre-war Hungarian army). Secretary of State for Defense Erno Raffay justified this measure, saying that the new government wanted a depoliticized army and did not need officers who tried to imbue recruits with the 'socialist-internationalist' value system.[39] Shortly thereafter, in August 1990, the MOD announced that some 900 erstwhile political officers would be transferred to other areas in the HA or discharged.[40]

The power struggle and jockeying for positions accompanying Hungary's political transformation affected other military positions as well. By February 1990 more than 50 generals and 400 colonels were retired; the average age of professional soldiers dropped to 35 years.[41] Many officers (1,700 in the first half of 1990 alone) left the service as a result of having better career opportunities in civilian life. The question of what to do with those officers who had been active in the HSWP was also addressed by the new political leadership.

At a session of the parliament's Defense Committee representatives debated the 'red or expert' issue and came to the conclusion that since 'it was impossible to dismiss the entire army', consequently, professional competence should be the decisive factor.[42] Defense Minister Fur said that while most officers had been HSWP members, it was impossible to say how many of them had been committed Communists. The new MOD, he added, was hopeful that the mentality of Communist officers could be altered, but those who could not change their ways would have to leave the armed forces.[43]

The need for the rapid replacement of officers active in the HSWP necessitated the revamping of military education and training within the framework of the army's transformation. Since the army's internal repressive function became irrelevant, officer training was altered to reflect this change.[44] In the Communist era as much as 30 percent of the instruction was taken up by Marxism-Leninism and other politico-ideological subjects although the dogmatism that had characterized these courses diminished after 1987.[45] Starting with the 1989–90 academic year, ideological training at the colleges was replaced by courses on military and security policy, international military law, and military history. At the Zrinyi Military Academy new subjects were introduced to ensure that education was based on the criteria of national interest.[46] Instead of socialist-internationalist values, officer training emphasized Hungarian political and military history, democratic values, and patriotism.

The structure of education at military colleges was also reorganized. The 1987 reform that reduced the training period to three years was unsuccessful as the pool of candidates did not improve – one high-ranking officer remarked that 'we could only attract mediocre students, and I am being tactful' – and the quality of training suffered.[47] Therefore, military leaders called successfully for the reintroduction of a four-year program and raising of admission standards. Field training mirrored the change in Hungary's military doctrine: only methods and elements of defensive warfare were practiced. In order to guarantee the continued preparedness of the officer corps, the MOD planned to test the knowledge and aptitude of officers in five-year intervals. Promotion would be conditional on performance in these examinations; those who failed risked being discharged.[48]

In the 1949–89 period approximately 2,600 Hungarian officers received their military college degrees in the USSR, 120 in Poland, and 65 in Czechoslovakia. In addition, around 4,000 HPA officers participated in postgraduate and other courses (2–10 months in duration) in the USSR.[49] While the training of Hungarian cadets in the Soviet Union was under review by the new government, the Soviet government also signalled that it was no longer willing to subsidize the education of foreign officers. A presidential decree permitted Soviet military colleges to charge for the training of foreign nationals, at the reported cost of US\$ 1,500 a month per student.[50] Only 20 percent of Hungarian officer candidates who studied in the USSR in 1989–90 – those close to completing their programs – enrolled in the 1990–91 academic year; the rest were recalled and transferred to other institutions. According to Defense Minister Für, Hungary would like to limit the training of its officer candidates in the USSR to a 'few specialized areas'. Instead, the MOD plans to send cadets to Great Britain, Germany, France, Italy, and the United States. Because of lack of funds, the MOD hope was that at least initially Hungarian cadets could be supported by the host institutions through special scholarships.[51]

The MOD would like the new army to attract the best and the brightest of young Hungarian men, but it is unclear what these hopes are based on.

In the recent past, only 60 percent of enrolled students graduated, largely because of inferior academic performance and disenchantment with the armed forces.[52] The prestige of the military career is at an all-time low and unlikely to increase, primarily because of the low income of professional soldiers. In the first half of 1990 1,700 officers requested their discharge, in spite of the MOD's efforts to improve the conditions of career soldiers.[53] What must have been even more troubling to military leaders was that usually officers with the highest qualifications left the service as they were the most attractive for prospective civilian employers. Professional military personnel were not permitted to take on a second job but their wage increases had not kept up with the high inflation rate of recent years. As a result, approximately 10 percent of active officers live under the official poverty line; in the case of NCOs this figure is even higher.[54] The MOD wants to raise the salary and benefits of its professional corps but the government's willingness and ability to remedy the situation at a time of profound economic difficulties is doubtful. The prestige and the relative material rewards of the profession is the lowest in Eastern Europe. At the same time the demands on line officers are immense; their life expectancy (58.9 years) is six years lower than that of other Hungarian males.[55] Every fourth officer retires for medical reasons.[56]

In addition, the army's arsenal is clearly substandard and because of its decreasing budget it even has trouble maintaining its equipment, a factor that is sure to repel technically inclined youths. For all these reasons, it is difficult to believe that the profession's reputation will be considerably improved in the foreseeable future. Thus, service academies expect to face recruitment problems in the future, therefore the system of the well functioning military high schools – an expensive solution that has had a limited impact – will probably be maintained for lack of other solutions. In the future, in contrast with earlier practice, graduates of these schools will have to pass the entrance examination administered by military colleges.[57]

Another factor contributing to the low prestige of the profession is that the armed forces – more precisely, the military leadership – has long been perceived by the population as the refuge of the incompetent and corrupt. A few recently published books only confirmed this belief.[58] Moreover, for decades Hungarians had viewed the military not as the guarantor of the nation's security but as a representative of foreign interests. It is possible that the 'nationalization' of the military may change the minds of some youths about a military career. Despite the severe budgetary problems, the MOD plans to demonstrate the importance of the military's national character by introducing new uniforms 'expressing the spirit of the

Hungarian Army' as early as 1992.[59] In addition, other external attributes such as manners of address ('comrade' was replaced by 'brother-in-arms' [*bajtars*] under Karpati only to be changed to 'sir' [*ur*] by Fur), ceremonial processions were altered to conform to pre-1945 practices.[60]

In short, by the end of 1990 the Hungarian army once again emerged as a national institution. Again, none of the theoretical approaches considered could anticipate these developments, consequently, none is relevant to Hungarian civil–military relations in the 1990s, for this is no longer a 'Communist party–state' but a constitutionally established democratic polity.

Part III   Democratization and Reorganization of the Armed Forces

The internal democratization and reorganization of the Hungarian armed forces are very important elements of the transformation of civil–military relations for they demonstrate the extent of military depoliticization. The result of this phenomenon was that by the end of 1990 the principles commanding the internal workings of the HPA had become in many ways similar to those of its democratic counterparts elsewhere.

A.   Internal Democratization

Although military leaders attempted to improve the lot of professional cadres in the 1988–90 period, in important respects their conditions had not changed. For instance, young officers and NCOs were often at the mercy of their superiors and the Code of Service obliged them to seek remedy of their problems from the same individuals who caused them. Although in the first half of 1990 a National Federation of Soldier's Associations was created, many line officers felt that this body could not solve their problems since it was controlled by their commanders. As a safeguard professional soldiers established the Association to Protect Soldiers' Interests in September.[61] The MOD did not debate the validity of the soldiers' complaints but rather insisted that relations between the ranks had to be governed by the Service Code. Defense Minister Fur suggested that both sides wait until the Constitutional Court rules on the matter.

In contrast, the service conditions of conscripts had further improved in the 1988–90 period. In early 1989 the HPA introduced monthly 'reception days' when conscripts could forgo the usual channels (i.e., requesting remedy for their complaints from their direct superiors) and discuss their grievances directly with their unit commanders. According to then Defense Minister Karpati, it was hoped this measure would disperse the soldiers' feeling of defenselessness.[62] With the abolition of political-ideological education conscripts were allowed to spend their free time as they saw fit. These were important measures not only because they made conscript life easier, but also because they signalled changes in the military establishment's attitude toward the civilian population.

Relations between the HA and the Churches had shown a marked improvement in the 1988–90 period. This process started in the mid-1980s with a few minor gestures extended to theological students serving in the HPA. Starting in 1990 they were required only to complete a one-month basic training preceding their studies. For the balance of their service, they would work as military chaplains following their ordination.[63] In September 1990 a delegation of Italian military chaplains visited the MOD to share their experiences. HA leaders had already familiarized themselves with the system of military chaplaincy in the Austrian and West German armed forces; an MOD spokesman said that the Ministry wanted to study the Italian and Swiss systems before committing itself to a proposal.[64]

The question of alternative (i.e., unarmed) military service was discussed seriously in the MOD for the first time in June 1988.[65] The Defense Law was modified to allow conscientious objectors to serve in the HPA without weapons, starting in 1989. In March 1989 the Minister of Justice suspended the prison sentences of the 70 young men who refused military service on grounds of religious beliefs and conscientious objection. In June, those opposed to armed service were offered two options: alternative service in the HA or work in the health and social welfare fields.[66]

The mandatory military service of conscripted soldiers was eased on several occasions starting with the early 1980s. The terms of service of the Hungarian armed forces changed in conjunction with the democratization process and the army's shrinking size. The length of service was reduced from 18 to 12 months in 1990, a proposal that was forwarded already by the Nemeth government in 1989. As a result of this measure 15,000 soldiers expecting to serve 18 months at the time of their entrance to the armed forces were discharged after only a year's service in August 1990. The total service time thus became 22 months (12 months full time and 10 months in the reserves).[67] The terms of alternative and civilian service were reduced from 28 to 22 months as well.

B.   Structural Reorganization

Already by 1987 the Hungarian forces were restructured along the lines of the brigade system. The most important decisions concerning the reorganization of the HPA's administrative setup were taken in late 1989. In December 1989, two days after a regular meeting of Warsaw Pact defense ministers in Budapest, Prime Minister Nemeth announced several changes in Hungarian defense policy. The government justified the measures by its new defensive security doctrine that required the reorganization of the military establishment.[68] This task entailed 'drastic and expedient' reductions in manpower and equipment within the Warsaw Pact in general and in the HA in particular. Clearly, some of these decisions were occasioned by Hungary's extremely difficult economic situation.

One of the most important facets of the reform package was the radical reorganization of the military command structure. In fact, nearly all employees of the Ministry proper had assumed new positions during the reorganization. The most significant change in the structure of the military command was that the MOD was divided into two separate entities: a Defense Ministry (MOD) with a relatively small staff of 135 in place of the earlier 1,500, and a so-called 'Command of the Hungarian Army' (CHA). In the new system the MOD is responsible for military policy and planning, doctrinal issues, the military's foreign contacts, and other administrative and theoretical matters. The CHA, the practical arm of the defense establishment, is charged with the tasks of supervising actual military training and development, exercises, and the like. The MOD is accountable to the Prime Minister and the government, while the Commander of the HA – in accordance with the new Constitution – is responsible to the President of the Republic, who is the Commander-in-Chief of the Armed Forces.[69]

Changes in military personnel were also implemented to accommodate the new organizational scheme and to retire and promote cadres in late 1989. Defense Minister Karpati retained his post until the national elections of March–April 1990. General Kalman Lorincz was appointed as the army's commander, a position that gave him the rank of State Secretary. General Laszlo Borsits was appointed as Lorincz's first deputy and Chief of Staff.[70] Several former deputy ministers were retired, among them General Lajos Krasznai, the erstwhile head of the HPA's MPA, who was transferred to the diplomatic corps.[71]

Shortly after the new appointments were publicized, observers pointed out that some of the military's new leaders had openly discussed their orthodox political views in the past and thus did not seem to fit the concept of radical military reform. The Nemeth government's answer to these charges was that personnel changes could best be characterized as 'generational', adding that many more cadres were soon to be retired.[72] The government also hinted that although all defense ministers in the WTO were military officers, because of the Hungarian reorganization it was now possible to appoint a civilian. In fact, quickly after the announcement of the reforms Karpati 'became' a civilian, having donned a suit in lieu of his uniform, and entered the reserves. In mid-May 1990, Jozsef Antall named Lajos Fur as his Minister of Defense. Fur, a prominent HDF politician and former university professor, had no experience in military affairs at the time of his appointment. Admittedly, not all military personnel were in favor of the reforms announced in December 1989. According to the MOD, some commanders unable to identify with the changes were dismissed or transferred. At the same time, as MOD spokesman Colonel Keleti conceded, some WTO leaders were perturbed by the swiftness and scope of the Hungarian military reforms.[73]

The main purpose of the command structure's reform was to render the armed forces accountable to the Hungarian government and the President of the Republic. This aspect of the reorganization – and it should be emphasized that it was introduced by the (reform)-Communist government – demonstrated a momentous change in civil–military relations. Whereas the military was previously subordinated to the Party, the December 1989 measures ensured that the armed forces would be controlled not by any party organization but by the government and, ultimately, the President. The implementation of this reform broke with the 40-year practice of the Communist Party's direct control of the armed forces.

C. Cuts in Manpower, Equipment, and Defense Allocations

The more favorable international environment – particularly the improvement of superpower relations and the absence of Moscow's disapproval – enabled Nemeth's government to implement considerable reductions in Hungary's armed forces.[74] In January 1989 the government announced that Hungary would cut its troop strength and equipment by 9 percent (9,300 men) in 1989–90.[75] In late November the Council of Ministers decided on another 20–25 percent of manpower by the end of 1991.[76] The result of these cuts will be a much smaller, lightly armed military. The HA's arsenal may improve in relative terms as the most obsolete weaponry will be discarded. In January 1990, the armed forces was composed of 106,800 men and 15,000 civilian employees. By the end of 1991, the number was to be reduced to 75,000 men, one-third of them career soldiers, plus

15,000 civilians, for a grand total of 90,000 – a reduction of over 30,000. According to Fur, the HA's manpower would stabilize at 0.6–0.8 percent of the population.[77]

By all accounts, the arsenal of the HPA has been decidedly mediocre but observers presumed that it was sufficient for Hungary's defense needs. The shocking inadequacy of the armed forces' equipment was revealed by some of the generals summoned before the *ad hoc* parliamentary committee examining the allegations in Colonel Bokor's book, *Petty Tyrants in Uniform*. This thin volume gave a grim portrayal of corruption and incompetence in the HPA that astounded the population. The parliamentary inquiry came to the conclusion that Hungary's defense capabilities were hopelessly insufficient.

General Mihaly Torok, for instance, explained that Hungary possessed neither good quality anti-tank guns to hold off an offensive nor equipment that could secure her borders.[78] In addition, the HA had not a single bomber, nor sufficient air defense capabilities to protect either the population or the ground forces, and whatever equipment it owned was on average 30 years old. The vast majority of armored carriers were often unable to leave their bases because of poor repair and obsolescence. Torok added that the reason for this situation was the distribution of tasks in the WTO, and that the Pact's antiquated offensive doctrine had rendered Hungary effectively impotent to defend itself. The defense of the country's air space, for example, was of 'tolerable' quality only when HA capabilities were complemented by those of the Southern Group of Soviet Forces (SGSF) stationed in Hungary.[79]

Hungary had never received the most modern equipment from the Soviet Union. According to General Janza, the Head of the MOD's Department of Economics, the weapons the HPA could buy from the USSR always lagged behind the Soviet military technology by 10–12 years.[80] Even though the Soviets sold relatively sophisticated equipment, such as MiG-29 airplanes, to countries like Egypt and India, Hungary never received any such equipment. Moscow's reluctance to entrust advanced weapons to its Hungarian ally caused a great deal of resentment among HPA officers.[81] Due to the drastically reduced defense budgets, it is unlikely that the MOD will be able to substantially improve the HA's arsenal in the foreseeable future. These problems were exacerbated by the fact that Hungary would have to pay in hard currency for the weapons and spare parts it buys from the erstwhile USSR beginning in 1991, since the two countries had agreed to conduct all trade in convertible currency. The HA has, nonetheless, expressed interest in acquiring new weapons, for instance T-72 tanks, from the arsenal of the former East German armed forces.[82] (Reportedly, Czechoslovakia and Poland are also eyeing the same tanks.) Hungary would like to obtain more modern surplus equipment from the United States as well.[83]

Nevertheless, diminishing government allocations make even these modest plans unlikely to succeed; indeed, it is doubtful whether the HA will be able to maintain its arsenal at the current level. On average military spending accounted for 4.1 percent of the GDP in the 1986–89 period.[84] The government's defense budget for 1989, adjusted for inflation, dropped by 17 percent.[85] The 1990 budget of the HA was slashed by 30 percent in real terms, compared to 1989. Only 35.8 billion forint (US$ 560 million) was set aside from the budget for defense purposes.[86] Initially, Fur contended that the armed forces would need a minimum of 75 billion forint (approximately US$ 880 million) in 1991 to maintain operations and to acquire some much-needed equipment. While annual per capita military expenditures were $80 in Hungary, they were three times higher in Czechoslovakia and one-and-a-half times higher in Romania.[87] Notwithstanding Fur's claims, defense only received 54.46 billion forint from Hungary's 1991 budget (of which the MOD had to generate 7.05 billion), some 30 percent less in real terms than in the previous year.[88]

Hungary's small defense industry has been very adversely affected by the economic crisis in general, and the drastic reductions in military spending in particular. Because of the elimination of state subsidies and the dramatic diminution of domestic and foreign orders, the divisions of most enterprises producing military equipment have been unprofitable since the mid-1980s.[89] The cuts in the army's manpower and equipment dealt an additional blow to the defense industry resulting in layoffs and enormous losses in revenue. The industry is in a profound crisis and its recovery is difficult to foresee.[90]

Part IV   Hungary, the Warsaw Pact, and Soviet Troop Withdrawals

The collapse of East European Communism was concomitant with the disintegration of the regional economic and military organizations. The CMEA was unceremoniously abolished in January 1991, the Warsaw Pact met the same fate on July 1. By the end of 1990, the WTO was reduced to a pro forma military organization as a result of the East European revolutions and the reunification of the two Germanys.

A. Hungary and the Pact

Until 1988 the questioning of Hungary's membership in the Warsaw Pact
was one of the few remaining taboos in the country. As a result of the
democratization process, which entailed the rapid liberalization of the
media, the issue of Hungary's Warsaw Pact membership soon became
one of the most frequently debated topics in the Hungarian media. The
publication of the views of Soviet Academician Oleg Bogomolov that a
neutral Hungary would not pose a threat to the security of the Soviet Union
gave further impetus to this discussion.[91] In his Council of Europe address
in the summer of 1989, Gorbachev renounced the Brezhnev doctrine and
said that 'any attempts to restrict the sovereignty of states – friends,
allies, or any others – are inadmissible'.[92] Hungarian politicians also
received signals from senior Soviet officials – Politburo member Yevgenii
Primakov, CPSU Spokesman Nikolai Shishlin and others – that the USSR
would tolerate WTO dropouts and 'Hungary could leave the alliance if it
chose to'.[93]

The process that culminated in Budapest's announcement of its intention
to withdraw from the WTO in June 1990 approximately corresponded to
the democratization of Hungarian politics. In April 1989 Foreign Minister
Horn had said that political changes in Hungary were valuable *within* the
WTO framework and withdrawal from the Pact was but an illusion.[94]
By mid-year, however, the official media began to publish articles and
interviews questioning Hungary's WTO membership. In June, for instance,
Professor Istvan Dioszegi, a respected diplomatic historian, was quoted as
saying that 'from a Hungarian perspective the alliance is devoid of any
reciprocity and is nothing else but the unilateral limitation of Hungarian
sovereignty'.[95] Still, the government, while allowing itself to criticize
certain aspects of the Pact – Foreign Minister Horn, for instance, said
that the WTO should concentrate on military cooperation rather than
on ideological or bilateral questions – was not officially considering
abandoning the alliance.

One of the first issues the new legislature discussed in May 1990 was
the withdrawal from the WTO. The AFD suggested that the government
decide the issue as quickly as possible.[96] International reaction to the
AFD's motion was decidedly cool.[97] Not unexpectedly, WTO leaders
rejected Western (and Hungarian) views that the Pact was in decline and
in a deep crisis. General Piotr Lushev, Commander-in-Chief of the WTO's
United Armed Forces stated in May that 'in today's Eastern Europe there is
no – and there can be no – other alternative mechanism that could influence
Europe's stability more efficiently than the WTO'.[98] In the spring of 1990,

the Budapest government began to study seriously the possibility of a unilateral withdrawal from the Pact. According to the Hungarian position, the Warsaw Pact contradicted the country's national interests, had become 'obsolete and superfluous', and 'its existence was not justified by the given circumstances of European development'.[99] At the Moscow PCC meeting in June 1990, Prime Minister Antall proposed the elimination of the Pact's military component by the end of 1991. More importantly, he announced Hungary's intention to leave the WTO's military arm in 1991 and stated that his government's ultimate objective was a negotiated full withdrawal from the Pact.[100] Following his talks with Soviet Defense Minister Dimitrii Yazov, Fur announced that he had informed his Soviet counterpart that Hungary would no longer take part in joint WTO exercises, would remove its armed forces from the Warsaw Pact Joint Command, and place them entirely under national authority.[101]

Hungary's Parliament voted overwhelmingly (232 for, none against, and 4 abstentions) for a full withdrawal from the Pact on June 26, 1990.[102] Soviet media reaction to the vote was negative but commentators did concede that 'the Hungarian people were brought to their knees under the flag of the WTO'.[103] In October, shortly before his visit to the United States, Antall urged Washington to fill the void in Eastern Europe left by Soviet retrenchment, expressing his preference for sustained American military presence in Europe despite the end of the Cold War. At the same time he confirmed that 'even if the military part of the Pact is not dissolved in 1991, we will withdraw from it'.[104] As it turned out, this was not necessary as the WTO quietly expired on July 1, 1991.

B. The End of Soviet Occupation

As political repression of the opposition weakened in the late 1980s, the sensitive issue of Soviet troops in Hungary began to surface ever more frequently.[105] After 1988, the once sacred subject had become a hotly debated issue and questions concerning the political, military, and strategic rationale for the approximately 65,000 Soviet soldiers stationed 'temporarily' in the country since 1945 had been publicly discussed on a number of occasions. In 1989 the USSR pulled out some 12,000 troops within the framework of Gorbachev's unilateral cuts of Soviet troops in Eastern Europe. The fate of the remaining Soviet soldiers and their equipment was the main topic of three rounds of talks between Soviet and Hungarian foreign and defense ministry officials in February and March 1990.[106] The agreement was signed on March 9 by the two foreign ministers, Eduard Shevardnadze and Gyula Horn, in Moscow.[107]

The Soviet Union agreed to withdraw all of its soldiers and equipment by the end of June 1991.

The lack of clear regulations was at least partly to blame for the serious difficulties concerning the departure of Soviet troops from Hungary. The first Hungarian-Soviet property agreement pertaining to Soviet bases was signed in 1948. Under its terms, Budapest had agreed to lease to the Soviet troops all buildings they occupied at the end of World War II but it retained ownership. In lieu of payments, the Soviets would renovate the buildings. In 1956 the invading Soviet forces occupied more buildings and bases than in 1948; an agreement was made regarding their financial status in 1958. This agreement invalidated the preceding documents. The ignorance of the high military leadership concerning important aspects of the Soviet forces stationed in Hungary quickly became apparent. General (Ret.) Janos Sebok conceded that he and his former colleagues in the MOD had not known that Hungary served as a supply depot for Czechoslovakia and the Ukraine. 'We were also not clear,' he said, 'about how many Soviet soldiers were stationed in our homeland.'[108]

In a short time the financial settlement of the Soviet troop pull-out became the most pugnaciously disputed issue between the two sides, eliciting a great deal of previously unimaginable ill-feeling, charges and counter-charges between the two sides. Budapest's MOD, after researching the issue, had reached several troubling conclusions. It became known, for instance, that in spite of the 1948 agreement stating that Moscow was to bear all costs for maintaining military bases and constructing new buildings, Hungary financed a large share of these expenditures between 1949 and 1953. The Soviet side, however, only compensated Hungary for 10 percent of the costs. The Hungarian MOD's financial support of the Soviet presence during this period was not regulated, and Budapest chose not to safeguard its own rights.

General Matvei Burlakov, Commander of the SGSF and the USSR's representative in charge of the withdrawals, estimated the value of the buildings the Soviet troops erected in Hungary at 10 billion forint (U.S>$ 135 million).[109] Moscow asked for compensation for their investments in and around the Hungarian bases. While the Hungarians did not directly refute the Soviet figures, they wanted to consider several important qualifications. For instance, Hungarian experts contended that many of the Soviet-built apartments conformed to Soviet (having, for example, communal baths and kitchens) rather than Hungarian building standards and thus were of little use to Hungary. Furthermore, the majority of not only the apartment buildings but also the barracks were in such poor condition that they were of almost no value to their new owners. Ideally, the MOD would have liked these buildings to be in the same condition as those maintained by the Hungarian forces.

As Soviet troops began to withdraw, many articles described the Soviet serviceman's life in Hungary. Despite Burlakov's frequent references to the 'friendship' existing between Soviet soldiers and the Hungarian people, this relationship could perhaps be best described as calculating and self-seeking, with a heavy dose of Russophobia on the Hungarian side.[110] Soviet military leaders vigorously denied that Hungarians and Soviet soldiers conducted 'business deals',[111] although scores of newspaper and magazine articles contradicted their disavowal. One such article graphically depicted the relationships between Hungarians and their Soviet 'friends' in the village of Hajmasker, site of the first base vacated by the Soviets.[112] Village residents expressed not only their annoyance about the noise of the Soviet military vehicles and the soldiers' occasional offenses but also mentioned the mutually advantageous commercial relationship that had existed between the village and the troops.[113] Soviet soldiers sold everything from overalls and boots to gasoline and television sets in exchange for Hungarian wine, brandy, soap, fruit and various food items, and, of course, cash.

The Soviets also sold machine guns and signal flares which they occasionally used to threaten their Hungarian 'friends' at a heavily frequented Veszprem county garbage dump.[114] Many denounced Soviet soldiers for selling ammunition, weapons, and explosives in the cities of Budapest, Gyor, Esztergom, and Szentendre.[115] Soviet servicemen in Hungary lived in relatively primitive conditions. The food rations for ordinary soldiers appear to have been very deficient. In an interview the former Commander of the Soviet base in Budapest, Colonel (Ret.) Georgii Lakhno conceded that the cultural level of Soviet officers 'remains very low'.[116] He acknowledged that disciplinary problems existed within the Soviet units in Hungary. In fact, because of the widespread thievery and general anti-social behavior, Soviet officers at some locations restricted their troops to base. Many Soviet soldiers never had the opportunity to see 'the world outside their barracks' during their 2-year tour in Hungary.

Notwithstanding all of these problems, the withdrawal of the Soviet troops from Hungary progressed on schedule. By the end of 1990 only 10–15 percent of the Soviet troops remained in Hungary and the withdrawal was completed in June 1991. A number of contentious issues still need to be resolved, however. As long as full documentation of the costs of the 45-year Soviet occupation remains unavailable, it is difficult to predict, through the barrage of claims and counterclaims, which side will have to compensate the other. One cannot help but feel that, in the end, the 'zero payment' alternative might be preferred, so that no money will be involved.[117]

C. Proliferation of Western Contacts

The HPA developed many important contacts with its Western counterparts during the 1980s. The successes of the Hungarian military diplomacy were likely the result of a well-planned 'Western policy program' starting in the mid-1980s and originated in the Foreign Affairs Department of the MOD. In 1988–90 these relations became more varied and substantial, signalling the army's growing distance from its WTO partners.

In 1989 alone, Hungary received three NATO defense ministers and a number of top-level military delegations. In May Dutch Minister of Defense Fritz Bolkenstein was the first NATO defense minister to visit Hungary.[118] In August HPA Chief of Staff General Pacsek paid visits to the U.S., the United Kingdom, Canada, and Switzerland.[119] He said that the HPA wanted to improve relations not only with European members of NATO but also with others 'out of gunshot range'. Pacsek announced plans for a two-year cooperation agreement between the HPA and the Canadian Armed Forces which would allow regular top-level meetings between Hungarian and Canadian military personnel. Budapest also hosted British Defence Secretary Tom King. Although King said that alliance structures had not yet shown any 'sign of genuine change', he stressed that confidence was increasing and that his visit had set an example, particularly in light of the Vienna CSCE talks.[120]

The HPA was also represented at various international meetings, such as the European Conference of Conscript Organizations held in Helsinki in August 1989. The Hungarian and Soviet delegations were the first from the WTO to attend this annual convention.[121] In December Hungary and France submitted a joint 'confidence-building proposal' at the CSCE talks in Vienna. This was the first time that a NATO and a WTO state jointly initiated a resolution. Moreover, a small Hungarian contingent (15 officers) participated in the United Nations peace-keeping forces observing the cease-fire agreement between Iraq and Iran.[122] In February 1990 the MOD and the Rand Corporation jointly organized a conference at which top U.S. and Hungarian experts examined civil–military relations in democratic political systems.[123]

Hungary, together with Canada, was also instrumental in the organization of the 'Open Skies' conferences that attempted to revive President Eisenhower's proposal to General Secretary Khrushchev at the 1955 Geneva summit meeting. The idea, characteristically dismissed by the

Soviet leader as 'legalized espionage', was to allow military airplanes to fly over each other's territory. Although agreements over technical matters could not be achieved between the 23 participants at the April 1990 Budapest meeting, the Hungarian and Canadian co-sponsors of the conference agreed that the long-term prospects of 'Open Skies' were good.[124]

In sum, since the mid-1980s the Hungarian military leadership has pursued an ambitious foreign relations agenda oriented toward Western states. Like Hungary's foreign policy toward the West, the country's military diplomacy, obviously supported by the government and the (Communist) party leadership, was very fruitful. The successes achieved by Hungarian military diplomacy must, however, be put in their proper perspective. The tangible results of the policy were some minor agreements holding the promise of 'regularized contacts' and the creation of a few (academic) exchange programs. These accomplishments indicated a decade-long Hungarian commitment to disarmament and demonstrated an attempt to ease the tension between the two alliances.

Summary

One could scarcely give a more succinct summary of the transformation of civil–military relations in Hungary than did Colonel Keleti, the capable spokesman of the MOD, offering the following in an interview in late 1990:[125]

> The political systemic change has now been completed in the Hungarian armed forces. One of the most important aspects of this is that the army is now a body free of party struggles, characterized by the primacy of national interests and the defense of national sovereignty. The Hungarian armed forces are getting out of the Warsaw Pact, an alliance that worked against its members' national interests. They are also realistically taking into account the events of the past forty to fifty years, rehabilitating (in some cases posthumously) the officers removed in 1956, restoring national traditions and former unit names in the military, and strengthening their ties with social organizations and the Churches. The armed forces are a part of Hungary's democratization process and have become the army of the people and the nation.

By the end of this period none of the existing models of East European civil–military relations had much relevance to Hungary. Not only did the

Communist Party disintegrate and essentially disappear from the political stage but *all* political organizations were banned from the armed forces. It is important to note that in contrast with some of its East European counterparts, the political transformation of Hungary was entirely peaceful and thus the HPA – which was not asked to come to the aid of the disintegrating Communist regime – played no role in it.

One of the first acts of the new legislation was the passing of a constitutional amendment which clearly stated that the highest authority over the armed forces was the freely elected President of the Republic. The military had become an institution subordinated to the Constitution and elected state officials. As a result of the transformation of the civil–military relations, the armed forces no longer had the opportunity to play their former role in politics. The political (i.e., Communist Party) structure in the armed forces was dismantled and military personnel were prohibited from engaging in any manner of party politics within the barracks. The military educational system was reformed to reflect the army's shifting loyalties, from the Party and the Warsaw Pact to the nation-state and the Constitution. In short, the primary consequence of the transformation of civil–military relations was the depoliticization of the armed forces. At the same time, the external relations of the military had also changed to mirror its regained independence from the Soviet Union and the Warsaw Pact.

The leaders of the Hungarian Army are in an unenviable situation. First, in order to attract the best and the brightest into the new officer corps, they need to convince the population, particularly the country's young men, that the new army is very different from the thoroughly politicized HPA. This will not be easy for some time to come since the middle and top ranks are currently dominated by officers with extensive ties to the Communist regime. These people, however, cannot easily be replaced due to the fact that despite their undesirable political connections to the past, their expertise is indispensable at the present time. Second, Hungary does not have the resources to address the army's financial problems. In the current socio-political and economic situation national defense occupies a rather low position on the government's list of priorities. Third, partly as a consequence of the preceding point and partly due to the country's former association with the Warsaw Pact, Hungary is in an extremely vulnerable security situation as it would be unable to defend itself from any one of its neighbors. It appears to be clear that without Western help – whether in the form of giving Hungary surplus military equipment and/or extending NATO's protective umbrella over the country – Budapest's security predicament will not be overcome in the foreseeable future. The first signals of cooperation on military issues between Czechoslovakia, Hungary, and Poland is indicative of the East Central European states' capability of genuine collaboration in this area.[126] Aside from enhancing their defensive capacities, such cooperation might also be looked upon very favorably by NATO's leaders in Brussels.

6 Civil–Military Relations in Eastern Europe, 1945–90: A Cross-National Analysis

The preceding chapters examined civil–military relations in Hungary and the applicability of some theoretical approaches to the Hungarian case. In this chapter the focus shifts to the entire region, more precisely, to the five non-Soviet Warsaw Pact (NSWP) states aside from Hungary (Bulgaria, Czechoslovakia, East Germany, Poland, and Romania). It is not and cannot be my purpose to offer comprehensive analyses of civil–military relations of Eastern Europe within the framework of this chapter. Instead, I merely seek to illustrate the fundamental argument that civil–military relations in Eastern Europe – despite important similarities – were very different throughout 1945–90 and the existing models thus far considered are incapable of accommodating the individual cases.

Part I Soldiers and Politics in Eastern Europe, 1945–88: Similarities and Differences

A. The Takeover Period and Soviet Interference

The period of 'sovietization' has been of particular import in my analysis because it illustrates the transformation of civil–military relations from non-Communist to Communist systems. Even though several models considered in Chapter 1 posited that the takeover period was nearly identical in all of the NSWP states, I try to point out some important deviations. For instance, it seems important to observe differences between military reorganization and the extent to which consolidation of power required penetration of indigenous military establishments. My hypothesis is that even in this phase – which is the historical stage when party–army relations across the region had shared more commonalities than in any other period – civil–military relations were different enough to question the utility of models claiming uniformity of experiences.

Even cursory examination of Eastern Europe's satellization reveals

Moscow's heavy-handed interference in the domestic policies of the region in general, and in the creation of their post-war armed forces in particular. Similarly to Hungary, the reorganization of the military did not figure prominently on the agendas of the emerging Communist regimes until about 1948, when the Soviet-induced large-scale military buildup commenced. In most cases the emerging Communist regimes were initially concerned with the consolidation of their power and concentrated on strengthening the security forces that could provide tangible support for them. In addition, restrictions imposed on the size of the region's armed forces were observed until 1948.

In Bulgaria, Soviet interference in military policy was strong and Soviet advisers had enjoyed a permanent presence as early as 1944. That year saw the deployment of Soviet political commissars in the Bulgarian army as the Balkan state joined the anti-fascist coalition and participated in the last stages of the war.[1] Romania is a different case to the extent that there was no single Soviet overlord supervising the sovietization of the armed forces – like General Biriuzov in Bulgaria – and the transformation was accomplished as a national process.[2]

Poland represents yet another pattern. The Polish People's Army (PPA) was created in 1945 although its origins could be traced back to 1943 when the First and Second Polish Armies were organized by Moscow on Soviet territory. Another albeit much smaller component of the PPA was made up of Communist partisans. In 1944–48 a small-scale civil war was fought between the Soviet-supported forces and the anti-Communist nationalist underground.[3] Communist victory and Soviet control over the PPA, however, was never really in question.

The East German case has several distinctive attributes which reflected the unique characteristics of its civil–military relations in the Soviet bloc. Clearly, the German Democratic Republic's (GDR) military was devoid of a *national* tradition and an alternative to ideology as a basis of military loyalties.[4] Indeed, the East German polity invested a tremendous effort in trying to *create* a nation to allure the population with the myth of a distinct cultural heritage and traditional value-system. Its National People's Army (NPA) was, in fact, an army without a nation and therefore, aside from the regime's Marxist–Leninist ideology, it had no other attachments. Apart from its important geopolitical and geostrategic position, this is an additional reason for the particularly direct and unmitigated control of Moscow over the NPA. The USSR supported indigenous East German military capabilities only reluctantly after the war, and the short-lived 1953 uprising confirmed Soviet misgivings. Moscow's doubts apparently remained well beyond the official creation of the NPA and dissipated only after the erection of the Berlin Wall in 1961.[5]

In many respects, the Czechoslovak case is the most similar to the Hungarian. In both countries the coalition governments were tolerated by the Kremlin until 1948. In Czechoslovakia this coalition period was more genuinely democratic and Communist influence on the military was less pronounced. The intensive politicization of the armed forces took place only after 1948 – in stark contrast with Hungary, where, as we have seen, the military was subjected to strong Communist interference already in 1945. In the 1945–48 period pro-Western officers still controlled important positions in the Czechoslovak People's Army (CSPA) and the Defense Ministry in Prague; in fact, at the time of the February 1948 coup only 15 percent of the top-ranking officers were Communists.[6]

The regimes realized the restructuring of the military establishments through different means; the end results, however, were comparable: heavily politicized Soviet-type armed forces. The purges of the militaries in the takeover period was an important similarity that fostered the process of the NSWP armies' sovietization. The 'purification' of East European militaries started in earnest in Bulgaria, where at least 2,000 'reactionary officers' were dismissed in July 1946, many of them accused of war crimes, imprisoned or executed.[7] In August 1946, more than 9,000 officers and 5,000 NCOs were dismissed from the Romanian People's Army (RPA) after the Communist takeover.[8] In Poland the appointment of Soviet Marshal Rokossovsky as Defense Minister foreshadowed the mass purges of 'national' elements in the PPA in 1948–49, although the process was not marked by the level of violence as it was in Bulgaria, Czechoslovakia, or Hungary.[9] In 1948 the CSPA was also thoroughly purged of those perceived of harboring anti-Soviet sentiments (approximately 4,000–6,000 professional soldiers were dismissed),[10] many top-ranking officers were prosecuted in show trials. (As in Hungary, some dismissed CSPA officers were reinstated during the military buildup of the early 1950s.) Everywhere in the region the purges brought about drastic deterioration in the quality of the officer corps. There was no East German army in 1953, but it is noteworthy that following the Soviet suppression of the 1953 uprising, 65 percent of the Barracked People's Police (BPP, the precursor of the NPA which was only established in 1956) officers left the service.[11]

As in Hungary, Soviet personnel were directly involved in the 'communization' of the armed forces in all NSWP states, although to varying degrees. In 1945–46, for instance, there were only 531 Soviet 'advisers' in the CSPA but 16,396 in the PPA.[12] Moscow's interference in Eastern Europe's military affairs was particularly extensive and intensive in 1948–53, an era of heavy arms buildup across the region. By 1950 the number of Soviet advisers increased precipitously (1,000 deployed in the CSPA alone).[13] The Kremlin in essence denied the national traditions and characteristics of the region's armies. Not only the military doctrines and organizational principles, but even uniforms and insignia were replaced by those of the Red Army.

After 1956 (when there were still 10,000 Soviet advisers in the PPA)[14] direct Soviet involvement in the domestic affairs of NSWP states had diminished. In that year the upheavals in Poland and Hungary signalled to Moscow that forthright interference was counterproductive and the leash on Eastern Europe needed to be loosened. Marshal Rokossovsky and thousands of Soviet citizens in Polish military uniforms were recalled. The number of Soviet military advisers in other NSWP states was also drastically reduced. Furthermore, the slow and careful process of 'renationalization' in some NSWP armies began with the late 1950s. As in the Hungarian case, at least outward signs of national characteristics (uniforms, marching songs, manners of address, etc.) were cautiously reintroduced in some of the East European armies, especially in Poland and Romania.[15] 'Renationalization' efforts in Czechoslovakia, on the other hand, did not commence until the mid-1960s, while in Bulgaria this policy was never really initiated.

An important facet of Moscow's control over the region was the stationing of Red Army units on the territory of *some* Eastern European states. Soviet troops had been stationed in East Germany and Poland since 1945. In 1958 they were withdrawn from Romania, apparently as a result of a cost-benefit analysis (which involved, among other factors, Bucharest's ability to manipulate the emerging Sino-Soviet split) in the Kremlin and at the urging of Emil Bodnaras, Romania's Defense Minister in 1948–57.[16] There is no evidence of the Soviet Army's presence in Bulgaria, although several authors have suggested that the possibility should not be discounted.[17] Moscow did not maintain troops in Czechoslovakia until the 1968 invasion.

One of the most significant aspects of the USSR's domination of the region was the Warsaw Pact. Established in May 1955, the Pact can be considered as a major component of Soviet policy intending to institutionalize the USSR's hegemony over Eastern Europe.

B.   The Communist Control of the Armed Forces

As noted above, the Marxist–Leninist party's control of the army had always been the *sine qua non* of civil–military relations in Communist systems. There are many similarities but also many profound differences between the East European Communist parties' management of their militaries. The reasons for these differences are many and, depending on the given case, include combinations of such factors as the distinctive political cultures of these states, the varying degrees of cohesion within the parties in question, the decline of Soviet pressure due to other priorities, and the army's identification with civil society despite party penetration.

To be sure, the overall structure of the Party's political domination was quite similar across the region. This pattern included party organizations within the armed forces supervised by a separate department of the Central Committee, the main political administration with its own army of political officers, heavy doses of Marxist–Leninist indoctrination at all levels of the military-education system, etc. Through these and other mechanisms the hegemonial parties intended to assure that their political control of the armed forces was rock solid. Apart from crises, the Party's relationship with the army appeared to be devoid of major tensions. The Commanders-in-Chief of the armed forces – in so far as this position was legally regulated at all – was none other than the leader of the local Communist party:[18] in the 1970s, for instance, these were Nicolae Ceauşescu, Edward Gierek, Erich Honecker, Gustav Husak, Janos Kadar, and Todor Zhivkov.

One of the main objectives of party control was to preclude the 'autonomization' of the military as an interest group to challenge or influence the Party's authority. The Party routinely disregarded military procedures in order to ensure political reliability. The best example, perhaps, is East Germany where the ruling Socialist Unity Party's (SED) control over the military was even more refined and pervasive than elsewhere in the Pact. In the NPA something similar to the dual command structure – adopted in the 'sovietization' stage by the Eastern European armed forces – survived. For all practical purposes the *Politapparat* was a second chain of command, a system that enabled East German political officers to appeal to their (political) superiors if regular commanders refused to take their suggestions.[19] Furthermore, in 1967 the SED created a Central Party Directorate at the company level to coordinate the activities of even the smallest party groups.[20] In Romania, the political leadership attempted to curtail the authority of senior officers by expanding the decision-making powers of local commanders at the expense of their superiors.[21]

In all NSWP states the Party's political control structure was fashioned after that of the CPSU with only slight variations. The most important departure from this pattern occurred in Romania, where in 1964 the MPA was abolished and replaced by a Higher Political Council to accentuate Romania's alienation from the rest of the WTO. MPA leaders had been first and foremost the regime's representatives in the armed forces although most defense ministers had also been political appointees. Some MPA leaders (Heinz Kessler in the GDR or Karpati in Hungary) became Defense Ministers. Nicolae Ceauşescu, the RPA's MPA Chief (1950–54), went on to occupy even higher positions. The exception was General Vaclav Prchlik of the CSPA, who represented the reformist movement in the pre-invasion Czechoslovak armed forces.

One of the important constraints on the MPAs' political-ideological work was the increasing professionalization of the military establishments, a phenomenon that was concomitant with the diminution of the political 'attentiveness' of career officers. In the 1950s and until the mid-1960s political reliability was clearly the most important condition of advancement in the region's militaries, witnessed by the meteoric rise of political officers to command positions.[22] As the technical and theoretical requirements of modern warfare increased, however, military education and training placed a premium on expertise, while ideological rigor became a somewhat less important criterion.[23]

At the same time, the more professionally oriented training tended to reduce the gap between the newly commissioned 'regular' and 'political' officers, resulting in the evolution of a more homogeneous officer corps. Officers began to exhibit 'apolitical attitudes', the meetings of party organizations in the armed forces 'had become stale', political work in the military had become superficial and routine: a plethora of articles and studies in all NSWP states decried these troubling phenomena at one time or another. The political elites of the NSWP armies attempted to counter this trend with periodic reorganizations and ideological campaigns (as in Poland 1957, 1970; East Germany 1976; Czechoslovakia throughout the post-1968 period, etc.) that nonetheless failed to yield the desired results.[24]

While professional credentials and reputation had gradually become more important conditions for promotion in Eastern Europe's militaries, they never replaced political reliability as the *ultima ratio* of success. A good illustration is the appointment of General Wojciech Jaruzelski, a professional soldier with impeccable political credentials to be sure, as Poland's Minister of Defense in 1968. By the 1970s and especially in the 1980s, political-ideological control over the military had become more subtle – especially in Poland and Hungary – and expertise was given more currency. The same could not be said for the East German case, however, which was marked by the continued politicization of virtually every aspect of military life, the process of professionalization notwithstanding.[25] The NPA elite, realizing the unwanted dichotomy between expertise and *partiinost'*, attempted to recruit professionally outstanding cadres to become political officers.[26]

An exception from the opposite end of the spectrum is the case of the CSPA, which had experienced a reverse path of development. The Czechoslovak military had never overcome the blow suffered by the 1968 invasion and the subsequent purging of the military. Although the CSPA was perhaps the most professional NSWP army preceding the invasion, during and after 1968 the many CSPA officers – particularly in the junior ranks – either resigned or were dismissed from the armed forces. As a result, the CSPA had faced a shortage of qualified political officers (and professional cadres in general) from 1968 onwards. In 1975, for instance, 15 percent of CSPA officers and 65 percent of warrant officers had not completed their secondary education.[27]

In crisis situations, however, the Party's control appeared to wane. This phenomenon was clearly noticeable in Poland, where the post-1956 liberalization trend was reflected in the reduction of the PPA's party apparatus and the previously high profile of political officers. In the Czechoslovakia of the mid-1960s, one of the foci of the reform movement within the CSPA was the issue of the Czechoslovak Communist Party's (CSCP) domination of the armed forces. Although MPAs had traditionally represented the conservative elements in NSWP militaries, an important exception is the CSPA's MPA, which became the institutional locus of the movement to limit party control of the military before the invasion.[28]

A further mechanism of the Party's control was the militarization of society. The high emphasis given to this effort was reflected by the stress on military education in the school system and the creation of paramilitary organizations. In every Eastern European country organizations (similar to DOSAAF) were established for pre-military training to endow youngsters with skills useful for the armed forces. This effort was particularly intensive in East Germany, but Czechoslovakia (especially after 1968) and the two Balkan states also did not lag far behind. In Czechoslovakia, for instance, even nursery-school children received a sort of 'military training' that taught them how to march briskly and to wear gas masks and protective clothing.[29] In 1989 – after some already implemented reductions in manpower – every 12th Bulgarian, 14th East German, 24th Czechoslovak, 26th Pole, 32nd Hungarian, and 36th Romanian adult was a member of either the regular or the reserve armed forces or one of the paramilitary organizations.[30] (The corresponding figures are 48 for Denmark, 61 for France, 89 for the United Kingdom and 215 for Canada.)[31]

C. Armed Forces in Politics: In Times Good and Bad

Let us now turn our attention to the extent of the Party's co-optation of
military personnel into political life. Did the military participate in politics
or did it play the role of the passive bystander, particularly in crisis
situations: in other words, how reliable were Eastern European armies in
the domestic context? How did these crises affect the armed forces? In
trying to answer these queries one quickly realizes that, again, no clear-cut
pattern emerges. In the following pages I shall compare the behavior of the
military in times of domestic tranquillity and in crisis situations. I argue
that in contrast with the contention of the models discussed in Chapter 1,
the practice of civil–military relations during four decades of Communism
in Eastern Europe points to periodic meddling by the armed forces in
politics.

In all of the NSWP states the representation of military personnel in
the highest policy-making bodies was less extensive than in the USSR.
Military presence on the Central Committee of the CPSU, for instance,
has averaged from 7 to 9 percent since 1972, while in Eastern Europe the
corresponding figure is only about 3 percent.[32] In fact, the representation
of the armed forces in top party bodies had tended to decline over time.
It is fair to say that the military's political role was significant only in
Bulgaria and Poland, and even in these countries only in certain periods.
The absence of a more prominent role is probably a consequence of the
fact that the military policy of these states was essentially determined by
the Kremlin and in the Soviet-dominated Warsaw Pact. Although starting
with the 1960s all but the Hungarian NSWP defense ministers were on
the Politburo – or in Romania's case, the Political Executive Committee –
this does not necessarily imply that they were influential members of that
body.

A special case is Poland in the 1980s. The imposition of martial law was
accompanied by the creation of the Military Council of National Salvation,
composed of 20 high-ranking military officers. After the election of
General Jaruzelski (member of the Polish United Workers' Party [PUWP]
Politburo since the 1960s) as first secretary of the PUWP in October 1981,
several military leaders were appointed to top political offices. Generals
Czeslaw Kiszczak and Florian Siwicki became Ministers of the Interior
and of Defense, respectively (they also became first alternate then full
Politburo members). General Michael Janiszewski headed the office of the
Council of Ministers after the imposition of martial law in December 1981.
Appointments to the party hierarchy included General Tadeusz Dziekan
who became head of the Central Committee's Cadres Department and

his deputy, Colonel Jerzy Wojcik.[33] Another unique case is that of East Germany, where distinguishing the lines of separation between civil and military functions of the NPA proves particularly difficult since the army actively participated in such quasi-military activities as patriotic education, civil defense, etc. The especially dense interpenetration of army and Party relationship in East Germany was also demonstrated by the routine transfer of retired NPA officers into various SED and government positions.[34]

In every NSWP state the vast majority of professional military personnel were Communist Party members. Party membership of professional cadres was the highest in the NPA (99 percent),[35] up to 90 percent in the BPA and the RPA,[36] 80 percent in the PPA,[37] and 75 percent in the CSPA.[38] These figures do not, of course, denote genuine allegiance to Communist ideals as the military's role in the 1989 revolutions and their aftermath demonstrated. Instead, they reflect the realization of East European officers that party membership was a necessary condition for advancement in the ranks. Party membership *per se* did not assure promotion, but without this manifestation of political loyalty career progress was well-nigh impossible.

Having said this much, we would expect the army not only to remain passive, but to side with the Party leadership and actively defend the Communist regime in times of political crises. We have already seen that the HPA was essentially paralyzed during the 1956 Revolution. Evidence shows that this was not an extraordinary phenomenon in Eastern Europe in 1945–88. The following is a brief review of the performance of NSWP armies in domestic crises.[39]

East Germany – 1953: There were no domestic crises in which the NPA was involved, although mention must be made of the demonstrations of June 1953, quelled by the Red Army. The protests were supposed to be handled by the BPP. Discipline in the BPP quickly broke down as officers ordered their men to drop their weapons rather than fire at the workers. After the Red Army's intervention some of these officers were summarily executed by the Soviets.[40]

Czechoslovakia – 1953, 1968: The CSPA was used against demonstrators during the violent clashes in the Bohemian city of Plzen after the monetary reform was introduced on June 1, 1953. Although there is little solid evidence of the CSPA's role in this event, it appears clear that it refused to put down the riot.[41]

During the 1968 invasion CSPA units were passive observers of the events. They were ordered by Defense Minister Ludvik Svoboda to remain in their barracks, probably because CSCP leaders feared that the army would resist the invading Warsaw Pact forces. Different segments of the CSPA did reveal their true colors before and after the heady days of August 1968. Contrary to the assumptions of theories on civil–military relations the CSPA attempted to influence political developments. The political division between the CSCP's reform and conservative wings was clearly observable in the miliary as well. Preceding the invasion, reformist (usually junior) CSPA cadres gained the upper hand; after August 1968 conservative (generally senior) officers had gained the upper hand.

Starting with 1966, an increasingly sharp debate emerged within the CSPA regarding the CSCP's political domination of the military and the blatant disregard of the WTO's (i.e., the Soviet) doctrine of Czechoslovak defense concerns. In many respects, the CSPA's officers became the cutting edge of the reform movement. The intra-military polemic culminated in the Memorandum issued by the Klement Gottwald Military-Political Academy in May 1968.[42]

Two important observations should be made about the reform movement in the CSPA.[43] First, some of the Memorandum's proposals (such as decreasing party control over the military, reorganization of the CSCP apparatus within the armed forces, etc.) were actually put into practice before the Soviet invasion. Second, in contrast with conventional wisdom that considered the MPAs the strongholds of conservatism in Communist armies, the Czechoslovak MPA was the bulwark of reformism before and during the Prague Spring. Following the invasion, the conservative faction of the CSPA officer corps came to the fore. In early 1969, some generals voiced their opposition to the then moderate leadership of Gustav Husak; rumors of an impending military coup circulated in Prague. Soviet support for the Husak regime solved this problem, and the conservative generals were 'sidetracked'.

Comparisons are often made with the post-Revolution phase of the HPA. Again, it must be stressed that the HPA *did not* disintegrate during the Revolution; its leadership did. Over 80 percent of the HPA officer corps signed the oath of allegiance to the Kadar regime. The CSPA, however, essentially lost its junior level officers corps *in toto*, as a result of the widespread post-invasion purges and the voluntary resignation of thousands of officers. Another important difference between the post-crisis HPA and CSPA is that while the HPA 'rebounded' quite quickly – perhaps aided by the relatively liberal policies of the Kadar regime – the CSPA never really recovered after 1968.

Poland – 1956, 1970, 1976, 1980: The military played an important role in all of the post-war political crises in Poland.[44] In the Poznan riots (June 1956) the Internal Security troops (KBW) were unable to suppress the disturbances, but the regular PPA units directed to help restoring order refused to fire on striking workers. In some cases, regular soldiers willingly handed over their weapons to the demonstrators.[45] The crisis was eventually solved by a KBW brigade with hundreds of casualties. One reason for Moscow's acceptance of Gomulka's return to power (October 1956) may well have been the perceived danger of armed Polish resistance to potential Soviet military action. As Ross Johnson pointed out, by opting for non-involvement, the PPA played something of the role of silent kingmaker.[46]

During the riots in the coastal cities of Gdansk, Gdynia, and Szczecin (December 1970) the PPA was again called upon to restore order. Several studies have characterized the PPA's involvement as limited.[47] According to recent evidence, however, the PPA's participation was more extensive than initially believed and included the utilization of 61,000 troops and a great deal of equipment.[48] Although the Polish military inflicted some casualties, it again performed its directed internal repressive function only partially and reluctantly. The PPA refused to carry out the orders of Polit-buro member Zenon Kliszko, who called for the utilization of immediate and overwhelming force to crush demonstrations. Subjected to divergent instructions from the political leadership – much as the HPA in 1956 – the PPA's generals evaluated the situation by themselves. The army's refusal to apply overwhelming force constituted a precedent, signifying that a Party leader could not save his position by relying on the armed forces. In fact, it is 'reasonable to assume' that in the power struggle following Gomulka's resignation the military actively backed Edward Gierek, the eventual winner.[49]

During the June 1976 crisis the PPA played a moderating role, cautioning PUWP leader Edward Gierek that 'Polish soldiers will not fire on Polish workers'.[50] The PPA was not utilized, its attitude during the crisis was markedly restrained; only a limited police forces were employed to counter the demonstrators. As Andrzej Korbonski and Sarah Terry pointed out, 'the Polish military once again reasserted its position as the key actor in the political arena whose veto or approval has ultimately proved decisive in time of emergency'.[51]

In December 1981, the PPA was once again a reluctant participant in the repression of the Solidarity movement.[52] Although a large part of the PPA was utilized, regular soldiers were generally used for purposes other than dealing with the demonstrators.[53] These included manning checkpoints and street patrols, securing uninterrupted communications and transportation, etc.[54] Once again, the actual suppression was the work of the security troops (ZOMO) supported only by the ominous presence of regular army units.

The track record of the PPA in these crises shows that it had achieved a measure of independence from the PUWP. At times, the army either did not carry out the directives of the Party elite or did so reluctantly. The PPA consistently failed to prop up the Communist regime and occasionally played a determining role in the settlement of domestic crises.

Some lessons are worth drawing from the performance of the NSWP forces in domestic crises:

1. Although it has been argued that one of the most important functions of the Eastern European military establishments was the repression of internal challenges to the Communist regime, actual experience shows that the armies were reluctant and even unwilling to discharge this duty. In fact, the available evidence suggests that when possible, the Party was disinclined to assign the 'dirty work' to the military and entrusted the security police units with it: the regimes appear to have had far more confidence in the loyalty of the security troops and 'people's' (that is, the Party's) militias, which were often better trained, equipped, and paid.

Although the armed forces seemed to be staunch supporters of the regimes in 'normal' circumstances, in crises they were disinclined to back up the Party with their weapons against the population. One important reason for the military's success in maintaining a measure of independence from the Party was that these armies were based on conscription and drafted soldiers could not be trusted to support the Party and fight against their own. Aside from its obvious doubts about the army's performance, the Party was also concerned with popular attitudes toward the military. The armed forces' legitimacy as a national institution would have been further eroded if it had been considered by the public as the able agent of domestic repression.[55]

2. Conventional wisdom held that the Communist military establishment would support the *status quo* and would be reluctant to actively interfere in politics. Nevertheless, the manifested reformist attitudes of important segments (in fact the *majority* of the officer corps) of the CSPA before and during the Prague Spring, and that of the PPA in 1956, mitigates this assumption. Clearly, the militaries of the regions had at times displayed reformist attitudes.

Other cases of military interference in politics are also noteworthy because they provide additional support to the argument that East European armies did not shy away from political involvement. It appears that the Communist Party's traditional fear of Bonapartism had not been irrational. In fact, the armed forces were implicated in several coups and coup attempts in Bulgaria, Czechoslovakia, Poland, and Romania. In the 1960s there were two cabals in Bulgaria, a country where military putschism has had a long-standing tradition. In 1958–61 rumblings were led by three former partisans with strong connections to the army.[56] In 1965, a handful of senior BPA officers conspired to overthrow Bulgarian Communist Party (BCP) leader Todor Zhivkov. Evidence suggests that the plotters opposed Zhivkov's unabashedly pro-Soviet policies and wanted to secure more independence for Bulgarian domestic and foreign policies. The cabal was discovered before the prepared plans could be put into action.[57]

I already mentioned the rumored coup attempt by some conservative officers in early 1969 in Czechoslovakia, who allegedly conspired to overthrow the 'moderate' regime of Gustav Husak. Some experts suggest, that this was the second coup attempt in Czechoslovakia within a year, for in early 1968 conservative officers attempted to utilize the CSPA to support Antonin Novotny's regime but were prevented from doing so by MPA Chief General Prchlik and officers loyal to him.[58] Robin Remington and others have argued that the imposition of martial law in Poland was a textbook case of a *coup d'etat*.[59] The PPA leadership was confronted with the erosion of the PUWP's legitimacy and a profound socioeconomic crisis and seized power to prevent the decomposition of the state and the collapse of the economy.

In 1987 up to seven RPA officers were arrested on suspicion of plotting against President Ceauşescu's regime.[60] In 1990, Romanian sources revealed that Ceauşescu's ouster had actually been fashioned after an aborted plot to remove him from power in 1984.[61] The putsch was planned to coincide with Ceauşescu's visit to West Germany in the summer but it did not materialize because the troops in question were dispatched to do agricultural work.

D. The Military in Communist Societies

Although the military traditions of Eastern European nations are very different – it is sufficient to refer only to the Prussian heritage of East Germans and the martial traditions of the Poles on the one hand, and the passivity and antimilitarism of Czechs and Slovaks (demonstrated in 1938, 1948, and 1968) on the other – during the interwar period the occupation of the military officer enjoyed a respected social status in all of these countries. For this reason alone, the loss of the profession's prestige in the Communist era in nearly all NSWP states is an interesting development. While this phenomenon was more prevalent in Czechoslovakia, Hungary, and Romania than in Bulgaria, East Germany, and Poland, a relative loss of the army's social status is observable everywhere in the region.

Perhaps the main reason for the military's declining esteem was that the population realized that the armed forces, similarly to the local Communist parties, were not the servants of national, but of supranational interests. Obviously the question of degree is important to observe as changes transpired among the various societies and in different periods, yet it is fair to say that the people considered Moscow to be the ultimate master of the military, and given the traditional Russophobia of Germans, Hungarians, Poles, and Romanians (and after 1968, of Czechs and Slovaks) this was a particularly disheartening state of affairs. Moreover, the fact that the individual armies identified themselves with their internal policing functions to varying degrees (i.e., more so in the GDR than in Poland) conditioned the people's judgment of their armed forces. Another cause for the armed forces' loss of prestige was the recurrent cleansing of the military of 'undesirable' officers. The mass removal of officers was not always politically motivated. In 1962–64 many NPA officers received their walking papers simply because of their inability to qualify in technical, administrative, and/or pedagogical skills.[62] In 1967–68, and following the Six Days' War between Israel and its Arab neighbors, the vast majority of PPA officers of Jewish origin were dismissed.[63] The post-invasion purges and resignations swept 19,000 officers out of the CSPA.[64]

The lack of efficiency of the NSWP regimes' indoctrination campaign was best illustrated by the ambiguous stances these armies took in crisis situations. This shortcoming was also shown by the fact that in order to attract promising candidates to military academies, the armed forces of the region relied on material incentives rather than on ideological motivation.[65] By the 1980s, however, the deterioration of the economic situation in all NSWP states was concomitant with the sinking living standards of military personnel. To make matters worse, professional soldiers could not take part in the activities of the second and third economies where these existed (particularly Hungary and Poland). Bulgaria seems to be an exception in this regard, as BPA officers and NCOs had consistently enjoyed living standards considerably (50–70 percent) higher than civilians of similar educational and professional levels.[66] On the other end of the spectrum, the Ceauşescu regime's neglect of the RPA was particularly conspicuous when contrasted with the superior treatment enjoyed by the security troops (Securitate).

A further reason for the decline of the military occupation's prestige was the low quality and quantity of the NSWP military arsenals. This was particularly true for the three armies of the WTO's southern tier (Bulgaria, Hungary and Romania) which received less, and more obsolete, equipment from the Soviet Union than the strategically more important northern tier (Czechoslovakia, East Germany and Poland). Until the late 1970s, the East European political and military elites were only indirectly involved in fiscal negotiations, since such decisions were usually made within the context of the Warsaw Pact.[67] In the 1980s, however, NSWP military spending was determined primarily by the available resources (that is, utilized national income) rather than other factors (i.e., Moscow's desiderata).[68] Military personnel were adversely affected by the reluctance of their governments to increase defense outlays according to Soviet wishes, a phenomenon that characterized especially the RPA and the HPA, from as early as the mid-1970s and the early 1980s, respectively.[69] On the other hand, Bulgaria and East Germany followed the WTO's guidelines on military expenditure until 1988.[70]

Yet another factor adversely affecting the prestige of the NSWP militaries was the practice of utilizing large sections of the armed forces as agricultural and industrial work-force.[71] The considerable amount of time spent on these activities hampered effective training and was useless from the military's perspective. Many professional cadres resented the practice of using the armed forces as a source of cheap labor. Thus, although the military made significant contributions to the national economies this adversely affected training, discipline, and the morale of draftees and professionals alike. In 1986, for example, nearly 50 percent of the RPA was diverted to economic activity and many tanks were employed as water transporters on cooperative farms.[72] In Bulgaria even a Higher People's Military-Construction Institute was established to train officers for service with the construction troops.[73]

The major consequence of the profession's diminishing prestige was the acute recruitment problem that all NSWP armed forces had had to face at one time or another. The replacement of professional cadres proved especially difficult following the political crises with military involvement. Recruitment rates dropped following the army's deployment, not only in internal scenarios, but also in *external* situations, as in Poland after 1968.[74] Respondents to a Czechoslovak opinion poll in the mid-1960s ranked military officers below sewage workers in perceived social status.[75] The CSPA's recruitment situation drastically deteriorated after 1968. To make the profession more attractive to the young, in 1970 the CSPA had to introduce schools that produced officers out of high school graduates in one year (those who did not complete high school could opt for a two-year program).[76] Still, major shortages of command personnel were reported even in the mid-1980s even though material incentives of the military career had been substantially increased.[77] On the other hand, the social prestige of Polish military officers had remained relatively high throughout the Communist era.[78]

Part II   East European Armies and Transition to Democracy

This section will analyze the militaries' role in the political upheavals of 1989–90. Again, my hypothesis is that the Hungarian case is a poor guide to understanding phenomena in the rest of the region. The spectrum of military activities in the region extends from essential non-involvement (Hungary, Poland) to very limited action (Czechoslovakia, East Germany), to a determinant role (Bulgaria and, especially, Romania). In other words, I shall try to disprove Adelman's assumption of minimal military involvement in politics.

A.   The NSWP Forces and the Collapse of Communism

The military played the least active role in the revolutionary changes in the two countries where the liberalization process had begun long before 1989: Hungary and Poland. In the other four NSWP states there were indications that the army might actively participate in the events. Remarkably, as the regimes of the region fell one by one (East Germany, Bulgaria, Czechoslovakia, Romania), the military's profile in the events correspondingly increased.

There is no evidence that the Polish military – aside from its top leaders who happened also to be PUWP and government leaders – actively opposed the transition from Communism to democracy. Throughout the transition period that started in Poland during the summer of 1988, nothing indicated PPA interference in the power struggle that culminated in the PUWP's surrender of power to the Solidarity-led government in August 1989. It is important to note that both Gorbachev and Jaruzelski pushed the PUWP to reintroduce Solidarity to the political game under the mistaken assumption that the Party could control the outcome. Once the June 1989 elections showed the fundamental weakness of the PUWP, the military's acceptance of Tadeusz Mazowiecki as Prime Minister was crucial.[79]

The CSPA was not involved in Czechoslovakia's political transition either. The Czechoslovak government resorted to the heavy use of security troops against demonstrators on November 17, 1989 in Prague, but no shots were fired. A few days later the CSCP's General Secretary – and the Commander-in-Chief of the CSPA – ordered the People's Militia to march toward the capital. In the end, the CSCP's 'private army' was not used against the demonstrators, probably because of opposition to the use of further force in the political leadership.[80]

It is important to note that, according to a presidential commission investigating the army's actions during Czechoslovakia's 'velvet revolution', the CSPA was ready to take action against demonstrators in Prague in November 1989. The Chairman of the committee said that the 'myth' that the army actually prevented a violent repression of the demonstration had to be refuted, and disclosed that then-Defense Minister Milan Vaclavik gave orders on November 23 for a possible use of force, and urged the CSCP leadership to put the army and the militia on alert.[81] In fact, the CSPA published a strongly-worded statement on the same day asserting that the army would 'defend Communism' and the 'achievements of socialism, freedom, and peace'.[82] The CSCP command resigned the next day, however, and the order was never given. The new CSCP General Secretary, Karel Urbanek, called on all army officers on November 30 to understand that the CSPA could not be used for 'external and internal reasons' and asked them 'not to cause him any trouble'.[83] In December, the new Defense Minister, Miroslav Vacek, said that the CSPA supported the democratization process, denied rumors of a potential coup by the army, and stated that the military would not be used against the people.[84] In October 1990, Vacek himself was dismissed for his ambiguous role during the revolution revealed by a presidential inquiry. He was replaced by Lubos Dobrovsky, a civilian with impeccable anti-communist credentials.

The East German army opted not to impede the astonishingly swift collapse of Communism. It is clear that the NPA did not want to fulfil the role of the suppressor of domestic conflict. Reports that the NPA was armed and put on alert to support regular police and security police (Stasi) units to quell the demonstrations in October 1989 prompted vigorous reactions from some members of the NPA.[85] As one NPA officer noted, the NPA and the border guards 'will use no force against the people'.[86] Although conservative elements in the army's leadership might have been tempted to support Honecker's disintegrating regime with military force, doubts about the NPA's reliability amidst domestic turmoil might well have prevented even an attempt at doing so.

The Bulgarian case, again, is unique for several reasons. Although to outside observers it appeared that the BPA had a well-nigh symbiotic relationship with the BCP, the loyalties of the BPA's officer corps were not to the party let alone to Todor Zhivkov, but to the army as an institution and to the military's access to resources.[87] Bulgaria's economic and social troubles brought about growing support for Zhivkov's removal from the military. Defense Minister (until September 1990) Dobri Dzhurov was an important participant of the cabal – by virtue of his assurance to the BCP leader's foes, that the BPA would neither support Zhivkov, nor take action on its own – that unseated BCP leader Todor Zhivkov in

November 1989. Indeed, according to Daniel Nelson, Dzhurov had 'held the key to power in late 1989 to early 1990'.[88] An influential member of the BCP's Politburo, he almost certainly enjoyed the tacit support of the Bulgarian armed forces. Nowhere in the region was the role of the armed forces in the collapse of the *ancien regime* as prominent as in Romania. In fact, the RPA was *the* decisive actor in the ouster, 'trial', and execution of its Commander-in-Chief, Nicolae Ceauşescu. It appears that before December 21, 1989, the RPA did carry out the orders of the higher military leadership to fire on demonstrators in Timisoara, Cluj, and Bucharest, although even at this time security troops played the major role in the crackdown. After this date, however, the military had refused to carry out orders and its non-compliance decided the fate of Ceauşescu's regime. At the top level, it was Defense Minister Vasile Milea who refused to reinforce troops in Bucharest in defense of the leadership. He reportedly commented that he had searched in vain in the military regulations for a paragraph requiring 'the people's army to fire on the people'.[89] Milea was executed by Ceauşescu loyalists on December 22.

At least some of the RPA's generals joined the revolution only hesitantly, and only after some of Romania's current leaders (e.g., President Ion Iliescu) appeared on national television and expressed their support for the uprising. Others could not be counted on to endorse the program of the emerging National Salvation Front (NSF). As Silviu Brucan, a prominent leader of the NSF in its early days, recalled, 'we had always been sure of the army, but not of all generals'.[90] Although some details about the RPA's role in the revolution may never be known, it is clear that not all RPA troops and officers supported the revolution and not all Securitate units fought on the side of the pro-Ceauşescu forces.[91] Nonetheless, the vast majority of the army leadership backed the NSF after December 22 and assured Romanians that the army would 'never stage a *coup d'état*' and 'never take power'.[92]

There are several lessons worth deducing from the NSWP armies' record in the 'velvet revolutions'. Interestingly, as the regimes of the region fell like so many dominoes, and as the process of the transitions began to accelerate, the militaries seemed to assume increasingly prominent roles. One way to explain this phenomenon could be that as events unfolded ever more rapidly, the military elites simply did not have sufficient time to reflect on the evolving political situation and deliberate what the armies' proper role might be (see figure of East European Armed Forces in the 1989 Transitions).

An important function of these armed forces was the defense of the Party from its internal enemies as evidenced by the military oath, the entire system of education and training, let alone the ongoing indoctrination

East European Armed Forces in the 1989 Transitions

ARMED INTERFERENCE

not considered	army's use considered	occurred
◀━━▶		
Bulgaria	Czechoslovakia	Romania
Hungary	East Germany	
Poland		

POLITICAL INTERFERENCE

absent			prominent
◀━━━▶			
Czechoslovakia		East Germany	Bulgaria
Hungary	Poland		Romania

campaign. Did the armed forces fail to prop up the tumbling regimes when asked to, or did the moral fibre of these polities disintegrate so rapidly that the request was never made? The answer, again, is not unambiguous. What does make a difference, however, is whether or not the armed forces had supported the emerging non-Communist order.

The East European armies, with the exception of the RPA, did not consciously decide not to support the old regime; the fact is that they never had to make that decision. In Poland and Hungary the parties never requested the military's intervention in the tumultuous events leading to the slow and gradual collapse of the regimes. The transition was entirely non-violent, not a window-pane was broken. It appears that the CSPA's senior officers were ready to support the disintegrating Communist regime but the changes had occurred so swiftly that these cadres never had a chance to make good on their promises. In Berlin, Erich Honecker seemed willing to call in the regular army but more realistic SED leaders opposed him. In any event, there were clear indications that the NPA would not have carried out the order had it been given. Bulgaria is yet another different case where the military elite actually supported the anti-Zhivkov reform Communists. As we have seen, the army was called in against the people in Romania, but after a few days of vacillation officers and soldiers took the side of the people.

Support or lack of support for intervention in the political processes should not, of course, be taken to denote the attitudes of the entire professional corps, much less those of the entire armed forces. Conscripted soldiers and the younger generation of officers and non-commissioned officers generally backed the reform movements. The older cadres – who had often spent decades in uniform and as a rule were more closely tied to the regimes – appear to have been more liable to favor the status quo. One of the questions that begs an answer, then, is why did a significant proportion of the senior officer corps – particularly of the two Balkan states – turn against their Communist leaders? The explanation may be found in the socioeconomic status of these forces. In Bulgaria, following decades of comparatively privileged existence, officers had had to face the evaporation of their perquisites as a result of continuous cutbacks. The RPA, on the other hand, had been the pariah of the Romanian defense establishment for some time.

Another important lesson one can derive from the events of 1989, is how little was the Communist Party capable of truly controlling the armed forces. In spite of all the effort expended on indoctrination, socialization, and material incentives, it appears that the armies were never really mastered by the Party. The East European armies' performance in 1989 plainly demonstrated, however, that such 'proofs' of reliability as party membership should hardly have been given much currency. The true colors of the soldiers were tested during the heady days of the regime changes, and the region's Communist leaders must not have liked the results very much.

B.   The Depoliticization of the NSWP Armies

The military's depoliticization denotes the obliteration of all Party mechanisms in the armed forces. This procedure includes the withdrawal of all party organizations from the armed forces, the termination of the MPA and the end of the political officer positions, the elimination of political indoctrination from the curricula of military colleges, etc. In short, it means putting an end to the Communist Party's domination of the armed forces and legally preventing other political organizations from doing so. This process began in all NSWP states soon after the revolutions but again, there are important differences to be observed. It appears that depoliticization has gone furthest in the states of East-Central Europe (East Germany, Poland, Czechoslovakia, and Hungary) where the transition to democracy has also been the most comprehensive. In the Balkans, however, just as questions remain about the extent of the political transformation, doubts are also to be entertained regarding the depoliticization of the armed forces.

It is clear that the political calamities profoundly affected civil–military relations in Eastern Europe. The institutionalized ties between the parties and the armies had basically disintegrated on the national level. Not unexpectedly, however, military elites were usually not supportive of the depoliticization efforts although overt opposition was not reported anywhere in the region. An important issue all new East European regimes have had to confront is how to ensure national defense without relying on the expertise of the Communists from the old regime. Obviously the entire officer corps could not be dismissed on the basis of membership in the Communist parties. In some cases new military oaths were introduced while in others those particularly closely allied with the former regime were discharged. It will take at least a couple of decades before the current pool of officers could be replaced with individuals trained by the new states, therefore, speedy reorganization of the military education systems is of great significance. The restructuring of the military establishment has been one of the more immediate measures undertaken by the post-Communist polities. By March 1990 Party organizations in the military were abolished in all of the NSWP states except for Poland where this was accomplished later in the year.[93]

Some important measures were implemented in the Polish Army already in 1989, but 1990 saw the process of the PPA's depoliticization to its conclusion. These reforms were necessitated by the persistent demands of the Solidarity-dominated government and the collapse of the PUWP. As a result of a political agreement, one of the few Communist ministers in Mazowiecki's government was Defense Minister Florian Siwicki. Siwicki, confirmed in September 1989, made several gestures to reduce political influence in the armed forces. In November 1989 the MPA was turned into a Main Education Administration with a subsequent cut in its manpower, political officers – just as in Hungary, initially – were renamed as 'education officers'.[94] Political education in military schools and colleges was abolished. In January 1990, party cells and the professional party apparatus in the PPA were dissolved.

Although the military leadership displayed some reservations about the obliteration of the socialists' 'privileged status' in the armed forces, its views had gradually changed. In fact, in January, the Warsaw MOD proposed a more radical plan to ban all political organizations from the military and prohibit party membership of all army personnel than did the government.[95] The Sejm passed these measures into law in February 1990. These achievements notwithstanding, there is evidence that the military's depoliticization was not as smooth as it might have seemed for outside observers. In late 1989 and early 1990 many officers and conscripts complained that little had changed in the practical aspects of military service and the implemented reforms amounted to little more than cosmetic changes.[96] There is reason to believe, however, that the Polish army's depoliticization had been completed by the end of 1990. In the December 1990 presidential elections the army was not involved, no campaigning took place in military sites, and the army's news organs attempted to portray the candidates objectively.[97]

The depoliticization of the East German armed forces was particularly rapid. Limited reform proposals in the NPA were already prepared in 1988–89 although no serious steps were taken to implement them until the events that swept away Honecker's regime. In November 1989 Defense Minister Heinz Kessler was arrested and replaced by Admiral Theodor Hoffmann. (Hoffmann, in turn, was succeeded five months later by Rainer Eppelmann, a one-time conscientious objector who renamed his office 'Ministry of Defense and Disarmament'.) The education system was quickly overhauled and a series of major measures were introduced to halt the exodus of draftees to West Germany, without success.[98] By February 1990, all organizations of political control disappeared from the NPA, political officers 'became' re-education officers, traditional address (i.e., *Frau* and *Herr*) replaced 'comrade' (*Genosse*), etc. By early 1990, however, the NPA had essentially disintegrated. The reunification of the two Germanys and the NPA's integration into the Bundeswehr poses further problems for the former NPA professional corps.

In Czechoslovakia the military oath was changed, the instruction of Marxism-Leninism at military schools was abolished, travel restrictions on army personnel were lifted, and all Party organizations in the armed forces were abolished already in December 1989.[99] The only organizations allowed to exist in the new armed forces are the separate trade unions created by professional soldiers, draftees, and civilian employees. The new defense law of 1990 changed the name of the CSPA to Czechoslovak Army (CSA) and codified many important changes in the military. It reduced compulsory military service from 24 to 18 months, provided for the option of unarmed duty, prohibited the drafting of women in peacetime, omitted references to the Soviet Union and the 'building of socialism', and guaranteed 'full freedom of religion' to soldiers.[100] The new law also imposed strict limitations on the use of army units as a cheap labor force and stated that soldiers might only be used during natural catastrophes. Czechoslovakia's new defense law singled out only one scenario where the armed forces could be used in internal security actions: in a case of direct and violent attack on the constitutional system of the country. The decision to use the military rests with its Commander-in-Chief, the President of the Republic.[101]

The democratization of the Romanian armed forces had been an onerous process that had not always met with the support of the post-Ceauşescu Romanian leadership. Professional cadres of the RPA staged demonstrations in January and February 1990 calling for greater academic autonomy at military colleges. In February, the Action Committee for the Democratization of the Army (CADA) was created by armed forces personnel. Their main demands were the acknowledgement of the true role of the RPA in the December uprising, the removal of compromised military officers and generals from the service, the appointment of a civilian, non-partisan defense minister, and the depoliticization of the armed forces.[102] The Committee's leaders, after a long stand-off, achieved the dismissal of Defense Minister Militaru who was replaced by General Victor Stanculescu, formerly the minister responsible for economic affairs in the NSF government and a deputy defense minister under Ceauşescu.

Not surprisingly, the appointment of Stanculescu – who purged some of the most outspoken officers associated with CADA – did not appease the CADA members who charged that he was implicated in the mass shooting of civilians in Timisoara.[103] Following continuous protests from both opposition and military circles, he was finally replaced by Major General Constantin Spiroiu in May 1991. Since early 1990, the NSF government instituted a new oath of allegiance for all armed forces personnel, to defend the homeland and observe the laws of the country.[104] The military leadership had demonstrated its intent to depoliticize the armed forces in a number of authoritative statements, emphasizing that the army was the defender of national interests and its function was not to serve as the support base for any particular regime, party, or government organization.[105] Although questions regarding the irregularities of the May 1990 elections were raised by the opposition and Western observers, the armed forces – assigned to guard polling stations and ensure the safe transportation of ballot boxes and documents – were not implicated in the charges against the regime.

The Romanian Army is the only NSWP force to have seen action in the domestic context in the post-revolution era. In March 1990, the army stepped in to break up ethnic clashes between Hungarians and Romanians in the city of Tirgu-Mures. After the violence began, however, the army and the police let two days pass without making an attempt to protect those targeted for violence, despite constant appeals for help from besieged Hungarians.[106] The army's role in the clashes supported one analyst's assertion that the Romanian 'military's loyalty is most clearly to the institutions of the state and not the people in the street'.[107]

The BCP's organizations were abolished in the Bulgarian army in February 1990 and BPA leaders repeatedly stated that political propaganda was 'impermissible' within the military.[108] In May, an official organization, the Bulgarian Legion 'Georgi Stoikov Rakovski' was formed in Sofia to promote professionalism, to foster a return to traditional military values, to support patriotic-national training in military schools, and to discourage political activity in the armed forces. Leaders of the Legion had written to the political leadership on several occasions expressing their anxiety about political forces attempting to subvert the army.[109] The Legion in some respects functions as a trade union aiming to secure better working conditions for professional military personnel. In late 1990 professional military cadres were forbidden to join political parties while draftees had to cancel their party memberships for the duration of their military service.

In contrast to the rest of the region, Bulgaria's military became involved in debates about defense issues prior to the June elections. The BPA leadership threw its support to the Bulgarian Socialist Party (BSP, that is, the 'rejuvenated' BCP) although the Union of Democratic Forces appeared to enjoy the backing of the lower ranks.[110] In 1990 Bulgaria was characterized by a rather fluid political situation where the process of democratization seemed rather ambiguous and controversial. The BPA did not make a clear commitment to political democratization and seemed to be ill-prepared for a new democratic era.

C. NSWP States and the Warsaw Pact (1988–90)

The dramatic political changes in Eastern Europe and the reduction of tensions in East–West relations also affected the NSWP states' relations to the Warsaw Pact. Since during the course of the preceding chapters some of the issues pertaining to the Warsaw Pact have already been dealt with, discussion here is limited to the 1988–90 period.

Until the summer of 1990 none of the Eastern European countries – except for Hungary and East Germany – indicated their desire to leave the WTO. (East Germany withdrew from the WTO on September 24, 1990 and joined NATO on West Germany's ticket ten days before official reunification.) For example, presenting his program to the Sejm, Prime Minister Mazowiecki said that his government would 'respect Poland's international obligations' arising from its membership in the Pact and the CMEA, while the similar Czechoslovak intent was written into the new Defense Law of April 1990.[111] Throughout the year, however, the reform of the Warsaw Pact that would stress its political character over its military one had gained a great deal of support in all of the NSWP states.[112]

The Hungarian announcement of the HPA's withdrawal from the Pact by late 1991 (at the June 1990 Moscow Pact meeting of the Political

Consultative Committee) failed to receive an enthusiastic cheer. The representatives of Poland and Czechoslovakia – both states, particularly Poland, have expressed their uneasiness at the re-emergence of a united Germany and were prudently trying not to antagonize Moscow – seemed to have thought the Hungarian decision hasty.[113] Bulgarian leaders, fearing Turkey from the south-east, continued to cling to Moscow as a source of security and opposed the Pact's dissolution.[114]

Perhaps not unexpectedly, the Czechoslovak and the Polish views of the WTO's viability had undergone rapid changes. The scrupulousness of these states was negated by Moscow's demonstrated willingness to consider the Pact's abolition. By November, the three Central European members of the remaining NSWP reached an agreement regarding the eradication of the military arm of the Pact. In September Poland's Foreign Minister Krzysztof Skubiszewski announced that his country 'no longer needed to be a member of the WTO'.[115] In the same months senior defense ministry officials from Poland, Czechoslovakia, and Hungary met to discuss military issues. A Polish officer said that the Soviets were not invited for the USSR had 'not advanced far enough as regards to democracy to be able to share their experiences with us'.[116] At the November 1990 Paris summit meeting Czechoslovak President Vaclav Havel stated that 'NATO has proved itself to be a guarantee of freedom and democracy . . . The Warsaw Pact . . . is an outdated remnant of the past'.[117]

At the other end of the spectrum, Bulgaria continued to insist that the Pact was a viable military instrument. Bulgarian desperation could be well illustrated by Foreign Minister Lyuben Gotsev's assertion that the Pact could be put to excellent use in peacetime in 'fighting international crime'.[118] At the end of NATO Secretary General Manfred Worner's visit in October 1990, Bulgarian President Zhelyu Zhelev stated that the Pact should only be a 'political consultative council in the future' and that Bulgaria, too, was 'looking for security guarantees through a system of agreements with all partners, in the framework of new European and world security structures'.[119] Romania was less vocal about its position *vis-à-vis* the WTO and Bucharest did not oppose the abolition of the Pact's military arm.[120]

In November Soviet Chief-of-Staff General Mikhail Moiseyev conceded that the military structures of the Pact would be superseded and it would be transformed from a military-political alliance, into a consultative–political organization. Moiseyev envisioned the operations of this new 'Pact' subordinated to 'the creation of the Paneuropean security system'.[121] By the end of 1990, then, the Warsaw Pact had become largely irrelevant as a multilateral actor in European security matters. In all NSWP states the pursuance of national interests in defense matters had once again emerged as superior to those of the alliance illustrated by the emerging *national* defense doctrines.[122] The WTO was unceremoniously abolished on July 1, 1991.

The collapse of the Communist system in Eastern Europe and the loss of Soviet influence over the region inescapably pushed the previously taboo issue of the Red Army's presence to the fore. As a result of bilateral negotiations the withdrawals of Soviet troops began from the occupied countries (Czechoslovakia, East Germany, Hungary, and Poland). The Soviet Army's pullout from the region is to be completed in 1994, when the last units are scheduled to leave the eastern part of reunified Germany.[123]

Summary

The 45-year history of civil–military relations in Communist Eastern Europe exposes the inability of Marxist–Leninist parties in this region to secure the loyalty of the armed forces. Although the degree of reliability of these armies was certainly different across the region, in domestic emergencies they usually shied away from turning against the enemies of the regime. During the political transitions of 1989, again, this conclusion was supported by the performance of the NSWP armies. By this time, some of the Communist regimes (in Czechoslovakia and East Germany, for instance) seemed to lack the confidence to utilize the armed forces during domestic crises, and counted on the militias to protect them.

In spite of the political indoctrination, socialization, and generally better-than-average living standards, the majority of armed forces personnel did not feel sufficiently allied with the regime to fight for it. Perhaps the most important reason for this notion was that the army was ultimately controlled by supranational military and ideological interests. Still, in crisis situations the military seemed reluctant to carry out its obligations and nationalist values turned out to be stronger than internationalist ones.

The record of the East European armed forces in the transitions and the post-Communist period underscores the profound disparities between the countries of the region. It appears that the countries of East Central Europe are well on the way to completing the democratization of their armed forces. Although this effort has not been devoid of difficulties these armies appear to be depoliticized and loyal to the constitutional order taking shape in their respective societies. The situation in the Balkans seems to be quite different. Until the end of 1990 at least, the Bulgarian and Romanian armies had not made an unambiguous commitment to political democratization. In sum, then, just as the political transformation of East Central Europe has been more convincing and comprehensive than in south-eastern Europe, the depoliticization process of the armed forces in the former region has also been more assuring.

In this chapter, I attempted to call attention to the many disparities of civil–military relations during the Communist period in Eastern Europe. As we have seen, not only the Hungarian case differed from the contentions of the models but also the experiences of other states in the region.

Conclusion

In this section I aim to accomplish three tasks. First, to recapitulate some of my findings pertaining to civil–military relations in Hungary. Second, to briefly reconsider the utility of the existing theoretical corpus to East European Party–army relations. Finally, to offer some testable generalizations that hold valid in *all* six East European cases and to state some of the most important disparities.

Civil–Military Relations in Hungary: an Assessment

Under Horthy's regime, the military was discouraged from taking an active part in politics although the ensuing world war and Hungary's participation in it indirectly led to limited (and by the end of the war enhanced) military interference. After the war, the Communists quickly managed to subordinate the armed forces whose power as a political actor became negligible. Although the Party hoped to ensure the unswerving loyalty and ideological zeal of the armed forces, it had confronted continuing problems in attaining this objective.

The HPA – aside from the pusillanimous disdain of some senior cadres – did not oppose the changes that ushered in the democratic system in the late 1980s. Just as in 1956, when the largest part of the army remained passive, in 1988–90 the military did not resist the changes. To the contrary, army spokesmen repeatedly assured the population that the military had no intention to intervene in political processes.

This study attempted to underline some of the important socio-political phenomena that affected the armed forces during the decades of Hungarian Communism. Thus, one of my concerns was to emphasize the diminution of the social esteem enjoyed by the armed forces in pre-Communist times. The prestige of the profession quickly evaporated after World War II because the population perceived the army as the servant of alien (i.e., Communist) domestic and foreign (i.e., Soviet) interests. The repercussions of this notion were persisting recruitment and replacement problems and widespread disaffection with the armed forces.

Another important theme of this work is the issue of Soviet control over the armed forces. During Stalin's lifetime the Communist leaders in Budapest were only nominal masters of the HPA whose real commanders dwelled in Moscow. The gradual but slow autonomization of the HPA (and of the Hungarian political leadership) began following the suppression of the 1956 Revolution although this process was not free of occasional relapses in either the politico-economic or the military spheres. In fact, this 'nativization' was a more arduous procedure in the armed forces which were controlled more closely by the Party than other societal groups. Furthermore, the HPA's leaders were conservative individuals not keen on political or ideological changes in their bailiwick.

The second transition period resulted in the Party's withdrawal from and the subsequent depoliticization of the armed forces. Some of the most important by-products of Hungary's – and Eastern Europe's – political transformation were the revelations of widespread corruption and incompetence of the country's leaders, an endemic facet of Communist systems everywhere. The shocking excesses of the HPA leadership received a generous share of this attention. Few observers remarked, however, that Czinege and his colleagues could not have succeeded without a system that tolerated their activities. As these disclosures filled the pages of the newly uncensored journals and books, Hungarians were astonished not only by the details of the erstwhile HPA leaders' possessions and persuasions but also where their stewardship had taken the armed forces.

The confirmation that military policies were determined first of all by the Kremlin and secondly by the HSWP with only nominal participation from the state should not have come as a surprise. What *did* shock the people was the Party's and the military's documented disregard of the legal system. Citizens learned that control over the armed forces was not regulated by law, because such formalities were irrelevant and superfluous niceties. After all, everyone knew who was in charge. It was also clearly revealed that the 'alliance' that was supposed to defend Hungary from the imperialist West in essence robbed Hungary of its defensive capabilities and rendered it impotent to fight any external enemy. At the same time, the fact that one of the most important functions of their army was protecting the rulers from the ruled was hardly a sensational revelation to the population.[1]

The second transformation of civil–military relations in Hungary was faster and less spectacular than the first. Even so, by late 1990 civil–military relations were drastically altered. Not only did the Communists lose their political influence in the armed forces, but activities by all political organizations were prohibited in the military. A constitutional amendment clearly stated that the highest authority over the armed forces was the freely elected President of the Republic.

As in the past, in the future Hungary's international situation will have significant implications on the country's military establishment and on civil–military relations. The political transformation of Eastern Europe and the collapse of the Soviet Union were concomitant with the surfacing and re-surfacing of security concerns across the region.[2] Budapest had succeeded in establishing special diplomatic relations with NATO in 1990, and became a member of NATO's Cooperation Council that was created in November 1991. Hungary's national security has been strongly affected by the civil war in Yugoslavia on its southern border and the subsequent emergence of Slovenia, Croatia, and Bosnia-Herzegovina as independent states. At the same time the troublesome treatment of Hungarian minorities in Serbia, Slovakia, and particularly in Romania has not been lost on politicians and security experts.

It could be argued that Hungary is in a security limbo of sorts. It is no longer a member of the Warsaw Pact – an alliance system that, while in many respects disadvantageous for its non-Soviet members, could guarantee the defense of its territory from external foes – but it is incapable of protecting itself from virtually any external threat. Perhaps it is not unreasonable to speculate that Hungary and its East Central European neighbors to the north might be admitted as full members of NATO within the next decade, something they all have expressed an interest in.

In the meantime, Hungary's politicians and soldiers have sought to enhance the country's national security by establishing bilateral military cooperation agreements with former Warsaw Pact allies neighbors.[3] The three East Central European states (often referred to as the 'Central European Triangle') have actively explored the possibilities of military cooperation since their first summit meeting in February 1991, in Visegrad, Hungary.[4] Together with Austria, Italy, and the former Yugoslavia, they have also been members of the Central European Initiative (CEI), a regional organization known as the 'Hexagonal Group' until its January 1992 summit meeting. Although the CEI is an organization oriented primarily toward economic and cultural cooperation it encourages the addressing of common security concerns as well.

The Utility of Models

One of the reasons why this study has concerned itself with the theoretical constructs is the, I think, mistaken assumption in the scholarly literature that there is an overall explanatory model for civil–military relations in Communist systems. It is important to note that the 'models' considered throughout this study would scarcely satisfy the rigorous methodological criteria to be observed by 'model-builders'.[5] At best, these statements are clusters of generalizations and, for the most part, unsubstantiated hypotheses. Even though Colton, Kolkowicz, and Odom devised their 'models' to pertain to the Soviet case, I submit that they might be applicable to Eastern Europe as well, since there are many fundamental similarities between party–army relations in the two regions under Communism. The most important difference is, of course, that the Soviet military was subordinated to the CPSU, whereas the East European armed forces were controlled not only by their respective parties, but also by the USSR and the Warsaw Pact.

Although all of the approaches are useful to the extent that they can offer valuable insights into the phenomenon, they fall short of offering an all-encompassing theoretical guide. Their utility is limited for they are relevant only to certain historical periods (e.g., the Stalin era) or cannot say meaningful things about all of the region's states.

For instance Kolkowicz's thesis stipulating Party–army conflict has only limited application to East European cases. As far as Hungary is concerned, the HPA failed to assume the role of an 'interest group.' Military representation in the party hierarchy was consistently nominal. In most of the region's states – apart from Hungary – defense ministers were rewarded with memberships in the ruling Politburo. This does not necessarily mean, however, that they were influential policy-makers. Heinz Hoffmann in East Germany and Dobri Dzhurov in Bulgaria were major political players, while Martin Dzur in Czechoslovakia and Vladimir Olteanu in Romania were not.

To take another example, Odom's point that intra-institutional disputes (i.e., between various segments or services of the military) transpire in the armed forces may well be borne out by evidence pertaining to the Soviet case but it has no validity for Hungary or East Europe. The only publicized conflicts within the East European armies concerned newly drafted soldiers and their peers who had already put in some service time and this friction was devoid of political overtones. In addition, in the multi-ethnic states of the NSWP (Bulgaria, Czechoslovakia, Romania) nationalist sentiments occasionally flared up among the troops. If we were to consider the security forces as a segment of the military establishment, then the intra-institutional conflict theory could have relevance to at least some East European cases. The best example is the protracted tension between the Romanian army and the Securitate which was clearly manifested during the heady days of late 1989.

Colton's approach differs from the other two by its stress on the army's political participation as the most important aspect of civil–military relations in the USSR. His is a more flexible construct insofar as it allows more variation in the degree of the army's participation in politics. Nonetheless, Odom's model with its stress on consensus accommodates the Bulgarian,

Czechoslovak, East German, Hungarian, and Romanian experiences more neatly. At the same time Colton's more elastic 'participatory model', can aid us in better explaining civil–military relations in Poland where the military elites had acquired a significant role in politics after 1956.

In spite of their shortcomings, all three approaches can contribute to our understanding of civil–military relations, even in the Eastern European context. Trying to apply the 'Soviet' models to civil–military relations in other Communist systems is a worthwhile undertaking particularly since these approaches are conceptually sounder and more sophisticated than the ones formulated specifically for the Eastern European cases.

Some of the approaches seeking to explain East European civil–military affairs discuss only one broad aspect of this relationship, therefore their explanatory power is quite limited; others aspire to embrace the entire subject area and cannot succeed in providing satisfactory answers to the many profound differences between civil–military relations in the region.[6] Herspring and Volgyes, for instance, place undue emphasis on political socialization and appear to ignore the constants in Party–army relations and concentrate on change instead. As Albright suggested, the basic flaw of this model is in its attempt to reduce the experiences of all East European states to a single pattern of change.[7] While the three phases of civil–military relations (transformation, consolidation, and system maintenance) are useful interpretive tools, when applied to the task of explaining actual behavior, their deficiencies are clearly revealed. For instance, these phases offer no guidance to elucidate the Czechoslovak case. Civil–military relations there progressed relatively smoothly through the phases of 'transformation' and 'consolidation' to 'system maintenance.' Yet, in this last stage, important segments of the Czechoslovak army not only manifested reformist attitudes but were in the vanguard of reform.

Adelman's 'historical developmental' approach stresses the extent of Soviet interference in Eastern Europe during the takeover period and posits that the military's influence subsequent to the 'sovietization' stage was minimal. Even the takeover period, however, was quite different in the East European countries. There is no need to reiterate these dissimilarities here, but it is worth noting that the problems the Soviets faced in the takeover of, say, Poland and Czechoslovakia were very dissimilar. And again, there seems to be an exception even in this regard, for the sovietization of the Romanian armed forces was largely accomplished by indigenous actors and was marked by Soviet restraint uncharacteristic elsewhere in the region. Moreover, the 'minimal political influence' that Adelman's model assigns to the armed forces of the region is an assumption that can easily be refuted by reference to the Polish case, and even to some other NSWP military establishments in certain historical periods (i.e., Czechoslovakia 1967–69, Romania and Bulgaria 1989–90). One must underscore that these approaches have greatly informed our quest for knowledge in the past decade. They have enabled us to focus on the crucial issues of civil–military relations and have offered many important insights and explanations. Perhaps the search for an omnipotent model was unsuccessful because it is almost impossible to state worthwhile generalizations that can encompass such divergent cases. Thus, after contrasting the contentions of these approaches with actual behavior it becomes clear that none succeeds in offering an acceptable model.

Similarities and Differences

In Communist states civil–military relations is a strictly controlled area of politics. Since the East European parties' military policies were 'inspired' by Moscow and the Warsaw Pact and not by national criteria, this was perhaps the aspect of politics with the most similarities and the fewest variances among states. A careful examination of civil–military relations in the six NSWP members is bound to demonstrate, however, that even in Party–army relations there are, indeed, very few rules that are germane to all of them. I have arrived at a synthesis consisting of a group of seven empirically testable generalizations that are applicable to all six former NSWP states.

1. Throughout the four decades of East European Communism Moscow's influence on Party–army relations was pervasive but Soviet control had slowly but perceptibly waned following the takeover and consolidation stages. In crisis situations, however, Moscow continued to reinforce its rule either directly (e.g., Czechoslovakia 1968) or indirectly (e.g., Poland 1980–81).

2. In all of these states, when the Communists gained power they inherited military establishments, at least a part of which were opposed to the new order. Therefore, at least initially, the parties displayed a great deal of suspicion of the armed forces. Purges against the undesirable segments of the armed forces occurred in every NSWP state, especially during the takeover period and after uprisings.

3. In all six states the Communist Party devised and operated several mechanisms to ensure the reliability of the armed forces (MPA, political officers, Communist Party organizations in the army, education system, recruitment and promotion, etc.).

4. Party membership of the professional military cadres, particularly officers, was extremely high (at or above 75 percent) everywhere in Eastern Europe.
5. In every NSWP state Communist parties maintained special security forces and/or militias and relied on them to do the dirty work in crisis situations, indicating their lack of confidence in the regular forces to repress internal uprisings.
6. The prestige of the military profession had suffered in all NSWP states under Communism, primarily because the peoples of the region considered the armed forces the defenders of foreign interests and an unpopular political regime; as a result, all East European militaries encountered recruitment problems at one time or another.

These commonalities do not lead to an all-encompassing theory of civil–military relations in Eastern Europe, however, because of the profound intra-regional disparities. Although these generalizations seem fairly obvious they can assist us in understanding the fundamental characteristics of civil–military relations in Communist Eastern Europe. At the same time, they amount to little more than tautologies and could hardly contribute much to specialized knowledge of the field.

Disparities, rather than similarities, are perhaps even more important to explore as they can help us better appreciate the profound differences in the region's civil–military relations. Let us consider a set of propositions identifying some of the most important areas in which Party–army relations in the region had diverged. For the sake of brevity, I shall point to the states occupying the opposing poles of the spectrum of significance, assuming that other cases fall somewhere in between.

1. The participation of the armed forces in policy-making: very important in Poland (1956–89, particularly after the declaration of martial law), insignificant in Hungary.
2. The party's cooptation of military personnel into the various levels of political administration: prevalent in East Germany, essentially non-existent in Czechoslovakia.
3. The importance of Soviet influence on military policy and the socialization of armed forces personnel, an issue that is closely related to affinities towards the alliance: very important in East Germany, negligible in Romania (after 1965).
4. The influence of professionalization on the officer corps as a factor adversely affecting the political control of the armed forces: a great deal of influence in Poland but substantially less in East Germany.

The set of discrepancies outlined above should caution our attempts to construct universal theories relating to this field. It is very difficult to make meaningful generalizations about a complex phenomenon in such a diverse region as Eastern Europe. Moreover, we should be aware that not all factors had affected civil–military relations in every state in the region and not necessarily at the same historical-developmental juncture. Instead of trying to build all-inclusive models, then, perhaps we should strive to make generalizations that yield useful insights into a given phenomenon and construct substantive typologies. The elaboration of such separate paths may well be more instructive than excessive concern with successive stages of development. A set of comparative questions, such as the ones suggested above, may help us in focusing our inquiry to understand the differences between the divergent cases before we attempt to distil uniformities and making generalizations.

With the declining Soviet role in the region's political, socioeconomic, and military life, another common feature will be erased. We are already seeing the major disparities between the post-Communist political paths of East European states. Considering the East European armed forces' role in the transition period and beyond, one can make a further generalization and state an important difference of experiences. On the one hand, the political changes in 1989–90 profoundly affected civil–military relations in the region and resulted in the disintegration of the multifaceted ties between the Party and the armed forces. On the other hand, the crucial disparities in the activities of the East European armed forces in the transitions of 1989–90 underscore the many differences I have tried to point out. In some cases, (e.g., Romania) the militaries were decisive actors; in others (e.g., Hungary), they remained interested but not particularly worried spectators of the unfolding events.

The record of the East European armed forces in the post-Communist period also demonstrates profound disparities between the countries of the region.[8] This notion further supports the argument that the states of Eastern Europe are just as different from each other as those on the Western part of the Continent. If most generalizations about the countries of this region were inadequate in the past, in the future they will be even more so.

Still, it is clear that since the revolutions of 1989 we have seen many important similarities in the socio-political performance of the new East-Central European regimes on the one hand, and between that of the south-east European polities on the other. If the patterns of political-institutional evolution and economic and social modernization are sustained in the region, I expect that we might be able to devise important typologies to help better explain the politics of this region.

Perhaps the quintessential question of future civil–military relations in Eastern Europe is similar to that of a now bygone era. What are the forces that will either keep military leaders in the barracks or push them willy-nilly onto the political stage? It seems that the new constitutional/legal frameworks in the East European states have already established the prerequisites of civilian oversight over the armed forces by subordinating the military to the state and not to any political party or movement. Whether the various political organizations and the armies will be compelled to play by the rules remains another question. The ignominious role of the Yugoslav/Serbian military in fomenting and perpetuating the civil wars in Croatia and Bosnia-Herzegovina serves as a timely warning to the emerging democracies of Eastern Europe. Completing the depoliticization of the military establishments, alleviating nationalist tensions, and ensuring the progress of democratization are essential for preventing that tragic scenario from occurring in the rest of the region.

Notes

Introduction

1. Guillermo A. O'Donnell and Philippe C. Schmitter, *Transitions from Authoritarian Rule* (Baltimore: Johns Hopkins University Press, 1986), p. 3.
2. Some of the exceptions are Dale R. Herspring, *East German Civil-Military Relations: The Impact of Technology* (New York: Praeger, 1973); Condoleezza Rice, *The Soviet Union and the Czechoslovak Army, 1948–83* (Princeton, NJ: Princeton University Press, 1984); and Jerzy J. Wiatr, *The Soldier and the Nation: The Role of the Military in Polish Politics, 1918–85* (Boulder, CO: Westview Press, 1988).
3. The NSWP states considered are Bulgaria, Czechoslovakia, East Germany, Hungary, Poland, and Romania.

1: Civil–Military Relations in Communist Systems

1. This view is supported among others by Amos Perlmutter, 'Civil-Military Relations in Socialist Authoritarian and Praetorian States: Prospects and Retrospects', in Roman Kolkowicz and Andrzej Korbonski, eds, *Soldiers, Peasants, and Bureaucrats: Civil–Military Relations in Communist and Modernizing Societies* (London: Allen & Unwin, 1982) especially pp. 323–324.
2. Some of the outstanding works following Samuel P. Huntington's *The Soldier and the State: The Theory and Politics of Civil–Military Relations* (Cambridge, MA: Harvard University Press, 1957) are S. E. Finer, *The Man on Horseback: The Role of Military in Politics* (New York: Praeger, 1962); Morris Janowitz, *The Professional Soldier: A Social and Political Portrait* (Glencoe, IL: Free Press), *The Military in the Political Development of New Nations* (Chicago: University of Chicago Press, 1964) and *Military Institutions and Coercion in Developing Nations* (Chicago: University of Chicago Press, 1977); Amos Perlmutter, *The Military and Politics in Modern Times* (New Haven, CT: Yale University Press, 1977); and Claude E. Welch and Arthur K. Smith, *Military Role and Rule: Perspectives on Civil-Military Relations* (North Scituate, MA: Duxbury Press, 1970).
3. See, for instance, David E. Albright, 'A Comparative Conceptualization of Civil–Military Relations', *World Politics*, Vol. 32, No. 4 (July 1980), pp. 557.

4.   S. E. Finer offered perhaps one of the most interesting typologies which is based on an analysis of political cultures in various systems. See examples of other typologies of civil–military relations in Edward Feit, *The Armed Bureaucrats* (New York: Houghton Mifflin, 1973); Janowitz, *The Professional Soldier*; and Eric Nordlinger, *Soldiers in Politics* (Englewood Cliffs, NJ: Prentice-Hall, 1977).

5.   For a detailed account of various typologies of civil–military relations, see Jerzy J. Wiatr, 'The Military in Politics: Realities and Stereotypes', *International Social Science Journal*, Vol. 37, No. 1 (1985), pp. 97–107.

6.   See David Easton, *A Framework for Political Analysis* (Englewood Cliffs, NJ: Prentice-Hall, 1965).

7.   Amos Perlmutter and William M. LeoGrande, 'The Party in Uniform: Toward a Theory of Civil–Military Relations in Communist Political Systems,' *American Political Science Review*, Vol. 76, No. 4 (December 1982), p. 779.

8.   Roman Kolkowicz, 'Toward a Theory of Civil–Military Relations in Communist (Hegemonial) Systems', in Kolkowicz and Korbonski, *Soldiers, Peasants, and Bureaucrats*, pp. 235–237.

9.   According to Alexiev's example, a Soviet officer may well not rationalize that his participation in the invasion of Czechoslovakia was Soviet national interest while a Polish officer participating in a hypothetical Soviet–Chinese war certainly would not do so. See his 'Party–Military Relations in Eastern Europe: The Case of Romania', in Kolkowicz and Korbonski, *op. cit.*, p. 202.

10. Thomas R. Dye and Harmon Ziegler, 'Socialism and Militarism', *PS: Political Science and Politics*, Vol. 22, No. 4 (December 1990), pp. 810–813. The authors used several approaches to determine the 'relative militarism' of democratic and Communist political systems. These included contrasting defense expenditure with GNP, military personnel per 1000 population, as well as comparing these variables before and after revolutions.

11. In many Communist countries the only possibility for youths to learn aeronautical skills or participate in target shooting was through these paramilitary organizations. Since these types of activities were generally popular among young people, through its monopoly of the means of such activities the party-controlled military attempted to attract them into its own ranks.

12. Perlmutter and LeoGrande, p. 780.

13. Timothy J. Colton, *Commissars, Commanders, and Civilian Authority: The Structure of Soviet Military Politics* (Cambridge, MA: Harvard University Press, 1979).

14. Carl Beck and Karen Eide Rawling, 'The Military as a Channel of Entry into Positions of Political Leadership in Communist Party States', *Armed Forces and Society*, Vol. 3, No. 2 (February 1977), pp. 201–202.

15.   Daniel N. Nelson, *Romanian Politics in the Ceausescu Era* (New York: Gordon Breach, 1989), p. 132.

16.   It goes without saying that the fear of Bonapartism or Praetorianism has not been confined to Communist political systems. See Finer, *The Man on Horseback*, pp. 104–109.

17.   Huntington, *The Soldier and the State*, p. 464.

18.   See Colton, *Commissars and Commanders*, especially Chapter 3.

19.   Kolkowicz, 'Military Intervention in the Soviet Union: Scenario for Post-Hegemonial Synthesis', in Kolkowicz and Korbonski, pp. 116–117.

20.   Amos Perlmutter, *Modern Authoritarianism* (New Haven, CT: Yale University Press, 1981), p. 56.

21.   As for instance in Poland in 1970. See A. Ross Johnson, Robert W. Dean, and Alexander Alexiev, *East European Military Establishments: The Warsaw Pact Northern Tier* (Santa Monica, CA: Rand, 1980), p. 52.

22.   The exception is Romania from where Soviet troops withdrew in 1958. Moscow's attempts to dominate Bucharest's military policy remained unfruitful afterwards.

23.   Janowitz, *The Military in the Political Development of New Nations* and Samuel P. Huntington, *Political Order in Changing Societies* (New Haven, CT: Yale University Press, 1968).

24.   Hannah Arendt, *The Origins of Totalitarianism* (London: Allen & Unwin, 1951); and Carl Friedrich and Zbigniew Brzezinski, *Totalitarian Dictatorship and Autocracy* (Cambridge, MA: Harvard University Press, 1956).

25.   Robin Alison Remington, 'Foreword', to Wiatr, *The Soldier and the Nation*, p. xii.

26.   H. Gordon Skilling and Franklyn Griffiths, eds, *Interest Groups in Soviet Politics* (Princeton, NJ: Princeton University Press, 1971).

27.   Roman Kolkowicz, *The Soviet Military and the Communist Party* (Princeton, NJ: Princeton University Press, 1967).

28.   Kolkowicz and others have argued that the political officers do not represent the military's interests but those of the party. See Kolkowicz, *The Soviet Military*, p. 11; and Herbert Goldhamer, *The Soviet Soldier* (New York: Crane Russak, 1975), p. 290. For this reason, Les Aspin contended that political troops should not be included in assessment of the Soviet military. See his 'How to Look at the Soviet-American Balance', *Foreign Policy*, No. 22 (Spring 1976), p. 106.

29.   William E. Odom, 'The Party–Military Connection: A Critique', in Dale R. Herspring and Ivan Volgyes, eds, *Civil–Military Relations in Communist Systems* (Boulder, CO: Westview Press, 1978), pp. 27–53.

30.   It must be mentioned that Odom rejected Timothy Colton's 'reading of an 'institutional congruence model' into his analysis, see *ibid.*, p. 48. Nonetheless, Odom's approach is referred to by that name in the literature.

31. See William E. Odom, 'A Dissenting View on the Group Approach to Soviet Politics', *World Politics*, Vol. 28, No. 4 (July 1976), pp. 542–568.
32. Odom, 'The Party–Military Connection', p. 43.
33. *Ibid.*, p. 48.
34. Colton's approach is most succinctly presented in his 'The Party–Military Connection: A Participatory Model', in Herspring and Volgyes, *op. cit.*, pp. 53–79.
35. See his *Commissars, Commanders*, especially Part Three.
36. Timothy J. Colton, 'Civil–Military Relations in the Soviet Union: The Developmental Perspective', *Studies in Comparative Communism*, Vol. 11, No. 3 (Autumn 1978), p. 217.
37. For a critical note on the three models, see Jonathan R. Adelman, 'Toward a Typology of Communist Civil–Military Relations', in Adelman, ed., *Communist Armies in Politics* (Boulder, CO: Westview Press, 1982), pp. 1–15.
38. Odom, 'The Party–Military Connection', p. 43.
39. Albright's model attempted to remedy this problem by introducing a seven-variable continuum but he was unable to account for the unequal importance of individual periods as well as for the interrelation between them. See his 'A Comparative Conceptualization . . . ', *op. cit.*, pp. 565–575.
40. See Adelman, 'Toward a Typology . . . ', *op. cit.*
41. An important distinction should be made in the cases of Bulgaria and Czechoslovakia. In these states there was a widespread popular support for Soviet policies following liberation.
42. Soviet troops have been stationed in East Germany and Poland since 1945. The withdrawal from both countries is in progress. The troop pullout was already been completed in the summer of 1991 from Czechoslovakia and Hungary, states the Soviets had occupied from 1968 and 1945, respectively. They were withdrawn from Romania in 1958 and were never deployed in Bulgaria.
43. Soviet troops suppressed popular uprisings in East Germany (1953) and in Hungary (1956). They were aided by the fraternal armies, with the exception of the Romanian army, in the invasion of Czechoslovakia (1968). Soviet troops were not put into action during Poland's crises (1956, 1970, 1976, 1981) although their deployment was contemplated in 1956 and 1981.
44. Command structures in the period of these armies' 'sovietization' can be considered as 'dual' in two ways. On the one hand, political officers were required to approve orders issued by regular officers with their signatures. On the other hand, Soviet officers within the native army signed the orders of native commanders. The latter system was characteristic of higher (on and above regimental) level of command. See, for instance, Bela Kiraly, *Honvedsegbol Nephadsereg* (Budapest: CO-NEXUS, 1989), pp. 139–177.

45. Christopher D. Jones, *Soviet Influence in Eastern Europe* (New York: Praeger, 1981), pp. 230–231.

46. For arguments supporting this conclusion, see Alexiev, 'Party Military Relations . . . '; Daniel N. Nelson, ed., *Soviet Allies: The Warsaw Pact and the Issue of Reliability* (Boulder, CO: Westview Press, 1984); Ivan Volgyes, *The Political Reliability of the Warsaw Pact Armies* (Durham, NC: Duke University Press, 1982). All of these authors, of course, point to the significant differences between the Soviet Union and each NSWP state. Some excellent studies that have discussed various issues of Warsaw Pact integration are Teresa Rakowska-Harmstone, Christopher Jones *et al.*, *Warsaw Pact: The Question of Cohesion* (4 volumes)(Ottawa: Operational Research Analysis Establishment/Department of National Defence, 1981, 1984, 1986); and Jeffrey Simon, *Warsaw Pact Forces: Problems of Command and Control* (Boulder, CO: Westview Press, 1985).

47. See Zoltan D. Barany, 'Soviet Control of the Hungarian Military Under Stalin', *Journal of Strategic Studies*, Vol. 14, No. 1 (June 1991), pp. 156–172.

48. It is noteworthy that in other Communist systems where the military was not subordinated to external domination, such as China or Vietnam, military representation in political organizations was also considerably larger than in Eastern Europe. See for instance William P. Ting, 'Coalitional Behavior Among the Chinese Military Elite', *American Political Science Review*, Vol. 73, No. 2 (June 1979); and William Turley, 'The Political Role and Development of the People's Army of Vietnam', in Joseph J. Zasloff and MacAlister Brown, eds, *Communism in Indochina: New Perspectives* (Lexington, KY: Lexington Books, 1975).

49. Ivan Volgyes, 'Military Politics and the Warsaw Pact Armies', in Morris Janowitz, ed., *Civil–Military Relations in Regional Perspectives* (London: Sage, 1981), p. 217.

50. This phenomenon was not unique to Eastern Europe since the military was utilized on a regular basis for economic activities in other socialist states, including the Soviet Union. In September 1990, for instance, Moscow's Mayor Gavriil Popov called for soldiers to man the city's bread factories temporarily. See *Newsweek*, September 17, 1990, p. 41.

51. Military representation in the all-important Central Committee has averaged 7 to 9 per cent in the USSR since 1952, while the corresponding figure in Eastern Europe has been closer to 3 per cent. See Volgyes, 'Military Politics . . . ', p. 198.

52. A. Ross Johnson, 'The Soviet–East European Military Connection: An Overview', in Herspring and Volgyes, eds, *Civil–Military Relation in Communist Systems*, p. 263.

53. See Zoltan D. Barany 'East European Armies in the Transitions and Beyond', *East European Quarterly*, Vol 26, No. 1 (March 1992),

pp. 3–12.
54. Dale R. Herspring and Ivan Volgyes, 'The Military as an Agent of Political Socialization in Eastern Europe', *Armed Forces and Society*, Vol. 3, No. 3 (Winter 1977), pp. 249–269.
55. Alexiev, 'Party–Military Relations . . . ', in Kolkowicz and Korbonski, eds, *Soldiers, Peasants, and Bureaucrats*, p. 201–202.
56. See his 'Toward a Typology . . . ', *op. cit.*, pp. 5–12.
57. Andrzej Korbonski, for instance, found that the historical developmental is 'not fully applicable to Poland'. See his 'The Polish Army', in Adelman, ed., *Communist Armies in Politics, op. cit.*, pp. 121–122.
58. For a useful methodological discussion concerning 'models', and theory building, see James A. Bill and Robert L. Hardgrave, Jr., *Comparative Politics: The Quest for Theory* (Washington DC: University Press of America, 1981), pp. 27–37.

2: The First Transition: Sovietization (1945–53)

1. The best of these in my view is still Bennett Kovrig's *Communism in Hungary: From Kun to Kadar* (Stanford, CA: Hoover Institution Press, 1979).
2. In addition to the death of almost one million people during World War II the property damages were also staggering: 50 percent of railways, 36 percent of bridges, 50 percent of livestock, 24 percent of industrial capacity, altogether one-third of the national wealth was destroyed. See *Tarsadalmi Szemle*, Vol. 44 (1989), special edition, p. 11. The $300 million reparation payments and the absence and deportation of hundreds of thousands further aggravated the already disastrous socioeconomic situation.
3. The lower figure is cited by Peter Gosztony, 'Die ungarische antifaschistische Bewegung in der Sowjetunion waehrend des Zweiten Weltkrieges', *Militargeschichtliche Mitteilungen*, Vol. 9 (1972), pp. 87–102; the higher by Ivan Volgyes, *Politics in Eastern Europe* (Chicago: The Dorsey Press, 1986), p. 70.
4. See Zoltan Vas's statement cited in Janos Kecskes, *'Vezeraldozatok', vagyis mit tesznek a kiskiralyok panikban* (Budapest: Tornado Damenija, 1990), p. 159.
5. For excellent analyses of the Paris Peace Conference from the Hungarian perspective, see Stephen Kertesz, *The Last European Peace Conference: Paris 1946 – Conflict of Values* (Lanham, MD: University Press of America, 1981); and Gyula Juhasz, 'Ut a parizsi bekehez', *Tarsadalmi Szemle*, Vol. 44, Nos. 8–9 (August–September 1989), pp. 13–18.
6. Zoltan D. Barany, 'Elections in Hungary', in Robert K. Furtak, ed., *Elections in Socialist States* (New York: Harvester-Wheatsheaf, 1990), pp. 71–72.

7. For an account of the meeting, see Charles Gati, *Hungary and the Soviet Bloc* (Bloomington: Indiana University Press, 1986), chapter 5.

8. Bennett Kovrig, 'Hungary', in Teresa Rakowska-Harmstone, ed., *Communism in Eastern Europe* (Bloomington, IN: Indiana University Press, 1984), p. 90.

9. *Legyozhetetlen ero* (Budapest: Kossuth, 1968), pp. 167–169.

10. *Ibid.*, p. 193.

11. Kovrig, *Communism in Hungary*, pp. 196, 265. It should be mentioned that in 1952, 69 Soviet-owned enterprises were transferred to Hungarian state ownership, and two years later the Soviet shares in joint-stock companies were sold back. Nonetheless, Hungary's uranium mines remained under direct Soviet control.

12. See the excellent article by the noted historian, Professor Mihaly Korom in *Petofi nepe*, April 20, 1990. Korom says that the Soviets, having grossly overestimated the size of the German forces defending Budapest, found only half the soldiers they had expected. But since the Soviets then had to satisfy quotas based on the overestimate in taking prisoners of war, these 'liberators' randomly abducted people from the street, seizing 70,000–80,000 civilians in the capital alone.

13. In fact, from 1949 to 1953 more Communists were executed than under the two and a half decades of Admiral Horthy's anti-Communist regime. See Paul Ignotus, 'The First Two Communist Takeovers of Hungary: 1919 and 1948', in Thomas T. Hammond, ed., *The Anatomy of Communist Takeovers* (New Haven, CT: Yale University Press, 1975), p. 398. The list of party leaders persecuted during this period includes Janos Kadar, Minister of Interior until June 1950. He was imprisoned between April 1951 and July 1954. It is worth noting that three other ministers of internal affairs died violent deaths in the totalitarian period: Laszlo Rajk, Kadar's predecessor (executed in 1949), Sandor Zold, Kadar's successor (committed suicide after killing his family in 1951), and Imre Nagy, who led the Ministry between November 1945 and March 1946 before Rajk's appointment (executed in 1958). One reason for the obvious occupational dangers of ministers of interior was the fact that they happened to know 'too much' about the regime's crimes. In addition, all four – with the exception of Zold – played a political role far more significant than their government positions suggested. For an excellent study of those (primarily World War II criminals) deported and translocated by police, see Tibor Zinner, "Haborus bunosok perei. Internalasok, kitelepitesek, igazolo eljarasok 1945–49', *Tortenelmi Szemle*, Vol 28, No. 1 (1985), pp. 118–141. For the recollections of a victim, see Mrs. Pal Jusztusz, 'Kistarcsa', *Mozgo Vilag*, Vol. 14 (November 1988), pp. 120–128. For those of a persecutor, see Gyula Kozak, 'Multbanezes', an interview with AVH Lt. Col. Vladimir Farkas in the same issue of *Mozgo Vilag*, pp. 90–119.

14. One could scarcely wish for a more reliable source than Janos Berecz,

a prominent Communist leader of the 1980s. See his *Ellenforradalom tollal es fegyverrel. 1956* (Budapest: Magveto, 1986), p. 26.

15. *Legyozhetetlen ero*, pp. 195–9.

16. Hungarian industrial production expanded by 210 per cent between 1949 and 1953. Corresponding figures are: Poland 158, Czechoslovakia 98, East Germany 92.3, Romania 144, Bulgaria 120. See Imre Nagy, *On Communism: In Defense of the New Course* (New York: Praeger, 1957), p. 185.

17. Mihaly Berki, *Hadsereg vezetes nelkul 1956* (Budapest: Magyar Media, 1989), p. 15.

18. Antal Ban, 'Hungary' in Denis Healey, ed., *The Curtain Falls: The Story of Socialist Eastern Europe* (London: Lincolns-Praeger Publishers, 1951), p. 67.

19. Stephen D. Kertesz, 'Hungary', in Stephen D. Kertesz, ed., *The Fate of East-Central Europe: Hopes and Failures of American Foreign Policy* (Notre Dame, IN: University of Notre Dame Press, 1956), p. 221.

20. J. Malcolm Macintosh, 'Stalin's Policies Toward Eastern Europe, 1939–48: The General Picture', in Thomas T. Hammond and Robert Farrell, eds, *The Anatomy of Communist Takeovers* (Munich: Institute for the Study of the USSR, 1971), p. 209.

21. See Revai's article 'On the Character of our People's Democracy', *Foreign Affairs* (Moscow), Vol. 28 (1949), pp. 143–152 for a detailed account of Hungary's 'development' and for acknowledgement of direct Soviet support.

22. Ferenc Vali, *Rift and Revolt in Hungary* (Cambridge, MA: Harvard University Press, 1961), p. 46.

23. Ivan Volgyes, 'The Military as an Agent of Political Socialization: The Case of Hungary', in Dale R. Herspring and Ivan Volgyes, eds, *Civil–Military Relations in Communist Systems* (Boulder, CO: Westview Press, 1978), p. 147.

24. Zoltan D. Barany and Ivan Sylvain, 'Hungary', in Rakowska-Harmstone *et al.*, *Warsaw Pact*, *op. cit.*, Phase II, Vol. 3, pp. 406–407.

25. For an excellent study of the Monarchy's professional soldiers, see Istvan Deak, *Beyond Nationalism: A Social and Political History of the Habsburg Officer Corps* (New York: Oxford University Press, 1990).

26. For a fine study on the social status of the military in this period, see Tibor Hajdu, 'A tisztikar tarsadalmi helyzete – 1848-18', *Valosag*, Vol. 30, No. 4 (April 1987), pp. 65–80.

27. *Ibid.*, p. 79.

28. Miklos M. Szabo, *A Magyar Kiralyi Honved Legiero a masodik vilaghaboruban* (Budapest: Zrinyi, 1987), p. 13.

29. For a detailed account of the limitations the Peace Treaty imposed on Hungary, see *A Magyar Bekeszerzodes es a becikkelyezo torveny*

szovege es magyarazata (Budapest: 'Ordo' Torveny-es Rendelettar, 1921), pp. 54–63.

30. For a perceptive essay on Gombos's policies, see Jozsef Vonyo, 'Diktatura – olasz modra: A Gombos-csoport az allamrol a harmincas evek elso feleben', *Valosag*, Vol. 31, No. 1 (January 1988), pp. 66–76.

31. See for instance, Miklos Horthy, *Emlekirataim* (Buenos Aires, 1953), p. 160.

32. See Lorand Dombrady, 'A hadsereg torekvesei a szinhazi cenzura bevezetesere a harmincas evek elso feleben', *Valosag*, Vol. 31, No. 1 (January 1988), pp. 52–65, especially p. 52.

33. The Hungarian defense budgets of the Gombos era showed large increases that the country could ill afford: 1933–34: 198.5 million pengo (m.), 1935–36: 211.4 m., 1936–37: 228.5 m., 1937–38: 303.7 m. See Lorand Dombrady and Sandor Toth, *A Magyar Kiralyi Honvedseg* (Budapest: Zrinyi, 1987), p. 100.

34. At a 1938 meeting with Hungarian Prime Minister Bela Imredy, Hitler remarked that 'Who wants to have dinner with us, must help in the cooking.' See Gyorgy Ranki, ed., *A Wilhelmstrasse es Magyarorszag 1933–44* (Budapest: Kossuth, 1968), p. 288.

35. Space does not permit a detailed analysis of Hungary's participation in World War II. For such studies, see Gyorgy Ranki, *A Masodik Vilaghaboru tortenete* (Budapest: Gondolat, 1976); and C. A. Macartney, *A History of Hungary 1929–45* (New York: Praeger, 1956 Vol. 1, 1957 Vol. 2).

36. For an engaging personal account of Hungary's involvement in the war against the Soviet Union, see Andras Simonffy, *Komporszag katonai* (Budapest: Magveto, 1981).

37. Admiral Nicholas Horthy, *Memoirs* (New York: Robert Speller and Sons, 1957), p. 193.

38. A dramatic portrayal of the defeat can be found in Istvan Nemeskurty, *Requiem egy hadseregert* (Budapest: Gondolat, 1968).

39. For an amusing description of life in Hungary during the winter of 1944, see Macartney, *A History of Hungary*, Vol. II, p. 340.

40. For a perceptive analysis of the few months of Szalasi's dictatorial rule in Hungary, see Eva Teleki, *Nyilas uralom Magyarorszagon* (Budapest: Kossuth, 1974).

41. *Szolgalati Szabalyzat a magyar kiralyi honvedseg szamara* (Budapest: Hadtudomanyi Konyvtar, 1931), Part I, pp. 29–32.

42. Cited in Dombrady and Toth, p. 68.

43. *Az Imredy-per* (Budapest: Hirado konyvtar, 1945), p. 27.

44. *Horthy Miklos titkos iratai* (Budapest: Kossuth, 1967), p. 248.

45. See Miklos Szucs, *Ezredes voltam 1956–ban a vezerkarnal* (Budapest: Szabad Ter, 1989), p. 35.

46. Volgyes, *The Political Reliability* . . . , p. 61.

47. Sandor Mucs and Erno Zagoni, *A Magyar Nephadsereg tortenete* (Budapest: Zrinyi, 1984), p. 17.

48. See Lorand Dombrady and Gabor Nagy, eds, *Fegyverrel a hazaert: Magyar ellenallasi es partizanharcok a masodik vilaghaboru idejen* (Budapest: Zrinyi, 1980), pp. 290–291.
49. Berki, *Hadsereg vezetes nelkul*, p. 9.
50. Peter Gosztonyi, *Legiveszely Budapest!* (Budapest: Nepszava, 1989), p. 183.
51. *A haza szolgalataban* (Budapest: Zrinyi, 1985), pp. 14–19
52. Istvan Pinter, *A magyar front es az ellenallas* (Budapest: Kossuth, 1970), p. 231.
53. See, for instance, Jozsef Revai's article in *Neplap*, January 30, 1945.
54. *Magyar Hirlap*, January 27, 1980.
55. *Hajdu-Bihari Naplo*, December 22, 1964.
56. Andras Kis, 'Nepi hadsereg szuletik, 1945', *Historia*, No. 1 (1985), p. 27.
57. For an interesting study on this first chapter of the new Hungarian army, see Andras Kis, *Az antifasiszta magyar katonai hagyomanyokrol (1945)* (Budapest: Akademiai, 1978).
58. On this point, see Denes Felkai, 'A magyar nephadsereg egeszsegugyi szolgalatanak kiepiteserol', *Hadtorteneti Szemle*, No. 1 (1984), pp. 150–152.
59. *Dokumentumok a magyar forradalmi munkasmozgalom tortenetebol 1935–1945* (Budapest: Kossuth, 1964), pp. 572–574.
60. Jozsef Revai wrote in January 1945: 'Those who do not take seriously the recruiting efforts of the Provisional Government are not good Communists.' See his article in *Neplap*, January 30, 1945.
61. See Sandor Mucs, *Politika es hadsereg Magyarorszagon 1944–48* (Budapest: Zrinyi-Kossuth, 1985), p. 30–31.
62. *Ibid.*, p. 44.
63. Kiraly, *Honvedsegbol Nephadsereg*, p. 119.
64. See Istvan B. Szabo's article in *Debrecen*, March 27, 1945; and *Kis Ujsag*, October 22, 1946.
65. Cited by Mucs, *Politika es hadsereg*, p. 114–115.
66. See the note prepared by Vilmos Zentai and Erik Bodrossy, cited in *ibid.*, p. 86.
67. Mucs and Zagoni, p. 204.
68. See the section by Gabor Nagy in Gabor Nagy and Lajos Moricz, eds, *Uj haza, uj hadsereg. Visszaemlekezesek as 1945–1947–es evekre.* (Budapest: Zrinyi, 1970).
69. Lajos Kossuth was one of the leaders of the 1848 Revolution and the War of Independence against the Habsburgs that followed. The HCP used his name to popularize military and other institutions.
70. For the text of the full speech, see Mihaly Farkas, *A beke arcvonalan* (Budapest: Szikra, 1949), pp. 339–367.
71. Nogradi, who was also a CC member, became First Deputy Minister of Defense as a result of his appointment to the MPA.
72. For an interesting account of the MPA's establishment, see

Erno Hancs, "A politikai focsoportfonokseg es a politikai tiszti intezmeny letrehozasanak elozmenyei a magyar nephadseregben (1948 aprilis-1949 februar)', *Hadtortenelmi Kozlemenyek*, Vol. 31 (1949), pp. 72–286.

73. See Bela Kiraly, 'Hungary's Army under the Soviets', *East Europe*, March 1958, p. 10.

74. See the interview with Gyorgy Zsombok Timar in Bulcsu Bertha, *Irok, szineszek, bortonok* (Budapest: Uj Ido, 1990), pp. 263–265.

75. *Ibid.*, p. 209.

76. See *A haza szolgalataban*, p. 97.

77. See *Uj Ember*, January 24, 1988; and *Magyar Nemzet*, October 12, 1988.

78. Mucs, *Politika es hadsereg*, p. 66.

79. Peter Gosztonyi, *Foltamadott a tenger . . . 1956* (Budapest: Nepszava, 1989), p. 33.

80. Karoly Szerencses, 'Mikor internaltak az emberi szellemet', *Hitel*, No. 6 (1990), p. 18.

81. *A magyar nepi demokracia tortenete 1944–62* (Budapest: Kossuth, 1978), p. 169.

82. Paul Zinner in his excellent *Revolution in Hungary* surmised that Farkas's exclusion from the Orgburo in 1951 'might be attached some significance' but there is no evidence that would suggest any ulterior motivation. Indeed, as Zinner says, Farkas did remain a member of the Politburo and the Secretariat.

83. See Kiraly, *Honvedsegbol Nephadsereg*, p. 125; and Kovrig, *Communism in Hungary*, p. 207.

84. *Nemzetgyulesi Naplo*, November 29, 1945–May 1946, Third Session, p. 82.

85. Kiraly, *Honvedsegbol Nephadsereg*, p. 109.

86. One good example is General Marcell Stomm who fought and fell prisoner on the Eastern Front. After he was returned from the Soviet Union in 1951, he stood trial and was sentenced to death for his alleged war crimes. Later the Presidential Council altered the sentence to life imprisonment. Stomm was released in 1954 and rehabilitated in 1989. See *Magyar Hirlap*, May 9, 1989.

87. See V. I. Lenin, *A haborurol, a hadseregrol es a hadtudomanyrol* (Budapest: Zrinyi, 1958), Vol. 2, p. 517.

88. Kovrig, *Communism in Hungary*, p. 207.

89. See Peter Gosztony, 'Die Ungarische Volksarmee', in Peter Gosztony, ed., *Zur Geschichte der europaeischen Volksarmeen* (Bonn-Bad Godesberg: Hochwacht, 1976), pp. 132–133.

90. For an informative interview about the function and methods of the Military Political Department, see Peter E. Kovary, 'Apam a katpolos', *Mozgo Vilag*, Vol. 15, No. 2 (February 1989), pp. 89–103.

91. See Berki, *Hadsereg vezetes nelkul*, pp. 11–12.

92. See Berki, *Hadsereg vezetes nelkul*, p. 45. Kovrig cites an interesting

anecdote that shows well the HCP's leadership's attitude toward the military leaders, who were themselves high party functionaries. 'When in late 1949 three senior Soviet military advisers casually asked what manner of a man was General Laszlo Solyom, the Hungarian communist chief of staff, Rakosi replied: 'English spy'. (Farkas later said Solyom was a French spy . . .) The visitors were visibly embarrassed by this absurd allegation . . . ' See Sandor Nogradi, *Tortenelmi lecke* (Budapest: Kossuth, 1970), pp. 401–403, 429; quoted in Kovrig, *Communism in Hungary*, p. 264.

93. *Magyar Nemzet*, February 19, 1990.
94. *Ibid*. See also the interview with Gyorgy Zsombok Timar in Bertha, *Irok, szineszek, bortonok*, pp. 261–262.
95. The section on military education draws on my article, 'Military Higher Education in Hungary', *Armed Forces and Society*, Vol. 15, No. 3 (Spring 1989), pp. 371–388.
96. See for instance, *Magyar Nemzet*, March 6, 1989.
97. Ivan Volgyes and Zoltan Barany, 'The Evolution of the Hungarian People's Army', in Jonathan Eyal, ed., *The Warsaw Pact and the Balkans: Moscow's Southern Flank* (London: Macmillan, 1989), p. 36.
98. *Nepszava*, July 10, 1990.
99. Szucs, *Ezredes voltam*, p. 40.
100. Erno Zagoni *et al.*, *Hadsereg, honvedelem* (Budapest: Zrinyi, 1968), p. 151.
101. *Fejer megyei Hirlap*, November 23, 1968.
102. Mucs, *Politika es hadsereg*, p. 55.
103. See Palffy's article, 'A Szovjet Hadsereg – a beke ore', in *Szabad Nep*, February 23, 1949.
104. For illustration of this point, see Istvan Hajduska, 'Igy el a felszabadito szovjet harcos kepe a magyar nep sziveben', *Szovjet Kultura*, May 1952, pp. 8–9; and 'Nephadseregunk peldakepe: A dicso Szovjet Hadsereg', *Szovjet Kultura*, September 1952, pp. 4–6.
105. Berki, *Hadsereg vezetes nelkul*, p. 16.
106. I do not see any evidence for the 'enormous benefits' and 'respect' allotted to the armed forces Ivan Volgyes writes about in his *The Political Reliability . . .* , p. 64.
107. Berki, *Hadsereg vezetes nelkul*, p. 18.
108. See Szucs, *Ezredes voltam*, pp. 24–42.
109. Mucs and Zagoni, *A Magyar Nephadsereg*, p. 198.
110. One such scandal broke out in the provincial city of Nagykanizsa, home to an infantry regiment. The officers' mess was run by a homosexual who demanded credits to be paid in the form of sexual favors. See Szucs, p. 36.
111. See, for instance, the telling anecdote in Kiraly's, 'Hungary's Army: Its Part in the Revolt', *East Europe*, June 1958, pp. 3–4.
112. Kiraly, 'The Hungarian Revolution and Soviet Readiness to Wage War Against Socialist States', in Kiraly *et al.*, eds, *The First War Between*

Socialist States: The Hungarian Revolution of 1956 and Its Impact (New York: Atlantic Research, 1984), p. 10.

113. Kiraly, 'Hungary's Army under the Soviets', p. 12.
114. See for instance, Gosztony, 'Die Ungarische Volksarmee', p. 129; Szucs, *Ezredes voltam*, p. 31.
115. Kiraly, 'Hungary's Army under the Soviets', pp. 12–13.
116. Vali, *Rift and Revolt in Hungary*, p. 1.
117. *The Observer*, May 27, 1951.
118. Ithiel de Sola Pool, *Satellite Generals* (Stanford, CA: Stanford University Press, 1955), p. 120.
119. Szucs, *Ezredes voltam*, pp. 49–50.
120. Raymond L. Garthoff, *Soviet Military Policy: An Historical Analysis* (New York: Praeger, 1966), p. 142.
121. Vali, *Rift and Revolt*, p. 72.
122. *Ibid.*, p. 74.
123. A. Ross Johnson, 'The Warsaw Pact: Soviet Military Policy in Eastern Europe', in Sarah M. Terry, ed., *Soviet Policy in Eastern Europe* (New Haven, CT: Yale University Press, 1984), p. 259.
124. For this point I am indebted to Dr Peter Deak, a noted Hungarian military expert.
125. Even Kiraly, the author who portrays advisers in the most negative light, admits some beneficial effects of the first group. See *Honvedsegbol Nephadsereg*, p. 146.
126. *Ibid.*, p. 143.
127. *Ibid.*
128. *Ibid.*
129. See, for instance, Tibor Gellert's Afterword to Kiraly's book, *Honvedsegbol Nephadsereg*, pp. 317–318.
130. Volgyes, *The Political Reliability*, p. 63.
131. Szucs, *Ezredes voltam*, p. 39.

3: Subordination (1953–68)

1. Again, see Kovrig, *Communism in Hungary*; Gati, *Hungary and the Soviet Bloc*; and Janos Radvanyi, *Hungary and the Superpowers* (Stanford, CA: Hoover Institution Press, 1972).
2. Kovrig, *Communism in Hungary*, p. 268.
3. See Nagy, *On Communism*, p. 252.
4. Bill Lomax, *Magyarorszag 1956* (Budapest: Aura, 1989), p. 64.
5. Vali, *Rift and Revolt*, p. 149.
6. Gosztonyi, *Foltamadott a tenger*, p. 40.
7. Vas, *Viszontagsagos eletem* (Budapest: Magveto, 1980), p. 525.
8. See Nagy's article in *Szabad Nep*, October 20, 1954.
9. He supposedly went there for health reasons but there can be no doubt that he used his time 'wisely', agitating the Kremlin leaders

against Nagy. The turn to the left that followed Rakosi's return was signalled by Jozsef Darvas's article – *Szabad Nep*, November 21, 1954 – warning about the strengthening of 'certain right-wing and petty-bourgeois tendencies'.

10. Sandor Balogh, 'Reformprobalkozasok (1953–56)', *Tarsadalmi Szemle*, Vol. 44, No. 8–9 (August–September 1989), p. 28.

11. Karoly Szerencses, 'Mikor internaltak az emberi szellemet', *Hitel*, No. 6 (1990), p. xx.

12. See Kalman Kulcsar, *A mai magyar tarsadalom* (Budapest: Kossuth, 1982), pp. 92–94.

13. See, for instance, Peter Veres, 'Oregek es fiatalok', *Irodalmi Ujsag* July 30, 1955, that started the avalanche of articles critical of the regime. Some of the excellent pieces that followed were Sandor Csoori, 'Fiatalok es oregek', *Irodalmi Ujsag*, August 6, 1955; Peter Kuczka, 'Egeszen nyiltan', *Irodalmi Ujsag*, August 13, 1955, and others. Poems, plays, and essays by Laszlo Benjamin, Tibor Dery, Laszlo Nemeth, Zoltan Zelk and others, also deserve mention.

14. For detailed descriptions of Rakosi's replacement, see Kovrig, *Communism in Hungary*, pp. 293–294; Gati, *Hungary and the Soviet Bloc*, p. 136; and Tamas Aczel and Tibor Meray, *Tisztito vihar: Adalekok egy korszak tortenetehez* (Munchen, 3rd edn, 1982), p. 361.

15. Bill Lomax, *Magyarorszag 1956* (Budapest: Aura, 1989), p. 47.

16. Apart from the books already mentioned on the Revolution, some of the best works are: Tamas Aczel and Tibor Meray, *The Revolt of the Mind* (New York: Praeger, 1960); Paul Kecskemeti, *The Unexpected Revolution: Social Forces in the Hungarian Uprising* (Stanford, CA: Stanford University Press, 1961); Melvin J. Lasky, ed., *The Hungarian Revolution: A White Book* (New York: Praeger, 1957).

17. Gosztonyi, *Foltamadott*, p. 106.

18. William Shawcross, *Crime and Compromise: Janos Kadar and the Politics of Compromise since 1956* (New York: E. P. Dutton, 1974), p. 15.

19. See Janos Berecz interviewed by Gyorgy Balo, 'Experiencing History', *New Hungarian Quarterly*, Vol. 27, No. 104 (Winter 1986), p. 29.

20. *Khrushchev Remembers*, edited and translated by Strobe Talbott (Boston: Little, Brown, and Co., 1970), p. 420.

21. See *ibid.*, p. 424 and Kovrig, *Communism in Hungary*, p. 314. To be sure, Munnich did not want the top position, referring to his long absence from the country (he was ambassador to Moscow).

22. See Laszlo Gyurko's 'Introductory Biography' to Janos Kadar, *Selected Speeches and Interviews* (Budapest: Akademiai, 1985), p. 100. At a March 1957 speech to the workers of Csepel, Gyorgy Marosan took 'credit' for calling the Soviet Army in. See *Frankfurter Allgemeine Zeitung*, March 25, 1957.

23. Gosztonyi, *Foltamadott*, p. 187.

24.   *A magyar nep demokracia*, pp. 298–299.
25.   See Gosztonyi, *Foltamadott*, pp. 222–237. One of the most infamous cases of Kadar's revenge was the execution of Peter Mansfeld. A fifteen-year-old (born on March 10, 1941) student during the Revolution, Mansfeld was arrested and detained until his eighteenth birthday, at which time he could be legally executed. The death sentence was carried out on March 21, 1959.
26.   See Vali, *Rift and Revolt*, pp. 439–440.
27.   See for instance the discussion of the 'Revai debate' in 1957 in Andrew Felkay, *Hungary and the USSR, 1956–88: Kadar's Political Leadership* (Westport, CT: Greenwood Press, 1989), pp. 105–108.
28.   HSWP Membership

December	1956	37,818	
January	1957	100,000	
April	1957	227,420	(11,496 primary organizations)
May	1957	283,000	
December	1959	402,456	(16,805 primary organizations)
December	1966	584,849	
December	1967	601,917	

CYL membership also grew rapidly: by December 1959 it reached 380,000 and by 1963 over 40 percent of young people were members of the organization.
Sources: Gosztonyi, *Foltamadott*, p. 188; *A magyar nepi demokracia*, pp. 308, 332; Felkay, *Hungary and the USSR*, p. 129; Kovrig, *Communism in Hungary*, pp. 335, 339; *Legyozhetetlen ero*, pp. 252, 269.
29.   Felkay, *Hungary and the USSR*, p. 159.
30.   For a comprehensive analysis, see Ferenc Donath, *Reform es forradalom* (Budapest: Akademiai, 1977).
31.   *A Magyar Szocialista Munkaspart hatarozatai es dokumentumai, 1956–62* (Budapest: Kossuth, 1964), p. 474.
32.   For a comprehensive treatment of economic debates in this period, see Ivan T. Berend, *Gazdasagi utkereses 1956–65* (Budapest: Magveto, 1983).
33.   See *Nepszabadsag*, January 22, 1957; and *A magyar nepi demokracia*, p. 134.
34.   Mucs and Zagoni, *A Magyar Nephadsereg tortenete* p. 221.
35.   *Ibid.*, p. 223.
36.   There was no reason given for the change at the top of the Defense Ministry. If possible, Bata was even less qualified for his position than his predecessor. See *ibid.*, p. 220.
37.   Berki, *Hadsereg vezetes nelkul*, pp. 27–28.
38.   Szucs, *Ezredes voltam*, p. 95. Party membership at the Miklos Zrinyi Military Academy, the elite institution of the HPA, was 92 percent in

1956.
39. See Berki, *Hadsereg vezetes nelkul*, p. 20.
40. See the interview with Gyorgy Zsombok Timar in Bertha, *Irok, szineszek, bortonok*, p. 259.
41. Berki, *Hadsereg vezetes nelkul*, pp. 23–24.
42. *Daily Telegraph* (London), August 15, 1955.
43. *The Manchester Guardian*, August 13, 1955.
44. *Sueddeutsche Zeitung*, January 24, 1956; *Daily Telegraph*, June 4, 1956.
45. See, for instance, 'Tankok fegyvertelen katonak ellen', *Otlet*, June 15, 1989, pp. 14–15.
46. "Magyar tiszti kepzes a Szovjetunioban', Hungarian Research, *Radio Free Europe*, March 5, 1957.
47. Imre Bokor, *Kiskiralyok munderban* (Budapest: Uj Ido, 1989), p. 16.
48. See, for instance, *Nepszabadsag*, March 11, 1990.
49. Kiraly, 'Hungary's Army: Its Part in the Revolt', p. 9.
50. Mucs and Zagoni, *A Magyar Nephadsereg*, p. 216.
51. See *Szabad Nep*, September 8, 1955 and August 23, 1956; and *A magyar nepi demokracia*, p. 274.
52. See Berki, *Hadsereg vezetes nelkul*, p. 29.
53. *Ibid.*, pp. 20–24.
54. *Time and Tide*, February 1, 1957.
55. For a comprehensive analysis of the Hungarian armed forces' equipment during the Revolution, see Dezso Ivan, 'A Magyar Nephadsereg legiereje 1956 oktobereben-novembereben', *Hadtortenelmi Kozlemenyek*, Vol. 102, April–June 1989, pp. 208–222.
56. See Istvan Kozma Toth, *Czinege Lajos munder nelkul* (Budapest: Zrinyi, 1990), pp. 49–50.
57. Berki, *Hadsereg vezetes nelkul*, p. 91.
58. Lomax, *Magyarorszag*, p. 134.
59. Berki, *Hadsereg vezetes nelkul*, p. 32.
60. See Mucs and Zagoni, p. 235; *A magyar nepi demokracia*, p. 279.
61. Gosztonyi, *Foltamadott*, pp. 96–97.
62. *Ibid.*, p. 89.
63. See Lomax, p. 133; and *ibid.*, pp. 172–173.
64. The freedom-fighters acquired their weapons from a variety of sources: the weapon storage of factories; army personnel with or without force; police and army armories. Budapest Police Headquarters, for instance, distributed 15,000 to 20,000 weapons to the rebels. See, Berki, *Hadsereg vezetes nelkul*, p. 169 and *Nepszabadsag*, June 16, 1989.
65. See Szucs, *Ezredes voltam*, pp. 70–72.
66. Gosztonyi, *Foltamadott*, pp. 117–119.
67. See Laszlo Foldes, *A masodik vonalban* (Budapest: Kossuth, 1984), p. 241.
68. See Laszlo Foldes, 'Ahogy en lattam 1956–ot', *Historia*, Vol. 4, No. 1

(January 1982), p. 23. Incidentally, there are major discrepancies between this article and Foldes' memoirs, *A masodik vonalban*.

69. Kiraly, 'Hungary's Army: Its Part in the Revolt', p. 12.
70. *A haza szolgalataban*, p. 129.
71. For a detailed description of the Kecskemet Division's activities during the Revolution, see Berki, *Hadsereg vezetes nelkul*, pp. 72–76.
72. See Kiraly, 'Hungary's Army: Its Part in the Revolt', p. 12.
73. Berki, *Hadsereg*, p. 82.
74. Radio Budapest, October 28, 1956, 1:20 p.m.
75. Mihaly Berki, 'A hadsereg 1956–ban', *Polgari Vedelem*, April 1989, pp. 27–28.
76. Ervin Liptai, 'A hadsereg az 1956. oktoberi es novemberi esemenyekben', *Tarsadalmi Szemle*, June 1989, p. 104.
77. When Mikoyan and Suslov returned on the same day to Moscow, their reports were uninteresting to the leadership as the latter probably already made up its mind about the invasion. See Gati, *Hungary and the Soviet Bloc*, pp. 146–148.
78. See *A Varsoi Szerzodes szervezete: Dokumentumok 1955–85* (Budapest: Kossuth, 1986), p. 13.
79. Among others the meeting was attended by Kadar, Munnich, Apro, and Karoly Kiss. All of them were members of the top party leadership following the repression of the Revolution. See Gosztonyi, *Foltamadott*, pp. 152–153.
80. Berki, *Hadsereg*, pp. 164–165.
81. See Gati, *Hungary and the Soviet Bloc*, pp. 148–150.
82. Jiri Valenta, 'The Soviet Union and East Central Europe: Crisis, Intervention, and Normalization', in Rakowska-Harmstone, ed., *Communism in Eastern Europe*, p. 338.
83. Jiri Valenta, 'Soviet Decision Making and the Hungarian Revolution', in Kiraly *et al.*, eds, *The First War between Communist States*, p. 270.
84. See Peter Gosztonyi, 'A magyar nephadsereg a forradalomban', in *Magyar Valtozasok* (Vienna: Integratio, 1979), pp. 36–59.
85. See *Nephadsereg*, February 22, 1986, p. 10.
86. These figures are cited by Gosztonyi, *Foltamadott*, p. 205.
87. See, for instance, Kiraly, *Honvedsegbol Nephadsereg*; Gosztonyi, *Foltamadott a tenger*.
88. *Nepszabadsag*, November 29, 1956.
89. Erno Zagoni, 'A munkashatalom megvedese es a Magyar Nephadsereg', *Parttorteneti Kozlemenyek*, No. 1, 1987, p. 21.
90. See Erno Zagoni, ed., *Az MSZMP es a szocialista honvedelem* (Budapest: Zrinyi, 1981), p. 27; and Arpad Szabo, *A magyar forradalmi honved karhatalom* (Budapest: Zrinyi, 1977), p. 110.
91. See *A magyar nepi demokracia*, p. 306. For a text of the original party resolution, see *A Magyar Szocialista Munkaspart hatarozatai*, pp. 25–26.

92. See Janos Kadar, *Hazafisag es kommunizmus* (Budapest: Kossuth, 1968), pp. 151–152.
93. For analyses of the Workers' Guard, see Jeremy King, 'The Workers' Guard: A Threat to Hungary's Reforms?' Hungarian Situation Report (hereafter HSR), *Radio Free Europe Research* (hereafter *RFER*), July 28, 1989; and Judith Pataki, 'National Assembly Disbands Workers' Guard', HSR, *RFER*, October 24, 1989.
94. *Az MSzMP honvedelmi politikajarol* (Budapest: Zrinyi, 1974), p. 26.
95. Berki, *Hadsereg vezetes nelkul*, p. 210.
96. It was the bitter irony of this situation that those who should have been punished – at least from the HSWP's point of view – were not and often rose to the highest positions in the HPA leadership. Colonel Istvan Olah, commander of a military high school in the capital during the uprising asked the permission of MOD Staff Colonel Szucs to attack Soviet units with his 15- and 16-year-old cadets on November 2. Szucs categorically rejected the request and told Olah to stay put and calm down. Szucs was persecuted after the Revolution; Olah became Minister of Defense in 1984. See Szucs, *Ezredes voltam*, p. 99.
97. See, for instance, *A haza szolgalataban*, p. 153.
98. For a text of the 'Officer's Declaration', see *Az MSZMP es a szocialista honvedelem*, p. 75–76.
99. *Magyar Nemzet*, July 9, 1990.
100. See *Khrushchev Remembers*, p. 425.
101. *Az MSzMP es a szocialista honvedelem*, pp. 30–31.
102. See Karoly Munk, 'A hadsereg partiranyitasanak megszilarditasat biztosito nehany fontos 1956–67–ben hozott intezkedesrol', *Honvedelem*, No. 6 (1966), p. 71.
103. See the interview with Chief of Staff Ferenc Ugrai and MPA Chief Pal Ilku in *Nepszava*, February 17, 1957.
104. *Pest Megyei Hirlap*, December 10, 1964.
105. Mucs and Zagoni, p. 269.
106. See Kozma Toth, *Czinege Lajos*, p. 74.
107. Kecskes, '*Vezeraldozatok*', pp. 134–135.
108. *Ibid.*, pp. 136–137.
109. *Ibid.*, p. 151.
110. Zinner, *Revolution in Hungary*, p. 147.
111. See Kozma Toth, *Czinege Lajos*, pp. 51–53; Bokor, *Kiskiralyok*, pp. 20–21.
112. See Kozma Toth, p. 67; Kecskes, pp. 92–93.
113. P. I. Efimov *et al.*, eds, *Boevoi soiuz bratskikh armii* (Moscow: Voenizdat, 1974), p. 81.
114. See Artur Zentai, 'Gondolatok a Magyar Nephadsereg fejlodesenek nehany kerdeserol', in *A tarsadalom es a hadsereg* (Budapest: Zrinyi, 1974), p. 93.
115. See Bokor, *Kiskiralyok munderban*, p. 100–102.
116. See Czinege's speech at the HSWP's 9th Congress in *Az MSzMP*

kilencedik kongresszusanak jegyzokonyve (Budapest: Kossuth, 1967), pp. 329–340.

117. *Az MSzMP es a szocialista honvedelem*, pp. 56, 134.
118. See Barany, 'Military Higher Education in Hungary', p. 372.
119. See, for instance, *Nepszabadsag*, February 7, 1963; *Nepszava*, July 6, 1965.
120. Zoltan Iszlai, *Emberek angyalborben* (Budapest: Zrinyi, 1985), p. 10.
121. It is worth bearing in mind that in the Hungarian educational system there is a clear distinction between college (*foiskola*) and university (*egyetem*). A degree from a college is considered clearly inferior to one earned at a university.
122. F. Rubin, 'The Hungarian People's Army', *RUSI Journal*, Vol. 121, No. 3 (September 1976), p. 62.
123. Jones, *Soviet Influence in Eastern Europe*, p. 204.
124. *The Military Balance, 1967–68* (London: IISS, 1967), p. 27.
125. *Az MSzMP es a szocialista honvedelem*, pp. 99–100.
126. Gosztony, 'Die Ungarische Volksarmee', p. 163.
127. For reports, see *Nepszabadsag*, May 14, 1965; and *Magyar Nemzet*, June 16, 1966.
128. See Czinege's speech at the HSWP's 9th Congress in *Az MSzMP kilencedik kongresszusanak jegyzokonyve*, p. 338.
129. See, for instance, *Nepszabadsag*, February 25, 1968.
130. *Az MSzMP es a szocialista honvedelem*, pp. 46–47.
131. *Nepszabadsag*, May 14, 1965.
132. See, for instance, *ibid.*, pp. 39–40.
133. For more information on the Hungarian defense industry, see Istvan Szilas, 'A hon vedelmenek vedelme', *Valosag*, August 1990, pp. 104–108.
134. Kecskes, '*Vezeraldozatok*', p. 175.
135. Peter Deak, 'A katonapolitikai helyzet alakulasa a masodik vilaghaboru utan – Magyarorszag szerepe a Varsoi Szerzodes vedelmi rendszereben', *Kulpolitika*, No. 5 (1987), p. 84.
136. See Johnson, 'Soviet-East European Military Relations', in Herspring and Volgyes, eds, *Civil–Military Relations*, p. 248.
137. Feher, 'Honvedelmunk helyzete', *op. cit.*
138. For a recent examination of the subject, see Keith Crane, *Military Spending in Eastern Europe* (Santa Monica: RAND, 1987).
139. *Ibid.*, p. 8.
140. Cited in Kecskes, p. 163.
141. Conversation with Dr Peter Deak.
142. For a fascinating description of this process, see Kecskes, pp. 142–149, 151–165. This discussion also draws on my talks with Dr Deak.
143. Since 1989 a massive amount of information has been published concerning the deeply-rooted and extensive corruption of military (and political) leaders of the Communist era. For some fascinating accounts, see Bokor, *Kiskiralyok munderban*, the volume that started

the avalanche of like publications; Kecskes's oft-cited book; in addition to literally hundreds of articles in the Hungarian press, particularly during the winter of 1989–90.

144. See Kozma Toth, *Czinege*, pp. 66–68.

145. *Magyar Hirlap*, July 28, 1989.

146. The Soviet accord with Hungary followed a series of similar arrangements signed with states where Soviet troops were stationed (East Germany, Poland, and Romania).

147. *Khrushchev Remembers*, pp. 513–515. Sergiu Verona's *Military Occupation and Diplomacy: Soviet Troops in Romania, 1944–1958* (Durham, NC: Duke University Press, 1992) offers an able analysis of the developments that led to Soviet troop withdrawals from Romania.

148. *Ibid.*, p. 427.

149. See *Petofi Nepe*, April 20, 1990.

150. See *Sueddeutsche Zeitung*, March 18, 1957.

151. See *Nepszabadsag*, February 19, 1958; *The New York Herald Tribune*, October 27, 1959; *The Christian Science Monitor*, November 24, 1959.

152. For a the WTO treaty's text, see Robin Alison Remington, *The Warsaw Pact: Case Studies in Communist Conflict Resolution* (Cambridge, MA: MIT Press, 1971), pp. 201–206; for a Hungarian version, *Szabad Nep*, May 15, 1955.

153. Zbigniew K. Brzezinski, *The Soviet Bloc: Unity and Conflict* (Cambridge, MA: Harvard University Press, 1967), pp. 458–459.

154. Christopher D. Jones, 'National Armies and National Sovereignty', in David Holloway and Jane M. O. Sharp, eds, *The Warsaw Pact: Alliance in Transition?* (London: Macmillan, 1984), p. 87. See also Jones's *Soviet Influence in Eastern Europe* and Rakowska-Harmstone *et al.*, *Warsaw Pact*.

155. Simon, *Warsaw Pact Forces*, p. xiii.

156. Jones, 'National Armies', pp. 92–96.

157. *Ibid.*, p. 94.

158. Michael Sadykiewicz, *Organizing for Coalition Warfare: The Role of East European Warsaw Pact Forces in Soviet Military Planning* (Santa Monica, CA: RAND, 1988), p. 6.

159. Johnson, 'Soviet Military Policy in Eastern Europe', p. 267.

160. For a useful compilation of data on WTO joint maneuvers between 1961 and 1982, see Simon, *Warsaw Pact Forces*, pp. 219–228.

161. See *Esti Hirlap*, April 21, 1962; *Nepszabadsag*, October 19, 1962; *Nepszabadsag*, August 20, 1966.

162. Volgyes, *The Political Reliability*, p. 85.

163. For an analysis of Kadar's dilemma during the Czechoslovak crisis, see Felkay, *Hungary and the USSR*, pp. 192–218.

164. *Nepszabadsag*, August 11, 1989.

165. "Husz ev multan', *Vilagossag*, No. 6 (June 1988), p. 348.

166. Cited in Kecskes, p. 193.

167. Csaba Bundula, 'Jogszerutlen kerelem', *Magyarorszag*, May 4, 1990.
168. *Dunantuli Naplo*, September 30, 1989.
169. According to a recently declassified report of the Czechoslovak Ministry of Interior, the five WTO armies altogether killed 82, seriously wounded 302, and slightly injured more than 500 Czechoslovak citizens. See *Obcansky Denik* (Prague), July 24, 1990.
170. Dr Deak submits that the invasion served to forge the HPA together. According to him, the 'Zala' exercise was held in secret on the orders of the HPA high command. The fact that it was kept secret signified a major success since no classified information remained classified, as a general rule. Deak described to me an example representative of the speed with which supposedly privileged information was spreading. In the early 1960s four commanders, one of them Deak, of the Tata Armored Regiment were called to the MOD and were told that their unit would be relocated to Nagyatad. The four officers and their driver went to Nagyatad cloaked in secrecy (switched license plates etc.) to survey the facilities. When they arrived back in Tata, Deak's wife told him that she had already heard from her hairdresser that the regiment was moving to Nagyatad.
171. For eyewitness reports, see Miklos Zelei, 'Az ismeretlen katona 1968–rol', *Kepes 7*, August 18, 1990; and the three-part series of the same journal published on August 18, 25, and September 1, 1990.
172. Beck and Rawling, 'The Military as a Channel of Entry', pp. 208–211.

4: Accommodation and Recalcitrance (1968–88)

1. See Simon, *Warsaw Pact Forces*, pp. 56–60.
2. John M. Caravelli, 'Soviet and Joint Warsaw Pact Exercises', *Armed Forces and Society*, Spring 1983, p. 413.
3. See Ildiko Lipcsey, 'Hungarians in Rumania: 1945–87', *The New Hungarian Quarterly*, Summer 1988, pp. 125–140.
4. Kovrig, *Communism in Hungary*, p. 411.
5. See William Welsh, 'Summary and Conclusions', in William Welsh, ed., *Survey Research and Public Attitudes* (New York: Pergamon, 1981), p. 492.
6. Gati, *Hungary and the Soviet Bloc*, p. 163.
7. For an excellent comparative study of opposition movements in the region, see Tony R. Judt, 'The Dilemmas of Dissidence: The Political Opposition in East-Central Europe', *East European Politics and Society*, Spring 1988, pp. 185–241.
8. For a brief overview of political reforms, see my 'The Bankruptcy of Hungarian Socialism', *Sudost-Europa*, Vol. 38, No. 4 (April 1989), pp. 197–205.
9. Zbigniew Brzezinski, 'The Crisis of Communism: The Paradox of Political Participation', *The Washington Quarterly*, Vol. 10, No. 4 (August 1987), pp. 168, 172.

10. *La Repubblica*, June 2, 1988; cited in Bennett Kovrig, 'Grasping the Nettle or Clutching at Straws'? Patterns and Prospects of Party Reform', paper presented at the conference on 'Eastern Europe and the Superpowers: A Region in Transition', at The Washington Institute, Washington, DC, September 1988, p. 6.

11. "Central Committee Communique Reviews Session', in *Foreign Broadcast Information Service – Eastern Europe* (hereafter *FBIS–EEU*), September 29, 1988, p. 34. On June 30, 1988 the HSWP's membership stood at 816,622.

12. *Nok Lapja*, May 28, 1988.

13. See John Van Oudenaren, 'The Soviet Union and Eastern Europe: New Prospects and Old Dilemmas', in William E. Griffith, ed., *Central and Eastern Europe: The Opening Curtain?* (Boulder, CO: Westview Press, 1989), pp. 102–130.

14. See for instance, *Pravda*, January 22, 1986. For the Hungarian reaction see *Nepszabadsag* and *Daily News*, January 23, 1986. For Western responses, see *Frankfurter Allgemeine Zeitung* and *Die Welt*, both on January 23, 1986.

15. See, for instance, *Pravda*, June 6, 1986.

16. *The Chicago Tribune*, June 9, 1986.

17. For a representative selection of Soviet articles praising the NEM, see Vladimir Gerasimov, 'Economic Reform in Hungary', *International Affairs* (Moscow), August 1987, pp. 134–143; *Moscow News*, September 27, 1988; *Izvestiya*, October 3, 1987; *Ekonomicheskaya Gazeta*, February 4, 1988.

18. Radio Budapest, February 23, 1987, 10:10 P.M.

19. See *Krasnaya Zvezda*, May 21, 1987; *Nepszabadsag*, April 21, 1988; and *The Financial Times*, April 22, 1988.

20. See Charles Gati, 'Reforming Communist Systems: Lessons from the Hungarian Experience', in Griffith, ed., *The Opening Curtain?* pp. 234–235.

21. *The Independent*, February 25, 1988.

22. *Ibid.*, May 24, 1988.

23. See his article, 'Blinded by Glasnost', in *ibid.*, December 22, 1987.

24. Cited in Matyas Szuros, 'Hungary, Europe, and the World', *The New Hungarian Quarterly*, Vol. 28, No. 107 (Autumn, 1987), p. 25.

25. For some Western accounts of Kadar's visits, see *The Financial Times*, December 8, 1976; *Corriera della Sera*, June 8, 1977; *Le Monde*, November 16, 1978; *Neue Zurcher Zeitung*, February 4, 1984; and *The Times*, November 5, 1985. A compilation of these articles in Hungarian can be found in *Mr. Kadar* (Budapest: Hirlapkiado Vallalat, 1989).

26. Cited in Simon, *Warsaw Pact Forces*, pp. 159–160.

27. *Nepszava*, March 2, 1985.

28. Janos Kadar, *Valogatott beszedek es cikkek: 1957–74* (Budapest: Kossuth, 1975), p. 456.

29. See Ivan T. Berend, 'A reform sorsforduloja az 1970-es evekben', *Valosag*, Vol. 31, No. 1 (January 1988), pp. 1–26. For an excellent politico-economic history of the post-Stalin era, see Berend's *The Hungarian Economic Reforms: 1953–88* (New York: Cambridge University Press, 1990).

30. For an analysis of inflation in Hungary, see Erno Huszti, *Antiinflacios utkereses – monetaris politika es gyakorlat Magyarorszagon* (Budapest: Kozgazdasagi es Jogi, 1987).

31. See Paul Marer, 'The Economies and Trade of Eastern Europe', in Griffith, ed., *Central and Eastern Europe*, pp. 37–74.

32. This section draws on my 'The Bankruptcy of Hungarian Socialism', *op. cit.*, pp. 209–210.

33. "Novekvo elegedetlenseg', *Jel-kep*, No. 2 (1988), pp. 154–162.

34. See *Statisztikai evkonyv 1984* (Budapest: Kozponti Statisztikai Hivatal, 1985), pp. 302–311.

35. Judith K. Pataki, 'Neurotic Disorders in Hungary', *Survey*, August 1987, p. 117.

36. *Dunantuli Naplo*, June 17, 1988. Between 1960 and 1984 the number of suicides doubled. See *Statisztikai evkonyv 1984*, p. 45.

37. Rudolf Andorka, 'Alkoholfogyasztas: mertekek es vegletek', *Tarsadalmi Szemle*, November 1988, pp. 87–96, especially p. 89.

38. *Nepszabadsag*, September 20, 1988. For a comprehensive treatment of the Hungarian 'poor-policy', see Zsuzsa Ferge, *Fejezetek a magyar szegenypolitika tortenetebol* (Budapest: Magveto, 1986), especially pp. 174–179.

39. *Magyar Hirlap*, July 7, 1988. For an excellent article on the subject, see Zsuzsanna Vajda, 'Szegeny vagyok, szegenynek szulettem?' *Valosag*, Vol. 30, No. 7 (July 1987), pp. 63–74.

40. A. A. Timorin, 'Sotsial'no-politicheskaia priroda i naznachenie sotsialisticheskikh armii', in S. A. Tiushkievich *et al.*, eds, *Voina i armiia* (Moscow: Voennizdat, 1977), p. 348.

41. For a further discussion of this point, see Christopher D. Jones, 'The USSR, the Warsaw Pact and NATO', in Ingmar Oldberg, ed., *Unity and Conflict in the Warsaw Pact* (Stockholm: The Swedish National Defence Research Institute, 1984), p. 49.

42. Cited in Kecskes, p. 186.

43. Erno Zagoni, 'A Magyar Nephadsereg helye a politikai rendszerben', *Honvedsegi Szemle*, May 1987, p. 4.

44. *The Military Balance, 1986/87*, p. 52.

45. *Ifju Kommunista*, September 9, 1979.

46. For an extensive treatment of the Workers' Guard, see Peter Gosztony, ed., *Paramilitarische Organisationen in Sowjet-block* (Bonn: Hochwacht, 1977), especially pp. 259–331.

47. *A Magyar Szocialista Munkaspart XII. Kongresszusa* (Budapest: Kossuth, 1980), p. 34.

48. *Partepites* (Budapest: Kossuth, 1972), p. 79.

49. *Az MSzMP es a szocialista honvedelem*, p. 200.
50. Volgyes and Barany, 'The Evolution of the Hungarian People's Army', p. 33.
51. *Az MSzMP es a szocialista honvedelem*, p. 257 (my emphasis). The text appeared in *Magyar Kozlony*, No. 25 (1976), pp. 281–291.
52. Erno Zagoni, 'Partunk honvedelmi politikaja', *Ifju Kommunista*, August–September 1971, p. 29. On this point, see also Ervin Czipo, 'Bevonulas utan – leszereles utan', *Partelet*, No. 6 (June 1985), pp. 86–90.
53. See Korom's recollections in Kecskes, '*Vezeraldozatok*' p. 132.
54. Needless to say, here we are only interested in the portion of the lists related to the armed forces. It is worth remembering, however, that the HSWP's list incorporated the important positions of all other areas (education, industry, trade unions, etc.) of political relevance.
55. My source is Kecskes, pp. 159–161. In February 1990 the Hungarian weekly *Vilag* published the 1971 and the 1985 lists in their entirety.
56. For an informative treatment of the WTO Technical Committee, see Jones, *Soviet Influence in Eastern Europe*, pp. 142–143.
57. Dale R. Herspring and Ivan Volgyes, 'Political Reliability in the East European Warsaw Pact Armies', *Armed Forces and Society* Winter 1980, p. 276. The authors point out that the three percent figure was usual in the Central Committees of all NSWP Communist parties although the corresponding figure in the Soviet Union has been higher, between seven and nine per cent since 1952.
58. Needless to say, these elections were democratic in theory only as they offered essentially no choice to the voters, who had to cast their ballots supporting candidates pre-selected for them by the PPF and the HSWP. For an analysis of the Hungarian electoral politics in the 1945–89 period, see my chapter 'Elections in Hungary', in Furtak, ed., *Elections in Socialist States*, pp. 71–98.
59. For instance at the 1985 national elections in the 6th electoral district (Budapest-Martonvasar) both elected candidates were professional soldiers: Division Commander Major General Mihaly Torok and Division Party Secretary Colonel Balazs Nagy. See *Fejer-megyei Hirlap*, April 30, 1985.
60. *Ifju Kommunista*, December 1970, p. 21.
61. Mucs and Zagoni, *A Magyar Nephadsereg*, pp. 308–309.
62. *Ibid.*, p. 288.
63. See, for instance, Czinege's speech at the March 18, 1982 conference of HPA leaders in *Nephadsereg*, March 28, 1982.
64. On the HPA's bureaucratization, see Sandor Simon, *A torzsekrol es munkajukrol* (Budapest: Zrinyi, 1987), pp. 105–114.
65. Bokor, *Kiskiralyok munderban*, p. 22.
66. *Ibid.*
67. *Ibid.*, p. 101.
68. Zentai, 'Gondolatok . . . ', p. 116.

69. See, for instance, Janos Kerekgyarto, 'A katonai forumok demokratiz-musa as a fegyelem ertekelese', *Honvedsegi Szemle*, September 1985, pp. 74–78.

70. Zentai, 'Gondolatok . . . ', p. 92; Mucs and Zagoni, *A Magyar Nephadsereg*, p. 304.

71. Emil Nagy, 'Korunk tarsadalmai es a hadsereg', in *A hadsereg es a tarsadalom*, p. 71.

72. See Bela Gyorgyi, 'A parttagok politikai aktivitasa a nephadseregben', *Partelet*, December 1986, pp. 81–86.

73. Mucs and Zagoni, *A Magyar Nephadsereg*, p. 305.

74. *Nephadsereg*, February 14, 1987.

75. According to the respondents of a RAND study, 'only 20 or 30 percent were convinced Communists'. See Alexander Alexiev and A. Ross Johnson, *East European Military Reliability: An Emigré-Based Assessment* (Santa Monica: RAND, 1986), p. 24.

76. The decision to introduce the 'trustee' system was made by the HSWP Politburo's October 13, 1981 meeting.

77. *Magyarorszag*, February 13, 1983; *Nephadsereg*, January 18, 1986.

78. *Nepszabadsag*, September 29, 1984.

79. *Nephadsereg*, May 30, 1987.

80. For an article discussing this issue from the HPA's point of view, see Gyorgy Keleti, 'Vallasos fiatalok a hadseregben', *Honvedsegi Szemle*, May 1987, pp. 6–13.

81. See, for instance, *Magyar Hirlap*, November 26, 1985; *Reformatusok Lapja*, December 15, 1985; *Uj Ember*, December 22–27, 1985.

82. *Magyar Kurir*, November 4, 1986, p. 569.

83. For a specific case, see *Magyar Hirlap*, May 29, 1987. In fact, Amnesty International's sole major criticism of Hungary's human rights record in the mid-1980s was that conscientious objectors to military service were at times imprisoned. See Felkay, *Hungary and the USSR*, p. 273.

84. See Mucs and Zagoni, *A Magyar Nephadsereg*, p. 279.

85. *Nepszabadsag*, April 22, 1988.

86. *Nepszabadsag*, December 5, 1976.

87. For this point I am indebted to Dr Peter Deak.

88. For the draftees' general health conditions, see Attila Juhasz, 'A sorkotelesek demografiaja, a katonai szolgalat kovetkezmenyei, es a katonai szolgalatra valo elokeszites', *A tarsadalom es a hadsereg*, pp. 246–286. The 1986 data were cited by Defense Minister Karpati, *MTI* (Budapest), June 12, 1986.

89. Istvan Magyar es Ivan Kemenczy, 'Kulonbozo magatartaszavarok pszichopatologiai elemzese', *A tarsadalom es a hadsereg*, pp. 355–360. See also, *Magyar Hirlap*, March 19, 1990.

90. For two insightful books on the subject, see Janos Habony, *A beilleszkedes es a bunozes* (Budapest: Zrinyi, 1986); and Odon Kisszekhelyi, *Kabulat minden aron?* (Budapest: Zrinyi, 1982).

91. On this subject, see Lajos Kecse, 'A vezetoi es a fegyelmi felelosseg', *Honvedsegi Szemle*, September 1985, pp. 70–74.
92. See, for instance, *Magyar Hirlap*, September 29, 1971; *Nephadsereg*, November 30, 1985 ; April 9 and May 16, 1987.
93. Janos Sandor and Laszlo Tiderle, 'A katonai alkalmassag elbiralasanak feltetelei', *Honvedsegi Szemle*, December 1985, pp. 87–90.
94. For a representative MPA pamphlet – which certainly underscores the criticisms regarding their quality – see *Legy parancsnok! Kemeny, fegyelmezett harcosokat nevelj!* (Budapest: HM Politikai Focsoportfonoksege, 1972).
95. For revealing accounts of the 'life and times' of Czinege and some of his subordinates, see Kecskes's book, and Kozma Toth, *Czinege Lajos munder nelkul.*
96. See Kozma Toth, pp. 76–77; and Kecskes, pp. 81–86.
97. For this point I am indebted to Dr Deak.
98. Bokor, *Kiskiralyok munderban*, p. 22.
99. *Ibid.*, p. 83.
100. Bokor, *Kiskiralyok*, p. 59. Bokor's emphases throughout. For an analysis of the book and the subsequent investigation, see my 'The Hungarian Army Revealed: Colonel Bokor's Sensational Book', RAD Background Report/221, *RFER*, December 20, 1989.
101. *Az MSzMP es a szocialista honvedelem*, p. 306. For a study book used by students in high school levels, see *Honvedelmi Ismeretek* (Budapest: Tankonyvkiado, 1984).
102. See Janos Farkas, 'Honvedelmi neveles-oktatas az iskolaban', *Honvedsegi Szemle*, December 1985, pp. 54–58.
103. *A honvedelmi neveles modszertani kerdesei* (Budapest: Zrinyi, 1980), p. 16.
104. Karoly Toth, 'Torz nezetek a honvedelmi nevelesben', *Honvedsegi Szemle* December 1985, pp. 60–63. See also Mihaly Kocsis, 'Tapasztalataink az altalanos iskolai oktatasrol', *Honvedsegi Szemle*, July 1982, pp. 47–49.
105. Personal interviews in Hungary.
106. *Pajtas*, August 29, 1983.
107. *Magyar Nemzet*, April 23, 1983.
108. Nagy, 'Korunk tarsadalmai', *op. cit.*, p. 60.
109. *Lobogo*, September 27, 1979.
110. *Nephadsereg*, January 31, 1987.
111. See, for instance, *Nephadsereg*, January 31, 1987, p. 3; February 14, 1987, p. 3; and June 6, 1987, p. 6.
112. *Magyar Hirlap*, March 3, 1984.
113. *Nepszabadsag*, August 20, 1987.
114. *Ibid.*
115. *Veszpremi Naplo*, September 22, 1984.
116. *Nephadsereg*, August 23, 1982.
117. *Ibid.*, August 29, 1987.

118.   *Ibid.*, June 6, 1987.
119.   F. Romhanyi, 'Hungary's Army Short of 'Worker' Officers', *Soviet Analyst*, No. 10 (October 1978), p. 7.
120.   In 1986, for instance, only one out of seven applicants was admitted to Kilian. See *Magyar Hirlap*, July 4, 1986.
121.   Volgyes, *The Political Reliability*, p. 77. A recent Rand study came to similar conclusions regarding the NSWP states. See Alexiev and Johnson, *East European Military Reliability*, p. 15.
122.   *Nephadsereg*, August 20, 1977.
123.   In fact, when in the early 1970s the proportion of working class applicants showed a modest decline, Defense Minister Czinege called for the reversal of this unfortunate trend. See Nagy, 'Korunk tarsadalmai es a hadsereg', p. 74.
124.   In an interview the then Deputy Minister of Defense Olah said: 'we have been worried by the fact that a good number of them [applicants to military colleges] have been applying because they could not get into other institutions of higher education, or had not even tried due to their weak marks in secondary school'. See *The Guardian*, February 5, 1973.
125.   *Nephadsereg*, May 1, 1987, p. 10.
126.   Jozsef Malomsoki, 'A tiszti allomany tarsadalmi helyzetenek nehany mutatoja', *Honvedsegi Szemle*, June 1987, p. 13.
127.   Iszlai, *Emberek angyalborben*, p. 12.
128.   *Pravda*, September 26, 1968.
129.   Robert L. Hutchings, *Soviet–East European Relations: Consolidation and Conflict, 1968–80* (Madison, WI: University of Wisconsin Press, 1983), p. 42.
130.   Neil Fodor's *The Warsaw Treaty Organization: A Political and Organizational Analysis* (New York: St. Martin's Press, 1990) offers a comprehensive examination of the structural changes throughout the existence of the WTO.
131.   Malcolm Mackintosh, 'The Warsaw Treaty Organization: A History', in Holloway and Sharp, pp. 50–51.
132.   Simon, *Warsaw Pact Forces*, p. 62.
133.   For analyses of the Pact's military administrative structure, see Jones, *Soviet Influence in Eastern Europe*, pp. 132–227; and Michael Sadykiewicz, *The Warsaw Pact Command Structure in Peace and War* (Santa Monica, CA: Rand, 1988).
134.   Hutchings, *Soviet–East European Relations*, pp. 140–141.
135.   See for instance, Dale R. Herspring, 'The Soviets and the Warsaw Pact', in Griffith, ed., *The Opening Curtain*, p. 138; and Johnson *et al.*, *East European Military Establishments*, p. 146.
136.   See Aurel Braun, 'Eastern Europe, the Warsaw Pact, and NATO: The Impact of Changes on Military Balance', in Nicholas N. Kittrie and Ivan Volgyes, eds, *The Uncertain Future: Gorbachev's Eastern Bloc* (New York: Paragon House, 1988), p. 164.

137. Several studies have reached this conclusion. See, for instance, Volgyes, *The Political Reliability*; Johnson *et al.*, *East European Military Establishments*; Daniel N. Nelson, ed., *Soviet Allies: The Warsaw Pact and the Issue of Reliability* (Boulder, CO: Westview Press, 1984); Rakowska-Harmstone *et al.*, *The Warsaw Pact*.

138. See Herspring, 'The Soviets and the Warsaw Pact', pp. 149–150. A distinction should, of course, be observed between the NSWP members' willingness to increase military budgets. In general, East Germany and Bulgaria were the most enthusiastic in heeding the Soviet call, while Romania and Hungary were at the other end of the spectrum.

139. See, for instance, A. Ross Johnson, 'Has Eastern Europe Become a Liability to the Soviet Union? (II) Military Issues', in Charles Gati, ed., *The International Politics of Eastern Europe* (New York: Praeger, 1976), p. 54.

140. *The Los Angeles Times*, June 29; *The Times*, July 4; *Nepszabadsag*, October 26; *Der Spiegel*, November 29 (all 1983).

141. See Kozma Toth, *Czinege Lajos munder nelkul*, pp. 79–83.

142. This point was brought to my attention by Dr Deak.

143. My source, again, is Dr Deak.

144. *Die Welt*, May 10 and *The Wall Street Journal*, May 28, 1984.

145. See Jane M. O. Sharp, 'Security through Detente and Arms Control', in Holloway and Sharp, eds, pp. 161–196. The Hungarian view was elaborated, among others, by Szuros in 'Hungary, Europe, and the World', *op. cit.*, pp. 16–26.

146. *The International Herald Tribune*, April 5; *Die Welt*, April 11; and *Die Weltwoche*, April 11, 1985.

147. *The Observer*, April 14, 1985.

148. Jones, *Soviet Influence*, p. 120.

149. Ivan Volgyes and Zoltan D. Barany, 'Hungarian Mobilization and Force Structure', in Jeffrey Simon, ed., *NATO–Warsaw Pact Force Mobilization* (Washington, DC: National Defense University Press, 1988), p. 391.

150. Cited in Mucs and Zagoni, *A Magyar Nephadsereg*, p. 329.

151. For representative articles, see *Nepszava*, July 24, 1970; *Nepszabadsag*, September 14, 1972; *Nepszabadsag*, June 30, 1984.

152. *Nepszabadsag*, October 11, 1970.

153. See, for instance, *Nephadsereg*, September 22, 1984; *Magyar Hirlap*, June 25, 1985; *Orszag-Vilag*, July 10, 1985; *Nephadsereg*, September 6, 1986; *Vasarnapi Hirek*, January 31, 1988.

154. From a report on the 'Danube-84' WTO exercise in *Nepszabadsag*, June 30, 1984.

155. Zagoni, 'Partunk honvedelmi politikaja', *op. cit.*, p. 28.

156. See his chapter, 'National Armies and National Sovereignty', in Holloway and Sharp, *op. cit.*, p. 94.

157. Kecskes, p. 72. See also *Jane's Defence Weekly*, June 4, 1988.

158. *Ibid.*, p. 95.
159. These examples were shared with me by Dr Deak.
160. See Volgyes, *The Political Reliability*, p. 85.
161. My view on this subject was also put forth in Barany and Sylvain, 'Hungary', in Rakowska-Harmstone *et al.*, *Warsaw Pact: The Question of Cohesion*, pp. 452–456.
162. See his 'The Measurement of East European WTO Reliability', in Nelson, *Soviet Allies*, pp. 2–41.
163. See Alexiev and Johnson, *East European Military Reliability*.
164. *Magyar Nemzet*, June 25, 1972.
165. RFE Special Report/SAS, September 22, 1972. According to this report, 23 HPA soldiers took part in a two-week course as the guests of the Austrian Army's rifle detachment in Saalfelden.
166. Radio Budapest, April 3, 1988, 9:30 p.m.
167. *Beketukor*, Vol. 4, Nos. 5–6 (1988), p. 12.
168. *The Baltimore Sun*, January 9, 1984; *Jane's Defence Weekly*, June 4, 1988.

5: The Second Transition: Democratization (1988–90)

1. *Magyar Nemzet*, August 29, 1988.
2. *Magyar Hirlap*, October 28, 1988.
3. *Magyarorszag*, March 3, 1989.
4. For detailed analysis of some of the reform proposals, see my 'Political Participation and the Notion of Reform: Electoral Practice and the Hungarian National Assembly', *East Central Europe*, Vol. 16, Nos. 1–2 (Summer 1989), pp. 107–122; and 'The Bankruptcy of Hungarian Communism', especially pp. 197–204.
5. See, for instance, Geza Kilenyi, 'A kormanyzati tevekenyseg tovabbfejleszteserol', *Tarsadalmi Szemle*, August–September 1987, pp. 54–63.
6. See, for instance, his article, 'Minden tarsadalmi ero erdekelt a megujulasban', *Partelet*, June 1988, p. 39–43; and the interview in *Newsweek*, July 18, 1988.
7. Pozsgay made this statement on Radio Budapest's popular 'Evening Dialogue' program, July 18, 1988, 7:05 p.m.
8. For an annotated list of political organizations, see my 'Hungary's Independent Political Groups and Parties', Background Report/168, *RFER*, September 12, 1989.
9. "Berecz: Nagy to Receive Proper Tomb', *FBIS–EEU*, October 21, 1988, p. 42.
10. For analysis, see Zoltan D. Barany and Louisa Vinton, 'Breakthrough to Democracy: Elections in Poland and Hungary', *Studies in Comparative Communism*, Vol. 23, No. 2 (Summer 1990), pp. 191–212.
11. For analyses of the elections, see my 'On the Road to Democracy: The

Hungarian Elections of 1990', *Sudost-Europa*, Vol. 39, No. 5 (May 1990), pp. 318–329; and Rudolf L. Tokes, *Vom Post-Kommunismus zur Demokratie: Politik, Parteien und die Wahlen 1990 in Ungarn* (Bonn: Konrad-Adenauer Stiftung, 1990).

12. For detailed electoral results, see *Magyar Nemzet*, March 30, and April 10, 1990. For the parties' views on the military, see *Magyar Honved*, March 19, 1990.

13. See, for instance, A. Melnikov's report about Hungary's implementation of the multiparty system in *Sovetskaya Rossiya*, March 12, 1989, p. 5.

14. *The Washington Post*, January 6, 1991. For a brief analysis of the CMEA's failures, see Gati, *The Bloc that Failed* pp. 124–135.

15. For the Nemeth government's foreign policy statement, see Gyula Horn, "Magyarorszag es az europai egyuttmukodes', *Kulpolitika*, Vol. 16, No. 1 (1989), pp. 3–11.

16. *Magyar Nemzet*, November 18, 1989.

17. *Nepszabadsag*, December 2, 1989.

18. Cited in Kecskes, '*Vezeraldozatok*', p. 207.

19. Radio Budapest, July 1, 1989, 0430 GMT.

20. See the interview with General Sebok in *168 ora*, June 23, 1989.

21. Kecskes, p. 211.

22. See, for instance, Gyorgy Sandor, 'Mit jelenthet az ifjusagi mozgalom megujulasa?' *Honvedsegi Szemle*, Vol. 43, No. 2 (March 1989), pp. 1–13; and Laszlo Rapcsanyi, 'Gondolatok a KISZ jelenerol es jovojerol', pp. 17–24 of the same issue.

23. See, for instance, Janos Mate, 'Meditaciok a parttestuletek munkastilusarol, munkarendjerol', *Honvedsegi Szemle*, March 1989, pp. 94–100; and Sandor Faar, 'Az alapszervi munka megujitasarol', pp. 100–108 in the same issue.

24. See *Magyarorszag*, April 7, 1989, p. 20.

25. See, for instance, *Nepszabadsag*, April 1, and August 30, 1989.

26. *Heti Vilaggazdasag*, May 27, 1989.

27. *Nepszabadsag*, September 2, 1989. For a military analysis of the new Code, see Kalman Lorincz, 'Az uj szolgalati szabalyzat bevezeteserol', *Honvedsegi Szemle*, Vol. 43, No. 3 (May 1989), pp. 17–21.

28. *Vasarnapi Hirek*, September 17, 1989.

29. *Magyar Hirlap*, September 11, 1989.

30. *Magyar Nemzet*, September 18, 1989. In 1989–90 hundreds of articles appeared in the press suggesting ways to assure that the army could not be utilized for the purposes of internal politics. See, for instance, Istvan Gyarmati, 'A hadsereg a demokratikus tarsadalomban', *Valosag*, April 1990, pp. 18–25.

31. See for instance, *Magyar Hirlap*, May 20, 1989.

32. *Nepszava*, February 24, 1990.

33. See for instance, *Magyar Hirlap*, March 11, 1990.

34. *Nepszava*, September 12, 1989.

35.   *Vasarnapi Hirek*, November 4, 1990.
36.   For short biographies of the representatives of the 1990 parliament, see *Szabadon valasztott* (Budapest: Idegenforgalmi es Propaganda Kiado, 1990), p. 154. For more details on Keri's life and career, see Ferenc Kubinyi, ' . . . *ketrecbe engem zartak* . . . ' (Budapest: Holnap, 1989), pp. 168–269.
37.   *Nepszava*, December 2, 1989.
38.   General Lorincz sought to dismiss such suspicion in an interview, two months before (!) Nemeth's announcement. See *Fejer megyei Hirlap*, September 30, 1989.
39.   See *Uj Dunantuli Naplo*, July 20, 1990.
40.   Radio Budapest, August 6, 1990, noon.
41.   *Magyar Hirlap*, February 24, 1990.
42.   *Magyar Nemzet*, May 10, 1990.
43.   *Vas Nepe*, June 2, 1990.
44.   *Vasarnapi Hirek*, November 4, 1990.
45.   See, for instance, *Magyar Nemzet*, August 18, 1990.
46.   *Uj Dunantuli Naplo*, July 20, 1990.
47.   *Nepszava*, April 9, 1990.
48.   See the interview with Fur in *Nepszabadsag*, September 10, 1990.
49.   See Peter Harkai, 'A Magyar Nephadsereg kadereinek kulfoldi katonai kepzese', *Honvedsegi Szemle*, January 1989, pp. 24–27.
50.   TASS (Leningrad), October 11, 1990.
51.   *Nepszabadsag*, September 10, 1991.
52.   *Nepszava*, April 9, 1990.
53.   *Magyar Hirlap*, June 21, 1990.
54.   For discussions of the low living standards of professional soldiers, see *Pont*, January 15 and January 29, 1990; and *Magyar Hirlap*, September 6, 1990.
55.   *Vilag*, August 10, 1989.
56.   See the interview with MOD spokesman Colonel Keleti in *Nepszabadsag*, July 30, 1990.
57.   *Zalai Hirlap*, January 25, 1990.
58.   See, for instance, Bokor, *Kiskiralyok munderban*; Kecskes, '*Vezeraldozatok*'; and Kozma Toth, *Czinege Lajos munder nelkul*. For Western analyses, see my 'The Hungarian Army Revealed', *op. cit.*, and *Die Presse*, February 5, 1990.
59.   *Nepszabadsag*, August 18, 1990.
60.   See the interview with General Antal Annus, in *Komarom-Esztergom megyei Dolgozok Lapja*, September 1, 1990.
61.   *Nepszabadsag*, September 17, 1990.
62.   *Magyar Hirlap*, May 20, 1989.
63.   Radio Budapest, August 6, 1990, 8 p.m.
64.   *Nepszava*, September 22, 1990.
65.   *Magyar Nemzet*, June 27, 1988. For an excellent analysis of conscientious objection, see Tamas Csapody, 'A szelidek ereje',

Forras, March 1990, pp. 73–82. For the opposition's view, see *Demokrata (samizdat)*, No. 5 (1988), pp. 13–19.

66. *Orszag-Vilag*, March 29, 1989.
67. *Nepszabadsag*, August 22, 1990. The HA at this time kept approximately 80,000 reserve officers on its registers.
68. For the text of the Prime Minister's speech, see *Magyar Nemzet*, December 2, 1990.
69. Questions regarding the President's authority in military affairs emerged in early 1991. See my 'East European Armies in the Transitions and Beyond', *East European Quarterly*, Vol. 26, No. 1 (March 1992), pp. 23–24. Furthermore, a new reform of the HA's structure has been widely debated since 1991. See *Heti Vilaggazdasag*, August 24, 1991; *Beszelo*, September 7 and 21, 1991; *Magyar Forum*, September 26, 1991.
70. Borsits retired and was replaced by Major General Janos Deak in September 1991.
71. Krasznai had a Party–military career, in many respects typical of the Communist era. A former civilian who had been First Secretary of the Pest County HSWP, he had been appointed as MPA Chief in December 1988 – with little military expertise – and given a military rank. See *Nepszabadsag*, December 2, 1989.
72. MTI (Hungarian Telegraph Service), December 1, 1989.
73. *The Independent*, December 21, 1989.
74. An article in the Soviet government's daily *Izvestia*, January 17, 1989 offered no criticism of the Hungarian defense cuts .
75. *Nepszabadsag*, January 31, 1989.
76. See my 'Major Reorganization of Hungary's Military Establishment', Background Report 230, *RFER*, December 28, 1989; and *Der Spiegel*, December 7, 1989.
77. *Magyar Hirlap*, November 29, 1990.
78. See Kecskes, '*Vezeraldozatok*', pp. 171–176.
79. These deficiencies became apparent during the fall of 1991 when the jets of the Yugoslav federal air force violated Hungarian airspace on several occasions. See *Nepszabadsag*, August 28, 1991 and *Magyar Hirlap*, November 9, 1991.
80. *Nepszabadsag*, May 8, 1990.
81. Personal interviews with Hungarian military officers in the summer of 1990.
82. *Nepszava*, September 27, 1990.
83. *Frankfurter Allgemeine Zeitung*, September 27, 1990; *Nepszabadsag*, December 7, 1990.
84. According to the *Weekly Bulletin* (July 20, 1990) of the MTI, the Hungarian defense budget had been reduced by 80 billion forints in the 1985–90 period. For an informed analysis of this issue, see Douglas Clarke, 'The USSR Cannot Expect Greater Military Efforts from Hungary', Background Report/13, *RFER*, January 27, 1989.

85. *The New York Times*, December 15, 1988, p. A12.

86. MTI (in English), December 15, 1989.

87. *Magyar Nemzet*, November 14, 1990.

88. Alfred Reisch, 'Armed Forces Reorganized and 1991 Defense Budget Passed', *Report on Eastern Europe*, March 15, 1991, p. 19.

89. *Magyar Nemzet*, July 22, 1989.

90. For an analysis of the financial situation of the Hungarian defense industry, see Jozsef Csabay, 'A magyar hadiiparrol, penzugyi szemmel', *Penzugyi Szemle*, No. 1, 1990, pp. 79–83.

91. See *Nepszabadsag*, February 9, and February 15, 1989.

92. *The New York Times*, July 7, 1989.

93. *The Baltimore Sun*, October 30, 1989.

94. *Magyar Hirlap*, April 24, 1989.

95. *Magyar Nemzet*, June 24, 1989.

96. See AFD Chairman Janos Kis' article in *Magyar Hirlap*, May 15, 1990; and *Weekly Bulletin*, May 23, 1990.

97. See, for instance, *The Independent* and *The Financial Times*, May 10, 1990.

98. TASS interview with Lushev published in *Nepszabadsag*, May 12, 1990.

99. *Nepszava*, June 7, 1990.

100. For a description of the meeting, see Alfred Reisch, 'Hungary to Leave Military Arm of Warsaw Pact', *Report on Eastern Europe*, June 29, 1990, pp. 20–25; and *Nepszabadsag*, July 14, 1990.

101. See Reisch, 'Hungary to Leave', *op. cit.*, and *The Economist*, June 16–22, 1990. The last major joint WTO exercise with Hungarian participation was 'Friendship-89' held in Czechoslovakia in February 1989. For a Hungarian analysis of the maneuvers, see Istvan Nyilas, 'A Baratsag-89 gyakorlat tapasztalatai', *Honvedsegi Szemle*, May 1989, pp. 9–16.

102. *The Times* (London), June 27, 1990.

103. Radio Moscow, June 27, 1990, 6:45 p.m.

104. AP dispatch from Budapest, October 8, 1990.

105. This section draws on two of my papers: 'A Hungarian Dream Comes True: Soviet Troops to Leave after 45 Years', *Report on Eastern Europe*, March 30, 1990, pp. 23–28; and 'Not a Smooth Ride: Soviet Troop Withdrawals from Hungary', *Report on Eastern Europe*, June 15, 1990, pp. 20–27.

106. For the state of Hungarian–Soviet negotiation on the troop withdrawals until the end of January 1990, see Zoltan D. Barany and Alfred Reisch, "Withdrawal of All Soviet Troops by End of 1990 Demanded', *Report on Eastern Europe*, February 9, 1990, pp. 22–26.

107. The text of the agreement was published in *Magyar Kozlony*, May 29, 1990, pp. 1190–1192.

108. *Mai Nap*, March 22, 1990. For the announcement that Hungary served as a supply base for Czechoslovakia, see *Magyar Hirlap*, March 8,

1990, and Radio Budapest, March 12, 1990, noon. It is unclear what Sebok's evidence was for the part of his statement regarding the Ukraine.

109. *Magyar Hirlap*, April 4, 1990.

110. The Soviet High Command was obviously satisfied with Burlakov's performance as in December 1990 he was appointed to oversee the withdrawal of some 380,000 Soviet troops from Germany. He was replaced in Hungary by General Viktor Silov. See Reuter (Berlin), December 13, 1990; and Radio Budapest, December 12, 1990, 5:00 p.m.

111. *Magyar Hirlap*, April 4, 1990. For a contrary claim, see *Kisalfold*, October 18, 1990.

112. *Rege*, March 7, 1990.

113. For a pictorial report of Soviet sale items, see *Nepszava*, March 28, 1990. The photos depict everything from service medals and Lenin busts to gas-masks and even an officer's cap priced at 2,000 forint.

114. *Veszprem megyei Naplo*, March 31, 1990. According to the article, Soviet soldiers regularly visited the garbage dump to search for saleable items in the rubbish. They also frightened Hungarian 'treasure hunters' by firing their handguns.

115. See for instance, *Komarom-Esztergom megyei Dolgozok Lapja*, April 17, 1990.

116. *Kepes 7*, April 7 1990.

117. Apparently this how the Hungarian leadership is calculating. See an interview with Fur in *Veszprem megyei Naplo*, June 30, 1990.

118. See *Nepszabadsag*, May 25, 1989, and *Mai Nap*, June 2, 1989.

119. *Magyar Hirlap*, August 28, 1989.

120. *Daily News* (Budapest), September 8, 1989.

121. AP (Amsterdam), August 4, 1989.

122. *Nepszabadsag*, October 13, 1988 and June 17, 1989.

123. Radio Budapest, February 12, 1990, 7:00 p.m.

124. See *Nepszava*, April 24, 1990 and May 11. For an incisive technical analysis, see Michael Krepon and Jeffrey P. Tracey, 'Open Skies and UN Peace-Keeping', *Survival*, Vol. 22, No. 3 (May–June 1990), pp. 251–263.

125. Cited in Alfred Reisch, 'Armed Forces Reorganized . . . ' *op. cit.*, p. 22.

126. For a fine discussion of this development, see Rudolf L. Tokes, 'From Visegrad to Krakow: Cooperation, Competition, and Coexistence in Central Europe', *Problems of Communism*, Vol. 40, No. 6 (November–December 1991), pp. 100–115.

6:   Civil–Military Relations in Eastern Europe, 1945–90: A Cross-National Analysis

1.   John D. Bell, *The Bulgarian Communist Party from Blabdev to Zhivkov* (Stanford, CA: Hoover Institution Press, 1986), p. 86.
2.   See Walter M. Bacon, Jr., 'The Military and the Party in Romania', in Herspring and Volgyes, eds, *Civil–Military Relations in Communist Systems*, p. 166.
3.   For a detailed study, see Rakowska-Harmstone, 'Poland', in Rakowska-Harmstone *et al.*, *Warsaw Pact*, Phase II, Vol. 2, pp. 47–61.
4.   Johnson *et al.*, p. vi.
5.   For a more detailed treatment, see MacGregor, *The Soviet–East German Military Alliance*, pp. 31–39.
6.   See Rice, *The Soviet Union and the Czechoslovak Army*, p. 43.
7.   Daniel N. Nelson, 'Political Dynamics and the Bulgarian Military', in Jeffrey Simon, ed., *European Security Policy after the Revolutions of 1989* (Washington: National Defense University Press, 1991), p. 484.
8.   Alex Alexiev, 'The Romanian Army', in Adelman, ed., p. 136.
9.   Andrzej Korbonski, 'Poland', in Rakowska-Harmstone, ed., *Communism in Eastern Europe*, p. 53.
10.   Harry Slapnicka, *Schwejk im Wandel* (Wien: Herold, 1970), pp. 57–58.
11.   J. Lolland, ed., *Zu Befehl Genosse Unterleutenant: Authentischeberichte aus den Alltag der Nationalen Volksarmee* (Stuttgart: Seewald, 1971), pp. 25–26.
12.   M. Monin, 'Internatsionalizm v Deistvi', *Voenno- Istoricheski Zhurnal*, 6 (1967), p. 12.
13.   Johnson *et al.*, p. 134.
14.   Adelman, 'Toward a Typology . . . ', in Adelman ed., p. 8.
15.   See Johnson *et al.*, p. 24; Alexiev, 'The Romanian Army', p. 154.
16.   For an excellent account of the Soviet withdrawal from Romania, see Verona's *Military Occupation and Diplomacy, op. cit.*
17.   Some sources suggest the possibility of a limited and covert Soviet military presence in southern Bulgaria, near the Turkish border. See Volgyes, *The Political Reliability*, p. 30; and Ashley, 'Bulgaria', p. 118.
18.   See, for instance, Michael Sadykiewicz and Louisa Vinton, 'Politicization in the Polish Military', *Report on Eastern Europe*, March 30, 1990, p. 30.
19.   See, for instance, J. Hacker *et al.*, *Die Nationale Volksarmee der DDR im Rahmen des Warschauer Paktes* (Munich: Bernard and Grafe, 1980), pp. 221–223.
20.   Dale R. Herspring, 'Civil–Military Relations in Poland and East Germany: The External Factor', *Studies in Comparative Communism*, Vol. 11, No. 3 (Autumn 1978), pp. 230–231.
21.   See Eyal, 'Romania: Between Loyalty and Nationalism', in Eyal, ed., p. 101.

22. For an excellent examination of the Czechoslovak case, see Jiri Valenta and Condoleezza Rice, 'The Czechoslovak Army', in Adelman, ed., pp. 134–137.

23. One of the best accounts of this development is Dale R. Herspring's *East German Civil–Military Relations* (New York: Praeger, 1973).

24. For some studies that reach this conclusion, see Johnson *et al.*, *East European Military Establishments*; Volgyes, *The Political Reliability*; and J. Hacker, *Die Nationale Volksarmee*.

25. For an excellent comparative study, see Dale R. Herspring, 'Technology and Civil–Military Relations: The Polish and East German Cases', in Herspring and Volgyes eds, pp. 123–144.

26. A. Vogel, 'Die Verantwortung der Grundorganisationen erhoehen – ein wichtiges Anliegen unserer Parteiarbeit', *Militarwesen*, August 1974, p. 101b; cited in Johnson *et al.*, p. 98.

27. I. I. Yakubovskiy, ed., *Boevoe sodruzhestvo bratskikh narodov i armii* (Moscow: Voenizdat, 1975), cited by Johnson *et al.*, p. 161.

28. See Johnson *et al.*, p. 146.

29. Arpad Abonyi, 'Czechoslovakia', in Rakowska-Harmstone *et al.*, *Warsaw Pact*, Phase 1, p. 108.

30. *The Military Balance, 1989–90* (London: IISS, 1989), pp. 45–51.

31. *Ibid.*, pp. 56–82.

32. Volgyes, 'Military Politics of the Warsaw Pact Armies', p.198.

33. See Jan B. de Weydenthal, 'Martial Law and the Reliability of the Polish Military', in Nelson, ed., *Soviet Allies*, p. 237; and Rakowska-Harmstone, "Poland", p. 153.

34. *Die NVA* (Bonn: Ministry of National Defense, 1978), pp. 99–100, cited by Johnson *et al.*, p. 103.

35. Henry Krisch, 'German Democratic Republic', in Nelson, ed., *Soviet Allies*, p. 170.

36. Ashley, 'Bulgaria', p. 151 and Eyal, 'Romania', p. 101.

37. Sadykiewicz and Vinton, 'Politicization of the Polish Military', p. 30.

38. This is a 1977 figure, cited by Christopher D. Jones, 'The Czechoslovak Armed Forces', in Jeffrey Simon ed., *NATO–Warsaw Pact Force Mobilization* (Washington, DC: National Defense University Press, 1988), p. 229.

39. This discussion draws on my 'Non-Soviet Warsaw Pact Forces in Domestic Context'.

40. See MacGregor, *The Soviet–East German Military Alliance*, pp. 32–33.

41. A. Ross Johnson, *Soviet–East European Military Relations: An Overview*, unpublished, January 1975, p. 46, cited by Ivan Volgyes, 'Military Politics of the Warsaw Pact Armies', p. 200.

42. For an excellent account of the Memorandum, see Rice, *The Soviet Union and the Czechoslovak Army*, pp. 133–138.

43. Johnson *et al.*, pp. 147–149.

44. Two excellent discussions of the Polish military's role in these crises are Ross Johnson's contribution to Johnson *et al.*, pp. 57–63; and

Robin Alison Remington's 'Polish Soldiers in Politics: The Party in Uniform?' in Constantine P. Danopoulos, ed., *The Decline of Military Regimes: The Civilian Influence* (Boulder: Westview Press, 1988), pp. 75–103.

45. See M. K. Dziewanowski, *The Communist Party of Poland* (Cambridge: Harvard University Press, 1976), p. 265.

46. Johnson *et al.*, p. 60.

47. See, for instance, Korbonski, 'The Polish Army', p. 117.

48. See Ryszard Jerzy Kuklinski, 'Wojna z Narodem Widziana od Srodka', *Kultura* (Paris), April 1987, p. 12; and Jerzy J. Wiatr, *The Soldier and the Nation*, pp. 118–119. During the riots 44 people were killed and 1,164 wounded.

49. See Wiatr, *The Soldier and the Nation*, pp. 119–120.

50. These words are attributed to Defense Minister Jaruzelski. Cited by Andrzej Korbonski, 'The Polish Army', p. 118.

51. Andrzej Korbonski and Sarah M. Terry, 'The Military as a Political Actor in Poland', in Kolkowicz and Korbonski, eds, *Soldiers, Peasants, and Bureaucrats*, p. 172.

52. For an excellent analysis of Polish Party–army relations in 1980–81, see Andrzej Korbonski's 'The Dilemmas of Civil–Military Relations in Contemporary Poland', *Armed Forces and Society*, Vol. 8, No. 1 (1981).

53. de Weydenthal, 'Martial Law . . . ', p. 227.

54. See Dale R. Herspring, 'The Soviets, the Warsaw Pact, and the East European Militaries', in Griffith, ed., *Central and Eastern Europe*, p. 142.

55. This phenomenon is particularly observable in Poland where the army's popularity remained consistently high, even during the Solidarity crisis of 1980–81. See Wiatr, *The Soldier and the Nation*, pp. 151–152.

56. Volgyes, *The Political Reliability*, p. 33.

57. For discussions of the 1965 coup attempt, see J. F. Brown, *Bulgaria Under Communist Rule* (New York: Praeger, 1970), pp. 173–181; the contribution of W. Oschlies in Peter Gosztony, *Zur Geschichte der Europaeischen Volksarmeen*, pp. 227–228; and J. L. Kerr, 'Dissidence in Bulgaria', RAD Background Report/156, *RFER*, July 10, 1978, pp. 1–2.

58. See, for instance, Valenta and Rice, 'The Czechoslovak Army', in Adelman, pp. 140–141; and Robin Remington.

59. See her introduction to Wiatr, *The Soldier and the Nation*, pp. xiii–xiv.

60. *The Daily Telegraph* (London), December 15, 1987. It is worth mentioning that this was the third time in 15 years that reports of an attempted coup surfaced. There is little hard evidence to substantiate these stories, however.

61. Michael Shafir, 'New Revelations of the Military's Role in Ceaușescu's Ouster', *Report on Eastern Europe*, May 11, 1990, pp. 24–27.

62. Johnson *et al.*, p. 106. See also Herspring, *East German Civil–Military*

Relations, pp. 98–101.

63. Wiatr, *The Soldier and the Nation*, p. 117.
64. The post-invasion purification of the CSPA was completed only sometime in 1975. See Rice, *The Soviet Union and the Czechoslovak Army*, pp. 188–189.
65. Alexiev and Johnson, *East European Military Reliability*, p. 15.
66. See Volgyes, *The Political Reliability*, p. 37.
67. Herspring, 'Civil–Military Relations in Poland and East Germany, p. 233.
68. See, Crane, *Military Spending in Eastern Europe.*
69. Bulgaria seems to be a special case in the southern tier as its defense spending hovered around 6 percent of its GDP, substantially more than the 3.5–4 percent figure in Hungary and Romania. See Condoleezza Rice, 'Defense Burden-Sharing', in Holloway and Sharp, eds, *The Warsaw Pact*, pp. 59–86; and Crane, *Military Spending in Eastern Europe.*
70. See, for instance, BTA (Bulgarian News Service), February 14, 1990; *The Times* (London), June 10, 1986; and Daniel N. Nelson, 'Watching the Pact Unravel: The Transformation of East European Political-Military Policies', *Berichte des Bundesinstituts*, 32/1990, pp. 6–8.
71. For a general treatment, see Douglas Clarke, 'The Warsaw Pact's Soldier-Farmers and Soldier-Builders', *Report on the USSR*, September 22, 1989, pp. 1–5. For more specific accounts, see for instance, Henry Dodds, "Perestroika in the Polish Army', *Jane's Soviet Intelligence Review*, July 1989; Jonathan Eyal, 'Romania: Looking for Weapons of Mass Destruction?' *ibid.*, August, 1989; and John Salford, *The Sword and the Ploughshare: Autonomous Peace Initiatives in East Germany* (London: Merlin Press, 1983).
72. Karen Dawisha, *Eastern Europe, Gorbachev and Reform: The Great Challenge* (New York: Cambridge University Press, 1988), p. 172.
73. John Jaworsky, 'Bulgaria', in Rakowska-Harmstone *et al.*, *The Warsaw Pact*, Phase II, Vol. 3, p. 309. For Bulgaria and Romania, countries with large and dissatisfied ethnic minorities, the utilization of the military as a labor pool was especially advantageous because ethnic youths – whom the regime was reluctant to equip with weapons – could become low-paid laborers.
74. The number of candidates to the most prestigious Polish institution, the Air Force Academy, declined from 100 percent in 1967, to 94 in 1968, 87 in 1969, and 47 in 1970. See, Johnson *et al.*, p. 59.
75. Of 28 professions listed, that of military officers was ranked by the respondents 25th. See, Jaroslav Krejci, *Social Change and Stratification in Postwar Czechoslovakia* (London: Macmillan, 1972), p. 99.
76. Johnson *et al.*, p. 161.
77. See, for instance, S.A.W., 'Army Officers, Big Brother Wants You', Czechoslovak SR/3, *RFER*, February 15, 1984. pp. 13–22.
78. See Wiatr, *The Soldier and the Nation*, pp. 131–142.

79. I am indebted to Professor Robin Remington for this point.
80. Jan Obrman, 'Changing Conditions for the Army and the Police', *Report on Eastern Europe*, January 26, 1990, p. 14.
81. Ceteka (Czechoslovak News Service) in English, November 6, 1990.
82. *The Times* (London), November 24, 1989.
83. Ceteka, November 6, 1990.
84. Barany, 'Non-Soviet Warsaw Pact Forces', p. 1.
85. Joseph S. Gordon, 'The GDR: From Volksarmee to Bundeswehr', in Simon, ed., *European Security Policy*, p. 161. See also the interview with Hans Modrow, the SED Secretary of the city of Dresden during the demonstrations, who reportedly called in the army in *Der Spiegel*, 7/1990 (February 12), pp. 98–100.
86. Cited by Gordon, *ibid.*
87. See Daniel N. Nelson, 'WTO Mobilization Potential: A Bulgarian Case Study', *Defense Analysis*, Vol. 5, No. 1 (1989), pp. 31–44, and 'The Bulgarian People's Army', in Jeffrey Simon, ed., *NATO-Warsaw Pact Force Mobilization*, pp. 449–478.
88. Nelson, 'Political Dynamics', p. 498.
89. *Adevarul* (Bucharest), January 15, 1990, quoted by Radio Bucharest, January 15, 1990, 4:40 p.m.
90. See the interview with Brucan in *Le Monde* (Paris), December 29, 1989.
91. Michael Shafir, 'The Revolution: An Initial Assessment', *Report on Eastern Europe*, January 26, 1990, p. 40.
92. See *La Repubblica*, January 2, 1990, translated in *FBIS-EEU*, January 5, 1990, p. 64; and *Nepszabadsag*, January 9, 1990.
93. See Ivan Scipiades, 'Vissza a starthoz', *Vilag*, March 1, 1990; and Radio Warsaw, August 8, 1990, 8:05 a.m.
94. For a comprehensive account, see Sadykiewicz and Vinton, 'Politicization and the Polish Army', pp. 31–35.
95. *Ibid.*, p. 32.
96. *Gazeta Wyborcza*, February 21, 1990.
97. See for instance *Polska Zbrojna*, December 11, 1990. This, incidentally, is army's 'new' daily that appeared first in October 1990, replacing the previous army daily *Zolnierz Rzeczypospolitej*. Actually, *Polska Zbrojna* was the Polish Army's popular daily in 1920–39.
98. Reuter (East Berlin), November 16, 1989.
99. See Jan Obrman, 'Changing Conditions for the Army and the Party', *Report on Eastern Europe*, January 26, 1990, pp. 12–15.
100. Jan Obrman, 'Changes in the Armed Forces', *Report in Eastern Europe*, April 6, 1990, p. 10.
101. AP dispatch, March 14, 1990. For an extensive analysis, see Thomas S. Szayna, 'The Military in a Postcommunist Czechoslovakia', Rand Note N-3412–USDP (Santa Monica, CA: Rand, 1992), pp. 28–32.
102. See Paul Gafton, 'Armed Forces Seek to Democratize', *Report on Eastern Europe*, April 6, 1990, pp. 37–41.

103. See Walter M. Bacon, Jr., 'Security as Seen from Bucharest', Occasional Paper No. 9111, Center for International Studies, University of Missouri-St. Louis, December 1991; and Reuter and AP dispatches (Timisoara), March 3, 1990.

104. Radio Bucharest, April 18, 1990, 7:30 p.m.

105. See Price, *op. cit*, p. 32.

106. Vladimir Socor, 'Forces of Old Resurface in Romania: The Ethnic Clashes in Tirgu-Mures', *Report on Eastern Europe*, April 13, 1990, p. 40.

107. Nelson, 'Watching the Pact Unravel', p. 19.

108. See, for instance, Radio Sofia, January 26, 1990, 7:30 p.m.

109. Duncan M. Perry, 'A New Military Lobby', *Report on Eastern Europe*, October 5, 1990, p. 2.

110. Nelson, 'Political Dynamics', pp. 29–31.

111. See Jan B. de Weydenthal, 'Poland and the Soviet Alliance System', in *Report on Eastern Europe*, June 29, 1990, p. 31; and Jan Obrman, 'Changes in the Armed Forces', p. 10.

112. See for instance, Price, 'The Romanian Armed Forces', p. 29.

113. See *Magyar Hirlap* and *Nepszabadsag*, June 7 and 8, 1990.

114. Nelson, 'Political Dynamics', pp. 38–39; and *Nepszabadsag*, June 8, 1990.

115. Reuter/AP dispatch (Warsaw), September 8, 1990.

116. PAP (Polish news service, in English), September 20, 1990. See also *Gazeta Wyborcza* of the same date.

117. Reuter dispatch (Paris), November 20, 1990.

118. NCA/Reuter dispatch, Sofia, November 14, 1990.

119. Radio Sofia, October 1, 1990, 6:30 p.m.

120. *Nepszabadsag*, October 24, 1990.

121. *Unita*, November 6, 1990.

122. Romania, of course, has had its own doctrine from the mid-1960s. For discussions of the new doctrines in Eastern Europe, see Michael Sadykiewicz and Douglas L. Clarke, 'The New Polish Defense Doctrine: A Further Step Forward', *Report on Eastern Europe*, May 4, 1990, pp. 20–24; Nelson, 'Watching the Pact Unravel', pp. 20, 26–35; Dobri Dzhurov, 'European Military Balance: Warsaw Treaty Organisation', *World Marxist Review*, Vol. 31, No. 4 (April 1989), pp. 20–23; PAP (Polish news service), December 16, 1990; and *Frankfurter Allgemeine Zeitung*, February 27, 1990.

123. A great deal of information is available regarding the details of the negotiations and the problems Soviet troop withdrawals from Eastern Europe entail, that are very similar to those discussed in Chapter 5 in the Hungarian context. (The last NSWP state to decide to request the withdrawal of the Soviet military was Poland. See the UPI dispatch [Warsaw], September 7, 1990.) For some useful accounts, see *The International Herald Tribune*, July 25, 1990; Jiri Pehe, 'The Ecological Damage Caused by the Soviet Troops', *Report*

on Eastern Europe, August 3, 1990, pp. 28– 32; Marc Fisher's piece in *The Washington Post*, September 11, 1990; Ian Johnson in *The Baltimore Sun*, December 2, 1990; and *The New York Times*, December 17, 1990.

Conclusion

1. Marton Vargha, 'Pacifista katonai doktrina', *Beszelo*, July 14, 1990. p. 25. See also, 'A hadsereg a demokratikus tarsadalomban', *op. cit.*, pp. 18–25.
2. For a more detailed discussion of this point, see Ivan Volgyes, 'Military Security in the Post-Communist Age: Reflections on Myths and Realities', *Studies in Comparative Communism*, Vol. 25, No. 1 (March 1992), pp. 89–95.
3. For a brief summary of Budapest's new security concerns, see Alfred A. Reisch, 'Foreign Policy Reorientation a Success', *Report on Eastern Europe*, Vol. 2, No. 51/52 (December 20, 1991), pp. 15–16.
4. See Tokes, 'From Visegrad to Krakow', *op. cit.*, pp. 104–109.
5. For discussions on theoretical constructs, see for instance, Sir Karl R. Popper, *The Logic of Scientific Discovery* (New York: Basic Books, 1959). For definitions of 'models' in the social sciences, see Bill and Hardgrave, *Comparative Politics*, *op. cit.*, pp. 27–29.
6. Again, the question, whether these 'models' are worthy of the name raises serious doubts. The answer, of course, depends on the definition one uses. I prefer Kenneth Waltz's definition and by his standards the models herein discussed would fail. See his 'Laws and Theories', in Robert O. Keohane, ed., *Neorealism and Its Critics* (New York: Columbia University Press, 1986), pp. 27–47, especially pp. 34–38. The same conclusion is reached if one uses the definitions of Bill and Hardgrave, *Comparative Politics*, *op. cit.*, pp. 27–29.
7. Albright, 'Civil–Military Relations: Developmental Contingencies', p. 295.
8. For a detailed examination of the region's post-revolution civil–military relations, see my 'East European Armies in the Transitions and Beyond', *op. cit.*

Select Bibliography

For the sake of brevity, no publications were included that are issued on a daily or weekly basis. Therefore, Radio Free Europe Research publications, while extensively used, are not incorporated into this bibliography. All sources can, of course, be found in the Notes.

Adelman, Jonathan R., ed., *Communist Armies in Politics* (Boulder, CO: Westview Press, 1982).

Adelman, Jonathan R., ed., 'Toward a Typology of Communist Civil–Military Relations, in Adelman, ed., *Communist Armies in Politics*, pp. 1–15.

Albright, David E., 'Civil–Military Relations: Developmental Contingencies', *Studies in Comparative Communism*, Vol. 11, No. 3 (Autumn 1978), pp. 292–309.

Albright, David E., 'A Comparative Conceptualization of Civil–Military Relations', *World Politics*, Vol. 32, No. 4 (July 1980), pp. 553–576.

Alexiev, Alexander, 'Party–Military Relations in Eastern Europe: The Case of Romania', in Kolkowicz and Korbonski, eds, *Soldiers, Peasants, and Bureaucrats*, pp. 199–231.

Alexiev, Alexander, 'The Romanian Army', in Adelman, ed., *Communist Armies in Politics*, pp. 149–166.

Alexiev, Alexander, and A. Ross Johnson, *East European Military Reliability: An Emigré-Based Assessment* (Santa Monica, CA: RAND, 1986).

Andorka, Rudolf, 'Alkoholfogyasztas: mertekek es vegletek', *Tarsadalmi Szemle*, Vol. 43, No. 11 (November 1988), pp. 87–96.

Arcidacono, Bruno, 'Az angolszasz hatalmak es a szovjet biztonsagi ovezet', *Valosag*, Vol. 33, No. 3 (March 1990), pp. 32–39.

Arendt, Hannah, *The Origins of Totalitarianism* (London: Allen & Unwin, 1951).

Ashley, Stephen, 'Bulgaria: Between Loyalty and Nationalism', in Eyal, ed., *The Warsaw Pact and the Balkans*, pp. 109–154.

Aspin, Les, 'How to Look at the Soviet-American Balance', *Foreign Policy*, No. 22 (Spring 1976), pp. 96–107.

Balogh, Sandor, 'Politikai reformprobalkozasok es kudarcaik 1953 es 1956 kozott', *Tarsadalmi Szemle*, Vol. 44, No. 8–9 (August–September 1989), pp. 19–35.

Bacon, Walter M. Jr., 'The Military and the Party in Romania', in Herspring and Volgyes, eds, *Civil–Military Relations in Communist Systems*, pp. 165–181.

Ban, Antal, 'Hungary', in Healey, ed., *The Curtain Falls*, pp. 61–83.

Barany, Zoltan D., 'Military Higher Education in Hungary', *Armed Forces and Society*, Vol. 15, No. 3 (Spring 1989), pp. 371–388.

Barany, Zoltan D., 'The Bankruptcy of Hungarian Socialism', *Sudost-Europa*, Vol. 38, No. 4 (1989), pp. 191–212.

Barany, Zoltan D., 'Political Participation and the Notion of Reform', *East Central Europe*, Vol. 16, Nos. 1–2 (Summer 1989), 107–122.

Barany, Zoltan D., 'On the Road to Democracy: The Hungarian Elections of 1990', *Sudost-Europa*, Vol. 39, No. 5 (1990), 318–329.

Barany, Zoltan D., 'Elections in Hungary', in Robert K. Furtak, ed., *Elections in Socialist States* (New York: Harvester-Wheatsheaf, 1990), pp. 71–97.

Barany, Zoltan D., 'Civil–Military Relations in Communist Systems: Western Models Revisited', *Journal of Political and Military Sociology*, Vol. 19, No. 1 (Summer 1991), pp. 75–99.

Barany, Zoltan D., 'Soviet Control of the Hungarian Military under Stalin', *Journal of Strategic Studies*, Vol. 14, No. 2 (June 1991), pp. 148–164.

Barany, Zoltan D., 'East European Armies in the Revolutions and Beyond', *East European Quarterly*, Vol. 26, No. 1 (March 1992), pp. 1–31.

Barany, Zoltan D., and Ivan Sylvain, 'Hungary', in Rakowska-Harmstone, *et al.*, *Warsaw Pact: The Question of Cohesion*, Phase II, Vol. 3 (1986), pp. 404–468.

Beck, Carl and Karen Eide Rawling, 'The Military as a Channel of Entry into Positions of Political Leadership in Communist Party States', *Armed Forces and Society*, Vol. 3, No. 2 (February 1977), pp. 199–218.

Bell, John D., *The Bulgarian Communist Party from Blabdev to Zhivkov* (Stanford, CA: Hoover Institution Press, 1986).

Berecz, Janos, *Ellenforradalom tollal es fegyverrel, 1956* (Budapest: Kossuth, 1986).

Berend, Ivan T., *Gazdasagi utkereses 1956–65* (Budapest: Magveto, 1983).

Berend, Ivan T., 'A reform sorsforduloja az 1970–es evekben', *Valosag*, Vol. 31, No. 1 (January 1988), 1–26.

Berend, Ivan T., *The Hungarian Economic Reforms, 1953–88* (New York: Cambridge University Press, 1990).

Berki, Mihaly, *Hadsereg vezetes nelkul, 1956* (Budapest: Magyar Media, 1989).

Bertha, Bulcsu, *Irok, szineszek, bortonok* (Budapest: Uj Ido, 1990).

Bill, James A. and Robert L. Hardgrave, Jr., *Comparative Politics: The Quest for Theory* (Washington: University Press of America, 1981).

Blaskovits, Janos, and Gyorgy Kiss, *Gondolatok az elso negyedszazadrol* (Budapest: Gondolat, 1970).

Bokor, Imre, *Kiskiralyok munderban* (Budapest: Uj Ido, 1989).

Braun, Aurel, 'Eastern Europe, the Warsaw Pact, and NATO: The Impact of Changes on the Military Balance', in Nicholas N. Kittrie and Ivan Volgyes, eds, *The Uncertain Future: Gorbachev's Eastern Bloc* (New York: Paragon House, 1988), pp. 155–202.

Brown, J. F., *Bulgaria Under Communist Rule* (New York: Praeger, 1970).

Brzezinski, Zbigniew K., *Political Controls in the Soviet Army* (New York: Research Program on the USSR, 1954).

Brzezinski, Zbigniew K., *The Soviet Bloc: Unity and Conflict* (Cambridge,

MA: Harvard University Press, 1967).

Brzezinski, Zbigniew K., 'The Crisis of Communism: The Paradox of Political Participation', *The Washington Quarterly*, Vol. 10, No. 4 (August 1987).

Caravelli, John M., 'Soviet and Joint Warsaw Pact Exercises', *Armed Forces and Society*, Vol. 9, No. 3 (Spring 1983), pp. 402–421.

Colton, Timothy J., 'The Zhukov Affair Reconsidered', *Soviet Studies* Vol. 29 (April 1977), pp. 185–213.

Colton, Timothy J., 'The Party–Military Connection: A Participatory Model', in Herspring and Volgyes, eds, *Civil–Military Relations in Communist Systems*, pp. 53–79.

Colton, Timothy J., 'Civil–Military Relations in the Soviet Union: The Developmental Perspective', *Studies in Comparative Communism*, Vol. 11, No. 3 (Autumn 1978), pp. 213–224.

Colton, Timothy J., *Commissars, Commanders, and Civilian Authority: The Structure of Soviet Military Politics* (Cambridge, MA: Harvard University Press, 1979).

Crane, Keith, *Military Spending in Eastern Europe* (Santa Monica, CA: RAND, 1987).

Csabay, Jozsef, 'A magyar hadiiparrol, penzugyi szemmel', *Penzugyi Szemle*, No. 1, 1990, pp. 79–83.

Dawisha, Karen, *Eastern Europe, Gorbachev and Reform* (New York: Cambridge University Press, 1988).

de Sola Pool, Ithiel, *Satellite Generals* (Stanford, CA: Stanford University Press, 1955).

de Weydenthal, Jan B., 'Martial Law and the Reliability of the Polish Military', in Nelson, ed., *Soviet Allies*, pp. 225–250.

Deak, Istvan, *Beyond Nationalism: A Social and Political History of the Habsburg Officer Corps* (New York: Oxford University Press, 1990).

Deak, Peter, 'A katonapolitikai helyzet alakulasa a masodik vilaghaboru utan', *Kulpolitika*, Vol. 14, No. 5 (1987).

Deane, Michael J., *Political Control of the Soviet Armed Forces* (London: Macdonald and Jane's, 1977).

Dombrady, Lorand, 'A hadsereg torekvesei a szinhazi cenzura bevezetesere a harmincas evek elso feleben', *Valosag*, Vol. 31, No. 1 (January 1988), pp. 52–65.

Dombrady, Lorand, and Gabor Nagy, eds, *Fegyverrel a hazaert: Magyar ellenallasi es partizanharcok a masodik vilaghaboru idejen* (Budapest: Zrinyi, 1980).

Dombrady, Lorand, and Sandor Toth, *A Magyar Kiralyi Honvedseg* (Budapest: Zrinyi, 1987).

Donath, Ferenc, *Reform es forradalom: A magyar mezogazdasag strukturalis atalakulasa 1945–75* (Budapest: Akademiai, 1977).

Dondo, Rezso, *Honvedelmi neveles* (Budapest: Tankonyvkiado, 1977).

Dye, Thomas R., and Harmon Ziegler, 'Socialism and Militarism', *PS: Political Science and Politics*, Vol. 22, No. 4 (December 1990), pp. 800–813.

Dzhurov, Dobri, 'European Military Balance: Warsaw Treaty Organisation', *World Marxist Review*, Vol. 31, No. 4 (April 1989), pp. 20–23.

Dziewanowski, M. K., *The Communist Party of Poland* (Cambridge, MA: Harvard University Press, 1976).

Easton, David, *A Framework for Political Analysis* (Englewood Cliffs, NJ: Prentice-Hall, 1965).

Efimov, P. I. *et al.*, eds, *Boevoi soiuz bratskikh armii* (Moscow: Voenizdat, 1974).

Eyal, Jonathan, ed., *The Warsaw Pact and the Balkans: Moscow's Southern Flank* (London: Macmillan, 1989).

Eyal, Jonathan, 'Romania: Between Appearances and Realities', in Eyal, ed., *The Warsaw Pact and the Balkans*, pp. 67–108.

Farago, Jeno, ed., *Mr. Kadar* (Budapest: Hirlapkiado, 1989).

Farkas, Mihaly, *A beke arcvonalan* (Budapest: Szikra, 1949).

Felkai, Denes, 'A Magyar Nephadsereg egeszsegugyi szolgalatanak kiepiteserol', *Hadtorteneti Szemle*, No. 1 (1984).

Felkay, Andrew, *Hungary and the USSR, 1956–88: Kadar's Political Leadership* (Westport, CT: Greenwood Press, 1989).

Fenyes Toth, Olga, *Nok a szovjet bortoneben* (Munich: Mikes Kelemen Kor, 1959).

Ferge, Zsuzsa, *Fejezetek a magyar szegenypolitika tortenetebol* (Budapest: Magveto, 1986).

Finer, S. E., *The Man on Horseback: The Role of the Military in Politics* (New York: Praeger, 1962).

Finer, S. E., 'The Morphology of Military Regimes', in Kolkowicz and Korbonski, eds, *Soldiers, Peasants, and Bureaucrats*, pp. 281–309.

Fodor, Neil, *The Warsaw Treaty Organization: A Political and Organizational Analysis* (New York: St. Martin's Press, 1990).

Foldes, Laszlo, *A masodik vonalban* (Budapest: Kossuth, 1984).

Friedrich, Carl and Zbigniew Brzezinski, *Totalitarian Dictatorship and Autocracy* (Cambridge, MA: Harvard University Press, 1956).

Garthoff, Raymond L., *Soviet Military Policy: An Historical Analysis* (New York: Praeger, 1966).

Gati, Charles, ed., *The International Politics of Eastern Europe* (New York: Praeger, 1976).

Gati, Charles, *Hungary and the Soviet Bloc* (Durham, NC: Duke University Press, 1986).

Gati, Charles, 'Gorbachev and Eastern Europe', *Foreign Affairs*, Vol. 65, No. 5 (Summer 1987).

Gati, Charles, 'Reforming Communist Systems: Lessons from the Hungarian Experience', in Griffith, ed., *Central and Eastern Europe*, pp. 218–240.

Gati, Charles, *The Bloc that Failed* (Bloomington, IN: Indiana University Press, 1990).

Godo, Agnes, and Bela Sztana, *A Horthy-rendszer katonai ideologiaja* (Budapest: Zrinyi, 1965).

Goldhamer, Herbert, *The Soviet Soldier* (New York: Crane Russak, 1975).

Gordon, Joseph S., 'The GDR: From Volksarmee to Bundeswehr?' in Simon, ed., *European Security Policy*, pp. 157–188.

Gosztony, Peter, 'Die ungarische antifaschistische Bewegung in der Sowjetunion wahrend des Zweites Weltkrieges', *Militargeschichtliche Mitteilungen*, Vol. 9 (1972), pp. 87–102.

Gosztony, Peter, 'Die Ungarische Volksarmee', in Peter Gosztony, ed., *Zur Geschichte der europaeischen Volksarmeen* (Bonn–Bad Godesberg: Hochwacht, 1976).

Gosztony, Peter, ed., *Paramilitarische Organisationen in Sowjet-block* (Bonn: Hochwacht, 1977).

Gosztonyi, Peter, *Legiveszely Budapest!* (Budapest: Nepszava, 1989).

Gosztonyi, Peter, *Foltamadott a tenger . . . 1956* (Budapest: Nepszava, 1989).

Gosztonyi, Peter, *Haboru van, haboru!* (Budapest: Nepszava, 1989).

Griffith, William E., ed., *Central and Eastern Europe: The Opening Curtain?* (Boulder, CO: Westview Press, 1989).

Gyarmati, Istvan, 'Egy lehetseges magyar honvedelmi koncepcio vazlata', *Tarsadalmi Szemle*, Vol. 45, No. 3 (March 1990), pp. 46–52.

Gyarmati, Istvan, 'A hadsereg a demokratikus tarsadalomban', *Valosag*, Vol. 33, No. 4 (April 1990), pp. 18–25.

Gyorgyi, Bela, 'A parttagok politikai aktivitasa a nephadseregben', *Partelet*, Vol. 31, No. 12 (December 1986), pp. 81–86.

Habony, Janos, *A beilleszkedes es a bunozes* (Budapest: Zrinyi, 1986).

Hacker, J. *et al.*, *Die Nationale Volksarmee der DDR im Rahmen des Warshauer Paktes* (Munich: Bernard and Grafe, 1980).

Hajdu, Tibor, 'A tisztikar tarsadalmi helyzete – 1848–1918', *Valosag*, Vol. 30, No. 4 (April 1987), pp. 65–80.

Hammond, Thomas T., ed., *The Anatomy of Communist Takeovers* (New Haven, CT: Yale University Press, 1975).

Hamori, Csaba, 'Akie az ifjusag, aze a jovo', *Partelet*, Vol. 33, No. 6 (June 1988), pp. 3–11.

Harkai, Peter, 'A Magyar Nephadsereg kadereinek kulfoldi katonai kikepzese', *Honvedsegi Szemle*, Vol. 43, No. 1 (January 1989), pp. 24–27.

A haza szolgalataban (Budapest: Zrinyi, 1985).

Healey, Denis, ed., *The Curtain Falls: The Story of Socialist Eastern Europe* (London: Lincolns-Praeger, 1951).

Herspring, Dale R., *East German Civil–Military Relations* (New York: Praeger, 1973).

Herspring, Dale R., 'Civil–Military Relations in Poland and East Germany: The External Factor', *Studies in Comparative Communism*, Vol. 11, No. 3 (Autumn 1978), pp. 225–236.

Herspring, Dale R., and Ivan Volgyes, eds, *Civil–Military Relations in Communist Systems* (Boulder, CO: Westview Press, 1978).

Herspring, Dale R., 'The Soviets and the Warsaw Pact', in Griffith, ed., *Central and Eastern Europe*, pp. 130–155.

Herspring, Dale R., and Ivan Volgyes, 'The Military as an Agent of Political Socialization in Eastern Europe', *Armed Forces and Society*, Vol. 3, No. 2 (Winter 1977), pp. 249–269.

Herspring, Dale R., and Ivan Volgyes, 'Political Reliability in the East European Warsaw Pact Armies', *Armed Forces and Society*, Winter 1980.

Holloway, David, and Jane M. O. Sharp, eds, *The Warsaw Pact: Alliance in Transition?* (London: Macmillan, 1984).

A honvedelmi neveles modszertani kerdesei (Budapest: Zrinyi, 1980).

Horn, Gyula, 'Magyarorszag es az europai egyuttmukodes', *Kulpolitika*, Vol. 16, No. 1 (1989), pp. 3–11.

Horthy, Admiral Nicholas, *Memoirs* (New York: Robert Speller and Sons, 1957).

Huntington, Samuel P., *The Soldier and the State: The Theory and Politics of Civil–Military Relations* (Cambridge, MA: Harvard University Press, 1957).

Huntington, Samuel P., *Changing Patterns in Military Politics* (New York: Free Press, 1962).

Huntington, Samuel P., *Political Order in Changing Societies* (New Haven, CT: Yale University Press, 1968).

Huszti, Erno, *Antiinflacios utkereses – monetaris politika es gyakorlat Magyarorszagon* (Budapest: Kozgazdasagi es Jogi, 1987).

Hutchings, Robert L., *Soviet–East European Relations: Consolidation and Conflict, 1968–80* (Madison, WI: University of Wisconsin Press, 1983).

Ignotus, Paul, 'The First Two Communist Takeovers of Hungary: 1919 and 1948', in Hammond, ed., *The Anatomy of Communist Takeovers*.

Iszlai, Zoltan, *Emberek angyalborben* (Budapest: Zrinyi, 1985).

Ivan, Dezso, 'A Magyar Nephadsereg legiereje 1956 oktobereben-novembereben', *Hadtorteneti Kozlemenyek*, Vol. 102 (April–June 1989), pp. 208–222.

Janowitz, Morris, *The Military in the Political Development of New Nations* (Chicago: University of Chicago Press, 1964).

Jaworski, John, 'Bulgaria', in Rakowska-Harmstone *et al.*, *Warsaw Pact*, Phase II, Vol. 3 (1986), pp. 291–340.

Johnson, A. Ross, 'Has Eastern Europe Become a Liability to the Soviet Union? (II) Military Issues', in Charles Gati, ed., *The International Politics of Eastern Europe* (New York: Praeger, 1976), pp. 37–58.

Johnson, A. Ross, Robert W. Dean, and Alexander Alexiev, *East European Military Establishments: The Warsaw Pact Northern Tier* (Santa Monica, CA: Rand, 1980).

Johnson, A. Ross, 'The Soviet-East European Military Connection: An Overview', in Herspring and Volgyes, eds, *Civil–Military Relations in Communist Systems*, pp. 243–266.

Johnson, A. Ross, 'The Warsaw Pact: Soviet Military Policy in Eastern Europe', in Terry, ed., *Soviet Policy in Eastern Europe*, pp. 255–284.

Jones, Christopher D., *Soviet Influence in Eastern Europe: Political Autonomy and the Warsaw Pact* (New York: Praeger, 1981).

Jones, Christopher D., 'National Armies and National Sovereignty', in Holloway and Sharp, *The Warsaw Pact*, pp. 85–110.

Jones, Christopher D., 'The USSR, the Warsaw Pact and NATO', in Ingmar Oldberg, ed., *Unity and Conflict in the Warsaw Pact* (Stockholm: The Swedish National Defence Research Institute, 1984).

Jones, Christopher D., 'The Czechoslovak Armed Forces', in Simon, ed., *NATO–Warsaw Pact Force Mobilization*, pp. 205–244.

Juhasz, Gyula, 'Ut a parizsi bekehez', *Tarsadalmi Szemle*, Vol. 44, Nos. 8–9 (August–September 1989), pp. 13–18.

Judt, Tony R., 'The Dilemmas of Dissidence: The Political Opposition in East-Central Europe', *East European Politics and Society*, Spring 1988, pp. 185–241.

Jusztusz, (Mrs.) Pal, 'Kistarcsa', *Mozgo Vilag*, Vol. 14 (November 1988), pp. 120–128.

Kadar, Janos, *Hazafisag es kommunizmus* (Budapest: Kossuth, 1968).

Kadar, Janos, *Valogatott beszedek es cikkek* (Budapest: Kossuth, 1975).

Kadar, Janos, *Selected Speeches and Interviews* (Budapest: Akademiai, 1985).

Kadar, Janos, *Vegakarat* (Budapest: Hirlapkiado, 1989).

Kecse, Lajos, 'A vezetoi es a fegyelmi felelosseg', *Honvedsegi Szemle*, September 1985, pp. 70–74.

Kecskemeti, Paul, *The Unexpected Revolution: Social Forces in the Hungarian Uprising* (Stanford, CA: Stanford University Press, 1961).

Kecskes, Janos, 'Vezeraldozatok', *vagyis mit tesznek a kiskiralyok panikban* (Budapest: Tornado Damenija, 1990).

Keleti, Gyorgy, 'Vallasos fiatalok a hadseregben', *Honvedsegi Szemle*, May 1987, pp. 6–13.

Keohane, Robert O., ed., *Neorealism and Its Critics* (New York: Columbia University Press, 1986).

Kerekgyarto, Janos, 'A katonai forumok demokratizmusa es a fegyelem ertekelese', *Honvedsegi Szemle*, Vol. 39, No. 9 (September 1985), pp. 74–78.

Kertesz, Stephen D., ed., *The Fate of East Central Europe: Hopes and Failures of American Foreign Policy* (Notre Dame, IN: University of Notre Dame Press, 1956).

Kertesz, Stephen D., *The Last European Peace Conference: Paris 1946* (Lanham, MD: University Press of America, 1981).

Khrushchev, Nikita S., *Khrushchev Remembers*, edited and translated by Strobe Talbott (Boston: Little, Brown, & Co., 1970).

Kilenyi, Geza, 'A kormanyzati tevekenyseg tovabbfejleszteserol', *Tarsadalmi Szemle*, Vol. 42, Nos. 8–9 (August–September 1987), pp. 54–63.

Kiraly, Bela, 'Hungary's Army under the Soviets', *East Europe*, Vol. 7, No. 3 (March 1958), pp. 3–15.

Kiraly, Bela, 'Hungary's Army: Its Part in the Revolt', *East Europe*, Vol. 7, No. 6 (June 1958), pp. 3–16.

Kiraly, Bela, 'The Aborted Soviet Military Plan Against Tito's Yugoslavia', in Vucinich, ed., *At the Brink of War and Peace*.

Kiraly, Bela, 'The Hungarian Revolution and Soviet Readiness to Wage War Against Socialist States', in Kiraly *et al*., eds, *The First War Between Socialist States: The Hungarian Revolution of 1956 and Its Impact* (New York: Atlantic Research, 1984).

Kiraly, Bela, *Honvedsegbol Nephadsereg* (Budapest: CO-NEXUS, 1989).

Kis, Andras, *Az antifasiszta magyar katonai hagyomanyokrol* (Budapest: Akademiai, 1978).

Kisszekhelyi, Odon, *Kabulat minden aron?* (Budapest: Zrinyi, 1982).

Kolkowicz, Roman, *The Soviet Military and the Communist Party* (Princeton, NJ: Princeton University Press, 1967).

Kolkowicz, Roman, 'Interest Groups in Soviet Politics: The Case of the Military', in Herspring and Volgyes, eds, *Civil–Military Relations in Communist Systems* (Boulder, CO: Westview Press, 1978), pp. 9–27.

Kolkowicz, Roman, 'Toward a Theory of Civil–Military Relations in Communist (Hegemonial) Systems', in Kolkowicz and Korbonski, eds, *Soldiers, Peasants, and Bureaucrats* (London: Allen & Unwin, 1982), pp. 231–251.

Kolkowicz, Roman and Andrzej Korbonski, eds, *Soldiers, Peasants, and Bureaucrats: Civil–Military Relations in Communist and Modernizing Societies* (London: Allen & Unwin, 1982).

Kopacsi, Sandor, *"In the Name of the Working Class"* (Toronto: Lester & Orpen Dennys, 1986).

Korbonski, Andrzej, 'The Dilemmas of Civil–Military Relations in Contemporary Poland: 1945–81', *Armed Forces and Society*, Vol. 8, No. 1, (1981).

Korbonski, Andrzej, 'The Polish Army', in Adelman, ed., *Communist Armies in Politics*, pp. 103–128.

Korbonski, Andrzej, 'Poland', in Rakowska-Harmstone, ed., *Communism in Eastern Europe*, pp. 50–85.

Korbonski, Andrzej, and Sarah M. Terry, 'The Military as a Political Actor in Poland', in Kolkowicz and Korbonski, eds, *Soldiers, Peasants, and Bureaucrats*, pp. 159–180.

Kovary, Peter, 'Apam a katpolos', *Mozgo Vilag*, Vol. 15, No. 2 (February 1989), pp. 89–103.

Kovrig, Bennett, *Communism in Hungary: From Kun to Kadar* (Stanford, CA: Hoover Institution Press, 1979).

Kovrig, Bennett, 'Hungary', in Rakowska-Harmstone, ed., *Communism in Eastern Europe*, pp. 86–114.

Kozak, Gyula, 'Multbanezes', *Mozgo Vilag*, Vol. 14, No. 11 (November 1988), pp. 90–119.

Kozma Toth, Istvan, *Czinege Lajos munder nelkul* (Budapest: Zrinyi, 1990).

Krejci, Jaroslaw, *Social Change and Stratification in Postwar Czechoslovakia* (London: Macmillan, 1972).

Krepon, Michael, and Jeffrey P. Tracey, ''Open Skies' and UN Peace-

Keeping', *Survival*, Vol. 22, No. 3 (May–June 1990), pp. 251–263.

Krisch, Henry, 'German Democratic Republic', in Nelson, ed., *Soviet Allies*, pp. 143–183.

Kubinyi, Ferenc, " . . . *ketrecbe engem zartak* . . . " (Budapest: Holnap, 1989).

Kuklinski, Ryszard Jerzy, 'Wojna z Narodem Widziana od Srodka', *Kultura* (Paris), April 1987.

Kulcsar, Kalman, *A mai magyar tarsadalom* (Budapest: Kossuth, 1962).

Kutika, Karoly, 'Szamolunk a KISZ-esekre, az ifjugardistakra', *Ifju Kommunista*, December 1970.

Larrabee, F. Stephen, 'Soviet Crisis Management in Eastern Europe', in Holloway and Sharp, eds, *The Warsaw Pact*, pp. 111–140.

Legyozhetetlen ero (Budapest: Kossuth, 1968).

Lenin, V. I., *A haborurol, a hadseregrol es a hadtudomanyrol* (Budapest: Zrinyi, 1958) 2 volumes.

Lolland, J., ed., *Zu Befehl Genosse Unterleutenant* (Stuttgart: Seewald, 1971).

Lomax, Bill, *Magyarorszag 1956* (Budapest: Aura, 1989).

Macartney, C. A., *A History of Hungary 1929–45* (New York: Praeger, 1956 [Vol. 1], 1957 [Vol. 2]).

MacGregor, Douglas A., *The Soviet-German Military Alliance* (Cambridge: Cambridge University Press, 1989).

Macintosh, J. Malcolm, 'The Red Army, 1920–36', in B. H. Liddell Hart, ed., *The Red Army* (Gloucester, MA: Peter Smith, 1968).

Macintosh, J. Malcolm, 'Stalin's Policies Toward Eastern Europe, 1939–48: The General Picture', in Thomas T. Hammond and Robert Farrell, eds, *The Anatomy of Communist Takeovers* (Munich: Institute for the Study of the USSR, 1971), pp. 200–215.

A magyar allam szervei 1944–50 (Budapest: Kozgazdasagi es Jogi, 1985), 2 volumes.

A magyar nepi demokracia tortenete 1944–62 (Budapest: Kossuth, 1978).

A Magyar Szocialista Munkaspart hatarozatai es dokumentumai, 1956–62 (Budapest: Kossuth, 1962).

A Magyar Szocialista Munkaspart XII. Kongresszusa (Budapest: Kossuth, 1980).

Major, Istvan, 'A 25 eves tiszthelyettes kepzesrol', *Honvedsegi Szemle*, Vol. 36, No. 9 (September 1982).

Malomsoki, Jozsef, 'A tiszti allomany tarsadalmi helyzetenek nehany mutatoja', *Honvedsegi Szemle*, Vol. 41, No. 6 (June 1987), pp. 12–19.

Marer, Paul, 'Intrabloc Economic Relations and Prospects', in Holloway and Sharp, eds, *The Warsaw Pact*, pp. 215–237.

Marer, Paul, 'The Economies and Trade of Eastern Europe', in Griffith, ed., *Central and Eastern Europe*, pp. 37–73.

Marosan, Gyorgy, *Nincs visszaut* (Budapest: ELTE AJTK, 1988).

Mastny, Vojtech, 'Stalin and the Militarization of the Cold War', *International Security* Vol. 9, No. 3 (Winter 1984/85).

Mate, Janos, 'Meditaciok a parttestuletek munkastilusarol, munkarendjerol', *Honvedsegi Szemle*, Vol. 43, No. 3 (March 1989), pp. 94–100.

The Military Balance (London: IISS, selected years).

Monin, M., 'Internatsionalizm v deistvi', *Voenno-Istoricheski Zhurnal*, No. 6 (1971).

Morocz, Lajos, 'Katonai doktrinank fobb tetelei', *Magyar Tudomany*, Vol. 33, No. 11 (November 1988), pp. 833–842.

Az MSzMP es a szocialista honvedelem (Budapest: Zrinyi, 1981).

Az MSzMP honvedelmi politikajarol (Budapest: Zrinyi, 1974).

Az MSzMP kilencedik kongresszusanak jegyzokonyve (Budapest: Kossuth, 1967).

Az MSzMP tizedik kongresszusanak jegyzokonyve (Budapest: Kossuth, 1971).

Mucs, Sandor, *Politika es hadsereg Magyarorszagon 1944–48* (Budapest: Zrinyi-Kossuth, 1985).

Mucs, Sandor, and Erno Zagoni, *A Magyar Nephadsereg tortenete* (Budapest: Zrinyi, 1984).

Munk, Karoly, *A fegyverszuneti szerzodestol a szocialista hadseregig* (Budapest: Zrinyi, 1964).

Nagy, Ferenc, *The Struggle Behind the Iron Curtain* (New York: Macmillan, 1948).

Nagy, Gabor, and Lajos Moricz, eds, *Uj haza, uj hadsereg* (Budapest: Zrinyi, 1970).

Nagy, Imre, *On Communism: In Defense of the New Course* (New York: Praeger, 1957).

Nelson, Daniel N., ed., *Soviet Allies: The Warsaw Pact and the Issue of Reliability* (Boulder, CO: Westview Press, 1984).

Nelson, Daniel N., 'The Measurement of East European WTO Reliability', in Nelson, *Soviet Allies*, pp. 2–41.

Nelson, Daniel N., *Romanian Politics in the Ceauşescu Era* (New York: Gordon and Breach, 1989).

Nelson, Daniel N., 'WTO Mobilization Potential: A Bulgarian Case Study', *Defense Analysis*, Vol. 5, No. 1 (1989), pp. 31–44.

Nelson, Daniel N., 'Watching the Pact Unravel: The Transformation of East European Political–Military Policies', *Berichte des Bundesinstituts*, No. 32 (1990).

Nelson, Daniel N., 'Political Dynamics and the Bulgarian Military', in Simon, ed., *European Security Policy after the Revolutions of 1989*, pp. 479–514.

Nemes, Janos, 'Rakosi iratok', *Mozgo Vilag*, June 1988, pp. 42–48.

Nemeskurty, Istvan, *Requiem egy hadseregert* (Budapest: Gondolat, 1968).

Nogradi, Sandor, *Tortenelmi lecke* (Budapest: Kossuth, 1970).

Nordlinger, Eric, *Soldiers in Politics* (Englewood Cliffs, NJ: Prentice-Hall, 1977).

Nyilas, Istvan, 'A Baratsag-89 gyakorlat tapasztalatai', *Honvedsegi Szemle*, Vol. 43, No. 5 (May 1989), pp. 9–16.

Odom, William E., 'A Dissenting View on the Group Approach to Soviet Politics', *World Politics*, Vol. 28, No. 4 (July 1976), pp. 542–568..

Odom, William E., 'The Party–Military Connection: A Critique', in Herspring and Volgyes, eds, *Civil–Military Relations in Communist Systems*, pp. 27–53.

Oldberg, Ingmar, ed., *Unity and Conflict in the Warsaw Pact* (Stockholm: The Swedish National Defence Research Institute, 1984).

Partepites (Budapest: Kossuth, 1972).

Perlmutter, Amos, *The Military and Politics in Modern Times* (New Haven, CT: Yale University Press, 1977).

Perlmutter, Amos, *Modern Authoritarianism* (New Haven, CT: Yale University Press, 1981).

Perlmutter, Amos, 'Civil–Military Relations in Socialist Authoritarian and Praetorian States: Prospects and Retrospects', in Kolkowicz and Korbonski, eds, *Soldiers, Peasants, and Bureaucrats*, pp. 310–331.

Perlmutter, Amos, and William M. LeoGrande, 'The Party in Uniform: Toward a Theory of Civil–Military Relations in Communist Political Systems', *American Political Science Review*, Vol. 76, No. 4 (December 1982), pp. 778–790.

Pinter, Istvan, *A magyar front es az ellenallas* (Budapest: Kossuth, 1970).

Price, George W., 'The Romanian Armed Forces', in Simon, ed., *European Security Policy*, pp. 457–478.

Radvanyi, Janos, *Hungary and the Superpowers* (Stanford, CA: Hoover Institution Press, 1972).

Rakosi, Matyas, 'Partunk feladatai a valasztasok kuszoben', HCP Seminar, Pamphlet No. 14, August 15, 1945.

Rakosi, Matyas, *Honvedelem, hazafisag* (Budapest: Honved Kiado Intezet, 1952).

Rakowska-Harmstone, Teresa, ed., *Communism in Eastern Europe* (Bloomington, IN: Indiana University Press, 1984).

Rakowska-Harmstone, Teresa *et al.*, *Warsaw Pact: The Question of Cohesion* (4 Volumes) (Ottawa: Operational Research Analysis Establishment/DND, 1981, 1984, 1986).

Ranki, Gyorgy, ed., *A Wilhelmstrasse es Magyarorszag 1933–44* (Budapest: Kossuth, 1968).

Ranki, Gyorgy, *A masodik vilaghaboru tortenete* (Budapest: Gondolat, 1976).

Remington, Robin Alison, *The Warsaw Pact: Case Studies in Communist Conflict Resolution* (Cambridge, MA: MIT Press, 1971).

Remington, Robin Alison, 'Foreword', to Jerzy J. Wiatr, *The Soldier and the Nation: The Roke of the Military in Polish Politics, 1918–85* (Boulder, CO: Westview Press, 1988), pp. xi–xviii.

Remington, Robin Alison, 'Polish Soldiers in Politics: The Party in Uniform?" in Constantin P. Danopoulos, ed., *The Decline of Military Regimes: The Civilian Influence* (Boulder, CO: Westview Press, 1988), pp. 75–103.

Revai, Jozsef, 'On the Character of Our People's Democracy', *Foreign Affairs* (Moscow), Vol. 28 (1949), pp. 143–152.

Rice, Condoleezza, *The Soviet Union and the Czechoslovak Army, 1948–83* (Princeton, NJ: Princeton University Press, 1984).

Rice, Condoleezza, 'Defense Burden-Sharing', in Holloway and Sharp, eds, *The Warsaw Pact*, pp. 59–86.

Romhanyi, F., 'Hungary's Army Short of 'Worker' Officers', *Soviet Analyst*, No. 10 (1978).

Rozsa, Laszlo, 'Aktivitas, kiallas, demokracia', *Tarsadalmi Szemle*, Vol. 31, No. 5 (May 1976).

Sadykiewicz, Michael, *Organizing for Coalition Warfare: The Role of East European Warsaw Pact Forces in Soviet Military Planning* (Santa Monica, CA: RAND, 1988).

Sadykiewicz, Michael, *The Warsaw Pact Command Structure in Peace and War* (Santa Monica, CA: RAND, 1988).

Salford, John, *The Sword and the Ploughshare: Autonomous Peace Initiatives in East Germany* (London: Merlin, 1983).

Schopflin, George, Rudolf L. Tokes, and Ivan Volgyes, 'Leadership Change and Crisis in Hungary', *Problems of Communism*, September–October 1988, pp. 27–40.

Seton-Watson, Hugh, *The East European Revolution* (New York: Praeger, 1965).

Shawcross, William, *Crime and Compromise: Janos Kadar and the Politics of Compromise Since 1956* (New York: E. P. Dutton, 1974).

Simon, Jeffrey, *Warsaw Pact Forces: Problems of Command and Control* (Boulder, CO: Westview Press, 1985).

Simon, Jeffrey, ed., *NATO–Warsaw Pact Force Mobilization* (Washington: National Defense University Press, 1988).

Simon, Jeffrey, ed., *European Security after the Revolutions of 1989* (Washington, DC: National Defense University Press, 1991).

Simon, Sandor, *A torzsekrol es munkajukrol* (Budapest: Zrinyi, 1978).

Simonffy, Andras, *Komporszag katonai* (Budapest: Magveto, 1981).

Skilling, H. Gordon, 'Interest Groups and Communist Politics Revisited', *World Politics*, Vol. 36, No. 1 (August 1983), pp. 1–28.

Skilling, H. Gordon, and Franklyn Griffiths, eds, *Interest Groups in Soviet Politics* (Princeton, NJ: Princeton University Press, 1971).

Slapnicka, Harry, *Schwejk im Wandel* (Vienna: Herold, 1970).

Slusser, Robert M., and Jan F. Triska, *A Calendar of Soviet Treaties 1917–57* (Stanford, CA: Stanford University Press, 1959).

Staar, Richard F., *Communist Regimes in Eastern Europe* (Stanford, CA: Hoover Institution Press, 1982).

Statisztikai evkonyv, 1956 (Budapest: Statisztikai Hivatal, 1956).

Statisztikai evkonyv, 1984 (Budapest: KSH, 1985).

Steele, Jonathan, *Eastern Europe Since Stalin* (London: David & Charles, 1974).

Szabadon valasztott (Budapest: Idegenforgalmi es Propaganda, 1990).

Szabo, Arpad, *A magyar forradalmi honved karhatalom* (Budapest: Zrinyi, 1977).

Szabo, Miklos M., *A Magyar Kiralyi Honved Legiero a masodik vilaghaboruban* (Budapest: Zrinyi, 1987).

Szabo, Tibor, 'A sorkatonak beilleszkedese es a politikai szervezetek munkaja', *Partelet*, Vol. 29, No. 2 (February 1984), pp. 78–82.

Szilas, Istvan, 'A hon vedelmenek vedelme', *Valosag*, Vol. 33, No. 8 (August 1990).

Szucs, Miklos, *Ezredes voltam 1956–ban a vezerkarnal* (Budapest: Szabad Ter, 1989).

Szuros, Matyas, 'Hungary and Detente in Europe', *The New Hungarian Quarterly*, Vol. 27, No. 103 (Autumn 1986), pp. 7–17.

Szuros, Matyas, 'Hungary, Europe, and the World', *The New Hungarian Quarterly*, Vol. 28, No. 107 (Autumn 1987), pp. 6–14.

A tarsadalom es a hadsereg (Budapest: Zrinyi, 1974).

Teleki, Eva, *Nyilas uralom Magyarorszagon* (Budapest: Kossuth 1974).

Terry, Sarah M., ed., *Soviet Policy in Eastern Europe* (New Haven, CT: Yale University Press, 1984).

Terry, Sarah M., 'Theories of Development in Soviet–East European Relations', in Terry, ed., *Soviet Policy in Eastern Europe*, pp. 221–254.

Timorin, A. A., 'Sotsial'no-politicheskaia priroda i naznachenie sotsialistichekikh armii', in S. A. Tiushkievich *et al.*, eds, *Voina i armiia* (Moscow: Voennizdat, 1977).

Tiushkievich, S. A. *et al.*, eds, *Voina i armiia* (Moscow: Voennizdat, 1977).

Tokes, Rudolf L., *Vom Post-Kommunismus zur Demokratie: Politik, Parteien und die Wahlen in Ungarn* (Bonn: Konrad Adenauer Stiftung, 1990).

Tokes, Rudolf L., 'From Visegrad to Krakow: Cooperation, Competition, and Coexistence in Central Europe', *Problems of Communism*, Vol. 40 (November-December 1991), pp. 100–115.

Toth, Sandor, *Budapest felszabaditasa 1944–45* (Budapest: Zrinyi, 1975).

Valenta, Jiri, 'The Soviet Union and East-Central Europe: Crisis, Intervention, and Normalization', in Rakowska-Harmstone, ed., *Communism in Eastern Europe*, pp. 329–259.

Valenta, Jiri, 'Soviet Decision Making and the Hungarian Revolution', in Kiraly *et al.*, eds, *The First War*.

Valenta, Jiri, and Condoleezza Rice, 'The Czechoslovak Army', in Adelman, ed., *Communist Armies in Politics*, pp. 129–148.

Vali, Ferenc, *Rift and Revolt in Hungary* (Cambridge, MA: Harvard University Press, 1961).

Van Oudenaren, John, 'The Soviet Union and Eastern Europe: New Prospects, Old Dilemmas', in Griffith, ed., *Central and Eastern Europe*, pp. 102–129.

Varga, Gyorgy T., 'Partapparatus Magyarorszagon 1948 utan', *Historia*, No. 1 (1988), pp. 28–31.

A Varsoi Szerzodes szervezete: Dokumentumok 1955–85 (Budapest: Kossuth, 1986).

Vas, Zoltan, *Viszontagsagos eletem* (Budapest: Magveto, 1980).

Verona, Sergiu, *Military Occupation and Diplomacy: Soviet Troops in Romania, 1944–58* (Duham, NC: Duke University Press, 1992).

Vitanyi, Ivan, 'Nepfrontgondolat es demokracia', *Tarsadalmi Szemle*, Vol. 44, No. 3 (March 1989), pp. 11–19.

Vogel, A., 'Die Verantwortung der Grundorganisationen erhoehen', *Militarwesen*, August 1974.

Volgyes, Ivan, ed., *Political Socialization in Eastern Europe: A Comparative Framework* (New York: Praeger, 1975).

Volgyes, Ivan, 'The Military as an Agent of Political Socialization: The Case of Hungary', in Herspring and Volgyes, eds, *Civil–Military Relations in Communist Systems*, pp. 145–164.

Volgyes, Ivan, 'Military Politics of the Warsaw Pact Armies', in Morris Janowitz, ed., *Civil–Military Relations in Regional Perspectives* (London: Sage, 1981).

Volgyes, Ivan, *The Political Reliability of the Warsaw Pact Armies: The Southern Tier* (Durham, NC: Duke University Press, 1982).

Volgyes, Ivan, 'Regional Differences within the Warsaw Pact', *Orbis*, Fall 1982, pp. 665–679.

Volgyes, Ivan, *Politics in Eastern Europe* (Chicago: Dorsey Press, 1986).

Volgyes, Ivan, 'Military Security in the Post-Communist Age: Reflections on Myths and Realities', *Studies in Comparative Communism*, Vol. 25, No. 1 (March 1992), pp. 89–95.

Volgyes, Ivan, and Zoltan D. Barany, 'Hungarian Mobilization and Force Structure', in Simon, ed., *NATO–Warsaw Pact Force Mobilization*, pp. 375–396.

Volgyes, Ivan, and Zoltan D. Barany, 'The Evolution of the Hungarian People's Army', in Eyal, ed., *The Warsaw Pact and the Balkans*, pp. 13–66.

Vonyo, Jozsef, 'Diktatura – olasz modra: A Gombos csoport az allamrol a harmincas evek elso feleben', *Valosag*, Vol. 31, No. 1 (January 1988), pp. 66–76.

Vucinich, Wayne S., ed., *At the Brink of War and Peace: The Tito–Stalin Split in a Historic Perspective* (New York: Brooklyn College Press, 1982).

Waltz, Kenneth N., 'Laws and Theories', in Robert O. Keohane, ed., *Neorealism and Its Critics* (New York: Columbia University Press, 1986), pp. 27–46.

Welsh, William, ed., *Survey Research and Public Attitudes* (New York: Pergamon, 1981).

Wiatr, Jerzy J., 'The Military in Politics: Realities and Stereotypes', *International Social Science Journal*, Vol. 37, No. 1 (1985), pp. 97–107.

Wiatr, Jerzy J., *The Soldier and the Nation: The Role of the Military in Polish Politics, 1918–85* (Boulder, CO: Westview Press, 1988).

Yakubovskiy, I. I., ed., *Boevoe sodruzhestvo bratskikh narodov i armii* (Moscow: Voenizdat, 1975).

Zagoni, Erno, 'Partunk honvedelmi politikaja', *Ifju Kommunista*, August-September 1971.

Zagoni, Erno, ed., *Az MSzMP es a szocialista honvedelem* (Budapest: Zrinyi, 1981).

Zagoni, Erno, 'A munkashatalom megvedese es a Magyar Nephadsereg', *Parttorteneti Kozlemenyek*, No. 1, 1987.

Zagoni, Erno, 'A Magyar Nephadsereg helye a politikai rendszerben', *Honvedsegi Szemle*, Vol. 41, No. 5 (May 1987), pp. 1–6.

Zagoni, Erno *et al.*, *Hadsereg, honvedelem* (Budapest: Zrinyi, 1968).

Zentai, Artur, 'Gondolatok a Magyar Nephadsereg fejlodesenek nehany kerdeserol', in *A tarsadalom es a hadsereg*, pp. 87–122.

Zinner, Paul E., *Revolution in Hungary* (New York: Columbia University Press, 1962).

Zinner, Tibor, 'Haborus bunosok perei', *Tortenelmi Szemle* Vol. 28, No. 1 (1985), pp. 118–141.

Index